MW01039322

Strike a Long Trot

Legendary Horsewoman
Linda Tellington-Jones

SHANNON YEWELL WEIL

TURTLE ROCK PRESS

©2013

Strike A Long Trot

Legendary Horsewoman Linda Tellington-Jones

Printed in the UNITED STATES OF AMERICA

Turtle Rock Press

First edition 2013

Cover Design by Kate Riordan

Edited by Kate Riordan

Includes bibliographical references

Horsemanship, Equestrian, Historical biographical

ISBN 978-0-9885212-0-9 (hardcover)

ISBN 978-0-9885212-1-6 (pbk.)

ISBN 978-0-9885212-2-3 (ebk.)

Library of Congress Control Number 2013936020

TABLE OF CONTENTS

ACKNOWLEDGEMENTS

Kate Riordan, thank you for your hours of editing, thank you dear friend. Your many contributions to Linda's life are invaluable and I salute you with the "Parade Wave."

Martha Merriam, this book would have been impossible without the bounty of archived letters, magazines, memorabilia and photographs that you have kept for decades. I am forever grateful to you for producing material that I didn't even know I needed. Thank you so much.

Susan Mayo of Susar Arabian Farm for your memories dating back to the Chadwick Stables in Rolling Hills. I am particularly grateful for your eyewitness account of Linda and Bint Gulida winning the 1961 Jim Shoulders 100-Mile Ride in Moore, Oklahoma.

Thank you goes to Jim Weil for allowing me the time to begin this project years ago and Julie Suhr for your helpful advice that launched this journey.

Valerie Pruitt Sivertson, thank you for assembling the detailed binder containing PCERF lessons, tests and examinations. You were smart to acquire mares from Margit Bessenyey and start breeding Hungarian horses.

Paula Stockebrand for sharing your wonderful PCERF memories and tales about Archie and Bunny. Lynn Blades for her reflections of Countess Margit Bessenyey and her accounts of riding the Hungarian horses. Alexis Flippen von Zimmer – thank you for your colorful memories that give depth to the description of PCERF.

Thank you to Pam Parker for her memories of endurance riding at Peaceful Valley, the Tevis Cup Ride and Ernie Sanchez. Diane Woodard Scott and Laurie Jurs for their recollections of PCERF. Thanks also to Roland Kleger for a lifetime of Tellington experiences.

Rob Edwards for his astute foresight to interview Wentworth Tellington for *Anvil Magazine* and for harvesting his observations, especially about Bint Gulida.

Phil Gardner, pioneer endurance rider, thanks for selecting me as his crew for the 1976 Great American Horse Race and for being a loyal friend all these years.

Mo Livermore, dear friend – you taught me how to write a good story. Thank you. Karen Puckett – eternal love.

Shannon Yewell Weil

Thank you goes to Ellen Nicholson Walker for her Hungarian Horse insight, to Cathy Rohm and her Arabian pedigree knowledge, Wendy Averill for Thoroughbred pedigree research, Phyllis Lambert, Cherie Evans Curry, Cherie Woodward and Steve Elliott for keeping the faith on this project. To Miss Pat Horan for being there for me. Diana Coco-Russell and John Russell for looking after me. And for swinging in on a vine at the last minute with various historic details, thanks goes to Diana Carter and to Sylvia Jordan who provided photographs of PCERF. A nod goes to my chickens for checking my daily progress.

Thank you Dave Stamey for your lyrical song "Mountain Wind" – I get it!

> Aspens are turnin', I think I'd better
> Head on down and find some warmer weather
> I strike a long trot to canyon's mouth
> Hit the valley gonna' head her south
> And leave behind this cold high mountain wind.

Thank you Wentworth Tellington who uncovered my confidence as a teenager and enlightened me to appreciate books. Your teachings are still relevant today and I am honored to share your influence with others.

Finally to Linda Tellington-Jones, thank you for asking me to tell this story of your incredible life.

DEDICATION

For Bint Gulida and Brado

and

Nancy Dau Yewell –

your love still lives in my heart.

INTRODUCTION

Linda Tellington-Jones

Often people ask me the question, "Do you ride?" This prompted the realization that many people are not familiar with my extensive equestrian competition background.

I knew that I needed to chronicle the part of my life that involved so many benchmarks in the evolution of my horsemanship and teaching skills. So I called my friend Shannon Weil, who is a former student and is the Pacific Coast Equestrian Research Farm historian. She had written a story about me and my champion Arabian mare, Bint Gulida, for the *Tevis Forum* publication a few years ago and I thought to myself, who better to write this book! I asked Shannon if she would be willing to craft a book about this early era of my life. She instantly replied, "Of course I would! I've been waiting for years for this call."

Dating back to the years when my first husband Wentworth Tellington and I established the Pacific Coast Equestrian Research Farm, a center for my School of Horsemanship, our main goal was to share our knowledge about horses in a structured format at the school and through writing articles and books. Remember that this was an era before the Internet and websites. During the 1950s when the primary use of horses shifted from transportation, war and agriculture to recreation and competition, information was sparse for the growing population of backyard horse owners.

More importantly, it was a time when people kept their knowledge about horses absolutely secret — so how could anyone learn? It was Went's idea to share his vast knowledge with the new generation of horse enthusiasts. By combining Went's U.S. Cavalry background with my competitive achievements and many years of experience as a riding teacher and United States Pony Club Instructor and judge, we made a great team. I give great respect to Went, who was adamant about sharing what we knew, a philosophy that I continue to practice today.

It is my honor to give this book my blessing, and to thank Shannon for her diligent time in sharing this story with you.

Blessings to you and your horses,

Linda

Linda Tellington-Jones
Kona, Hawaii
October, 2012

FOREWORD

As a student at her Pacific Coast School of Horsemanship over 40 years ago and a witness to part of her competitive career, Linda and I felt it was time to tell this story. Through my heart and eyes I am presenting the remarkable elements that made up the extraordinary life and times of Linda Tellington-Jones. It reveals how, as a fearless, athletic and intelligent young woman, she became not just a rider but also a champion, a brilliant teacher and a legendary horsewoman.

Linda's roots were as a farm girl in Edmonton, Alberta, Canada, where her loving family encouraged and nurtured relationships with animals of all kinds. A natural with horses, Linda was a first-class equestrian at a youthful age, earning the reputation as the go-to catch rider at national horse shows where she retired historic cup awards with her multiple wins.

Through her teamwork with U.S. Cavalry horseman (and then husband) Wentworth Tellington, she made a name for herself in the fledgling sport of endurance riding. Linda's wisdom about horses was also influenced by her grandfather, Will Caywood, himself a leading Thoroughbred racehorse trainer in both the United States and Russia. Will passed on to Went and Linda the equine healing and behavioral secrets he learned from a Gypsy named Orlo, his interpreter and companion on the Russian racetracks.

Linda and Went formed the Pacific Coast Equestrian Research Farm in California as a way to share their rich knowledge and insights with students from around the world. It's no wonder that their widely read *Western Horseman* articles were titled "Let's Go," since the ever-active Tellingtons were constantly on the move, seeking better ways to help horses and horsemen and horsewomen alike.

Riding her phenomenal Arabian mare, Bint Gulida, in 1961 Linda proved herself a formidable competitor at the Tevis Cup 100-Mile One-Day Ride. This challenging course traverses California's rugged Sierra Nevada mountains, and Linda sailed over the finish line in top-ten placement. At the time, it was unheard of for a horse to cover two 100-mile rides during a year of endurance competition. Linda and Bint Gulida proved it could be done, when a mere six weeks after Tevis they won and set a record at the Jim Shoulders 100-mile ride in Moore, Oklahoma that stood for seven years.

These accomplishments attracted the attention of Hungarian Countess Margit Sigray Bessenyey. Margit brought an element of magic into Linda's life, not only with her unprecedented wealth but also with her rare breed of Hungarian Furioso (Felver) horses that lived at her ranch in Montana.

Soon after meeting Countess Bessenyey, Linda met Countess Judith Gyurky, whose riveting tale of sacrifice during World War II tells of how she managed to save only a few of her prized Hungarian horses during that horrifying conflict. Judith's words describe fleeing Hungary on foot with 64 horses while being pursued by the Russian armies as they invaded her homeland. An emaciated handful of surviving horses became Judith's foundation stock after they arrived in Virginia where she had settled. Linda relates the story of how these two courageous Hungarian countesses fought to keep these Hungarian horses from total demise. Judith bred one of Linda's all-time favorite horses, a U.S. Olympic Equestrian Team reject named Magyar Brado. It was Linda who transformed Brado into the champion he was.

As the director of her Pacific Coast School of Horsemanship, Linda and students showcased the Hungarian horses by winning blue ribbons in horse shows, combined training events, dressage, fox hunts, hunter trials and steeplechase races at the esteemed shows at Pebble Beach, California. Linda also rode Hungarian stallion Brado to a top-ten finish at the world-renowned Tevis Cup Ride as well as other endurance rides.

This book chronicles the daily life at the residential Pacific Coast School of Horsemanship centered at the Pacific Coast Equestrian Research Farm. It explains the academic curriculum and techniques Linda used, and how she became a mentor for her fortunate students. Several of the students portray the impact that Linda had on their lives and the incredible opportunities they gleaned from attending this school. As students said in jest, "I wish I knew half of what Linda has forgotten." While digging through the archives for this book, the truth of that statement surfaced. I flushed out details and stories of her past that, sure enough, even Linda had forgotten.

It was a famous San Francisco astrologer who prophesized that Linda would be taken under the wing of royalty. Good fortune prevailed when Hungarian Countess Margit Bessenyey sought out Linda to train her own superb horses. The astrology chart also predicted that Linda would develop a new form of communication with animals; of course today Linda is known around the world for Tellington TTouch® Training Method, "a non-verbal language" with animals and humans.

After Linda and Wentworth divorced, Countess Bessenyey set Linda up in grand style at the Westwind Hungarian Horse Farm in Los Altos Hills, California. While living there Linda extended her now-hyphenated name when she was briefly married to Earl Birchell (Birch) Jones. Her new surroundings lasted only a few years before Linda was eager to widen her horizons. In 1974, after decades of training and showing horses and producing highly trained riding instructors, she was ready for a new shift in her life — Westwind closed its doors and she and Birch parted ways. Linda's life took on a new chapter when she moved to Europe with her partner, Roger Russell. Her desire to learn, rather than always teach, was assuaged when she began teaching weekend and weeklong trainings in German. They enrolled in the four-summer Feldenkrais professional training at the Humanistic Psychology Institute in San Francisco and over the next few years she and Roger began integrating the Feldenkrais Awareness Through Movement exercises into the riding workshops.

Finally, nine years after she closed her school, this book briefly delves into an adventure of a lifetime when Linda served as the International Rider Coordinator for the 1976 Great American Horse Race (GAHR), which ran its course from New York to California. She parlayed a sponsorship from the Icelandic government for a half a dozen German, Swiss and Austrian riders to introduce the unique Icelandic horses to America. After a chaotic saga, a small group of riders and their crews, spurred on by Linda and David Nicholson DVM, departed the GAHR and split off to form the 1976 Pony Express Race. This newly-formed group of dedicated riders followed the historic Pony Express Trail 1,960 miles from St. Joseph, Missouri to Sacramento, California.

Within these pages the reader will discover the impact Linda made on three breeds of horses – Arabians, Hungarians and Icelandics. This story of the first 40 years of Linda's life includes adventures, experiences and wisdom that led to the development of her own form of communication with animals and humans known today as Tellington TTouch® Training Method. Linda continues today to share her work worldwide with great enthusiasm and vision.

Please note: Many of the historical photographs show riders without helmets. Today Linda and I both practice and promote safe riding habits by securing and wearing a helmet at all times while riding horses.

Shannon Yewell Weil
Cool, California
October, 2012

CHAPTER 1

DISCOVERING PACIFIC COAST EQUESTRIAN RESEARCH FARM
THE SPRINGBOARD OF MY LIFE

How did I meet Linda Tellington-Jones? My friendship with her started in 1967 after my mother Nancy Yewell stared at me and proclaimed, "What am I going to do with you?"

I was two years out of high school and facing the social tumult of the Vietnam War era. We lived in a grand old Mediterranean house on Morada Place in Altadena, a Southern California town. Our busy home was filled with interesting people and often served as a safe haven for neighborhood kids. It was not uncommon for a gaggle of them to swing by our kitchen for some in-flight fueling from one of Mrs. Yewell's grilled cheese sandwiches and to soak in her welcome. My mother took time for everyone while balancing her own active life. Meanwhile, I struggled to find my own direction and wasn't gaining any significant traction.

My mother's gift of perfecting the art of entertaining and making people at ease made a strong impression on me. She was a beautiful woman with a keen sense of self and fabulous style. Anyone close to her can attest to her anthem of "never miss an opportunity," a theme driven by life experiences that contributed to her character.

Nancy unwaveringly led my father George and me straight into the heart of the Los Angeles contemporary art scene, leaving us with a first-rate education on the subject. The mechanical aspects of creations intrigued my father, an engineer and manufacturer by trade, while the artists, paintings, mixed media and the overall art scene left me smitten.

Dad loved sailing boats and spent a couple of summers as a crew member on the Trans Pacific Yacht Race (Transpac) from Los Angeles to Honolulu. During this time my older sister Susan lived in Northern California and was feverishly campaigning for one political cause or another. My younger brother Taylor was banging away on his guitar, playing music in a series of bands while attending Catalina Island School "26 miles across the sea" (cue the music). I was the only family member who had a passion for horses.

In the winter of 1966, my mother and I had a tête-à-tête about my future and she scheduled an appointment for me to meet with Mrs. Margaret Chadwick of the prestigious Chadwick School in Rolling Hills, California. Years earlier we had moved to Altadena after being forced to leave our ravaged landslide-broken home overlooking the Pacific Ocean in the magical community of Portuguese Bend (Rancho Palos Verdes) that sits just below Rolling Hills on the Southern California coastline. Many of my friends attended Chadwick School, so the notion of spending a day with Mrs. Chadwick was agreeable to me. In preparation for my visit, Mrs. Chadwick was already making plans to ship me off to Switzerland where she nearly had me enrolled in an American school there. Frankly, that plan had no appeal to me whatsoever.

I arrived at the Chadwick campus on the appointed Saturday morning and was greeted by a small-in-stature, lovely grey haired woman, the one and only Mrs. Chadwick. She welcomed me into her home and we spent most of our day in her book-filled office. She sat me down to take a battery of tests aimed at flushing out my natural aptitudes. She gave me her comforting and undivided attention. Her questions focused around topics of interest to me while she sorted out what possible goals I had in mind. Goals? How novel. I was just drifting through space in search of a well-lit exit sign.

Mrs. Chadwick kept elaborating on this idea of going off to school in Switzerland. "Just go watch French films and learn the language," she insisted, thinking that I would love it. This was a plan far loftier than I was prepared for or even able to grasp. "Yikes, not me. How can I escape this one?" was my reaction. Being sent away from the odd comfort of my ever wacky home made me feel as if life was careening out of my control.

My body language must have finally conveyed my paralysis to her Swiss plan because at the end of the day, everything stopped. She paused for a moment, sat back in her chair, looked at me and said in a serious tone, "You know, I think I have the perfect place for you." I braced myself for her next far-flung idea. "There is a school at a place called the Pacific Coast Equestrian Research Farm (PCERF) in Badger, California. It's all about horses. The directors are wonderful people and are former Chadwick teachers. Their names are Wentworth and Linda Tellington. I think that would be a perfect fit for you." That's it! As soon as she mentioned horses, I lit up and immediately wanted to learn more about this possibility. She jotted down the Tellingtons' address and we said goodbye.

Within two weeks I was holding a brochure from PCERF that had arrived in the mail. I studied every photo and carefully read each word, knowing full well I wanted to become a student there as soon as possible. My only question was, when could I go?

That spring my parents Nancy and George, sister Susan, brother Taylor and I took a house boating vacation on the Sacramento Delta in the mid-section of California. We had a great time while my vessel-loving father maneuvered the big, cumbersome, flat-bottomed watercraft in and around every nook and cranny on the Delta. We awoke one morning completely high and dry — the tide had drastically lowered without warning. After waiting patiently, the tide returned, the craft was liberated, and we were sent on our way. But my mind was on the side trip to Badger, home of PCERF, that was planned for the drive home. Finally we said goodbye to the houseboat and headed toward the Sierra Nevada foothills just east of Fresno.

Traveling south through the San Joaquin Valley, we found the road through the small town of Dinuba that emptied out into gently rolling ranch lands. Nature was showing off its glory; the landscape was dotted with wildflowers and singing birds. Gnarled barbed wire fences guarded green pastures busy plumping livestock. The narrow winding country road and old weathered barns completed a perfect Sunday afternoon in May. I loved the country life and was enjoying this jaunt since, after all, it was all about me! My dreams were coming true before my eyes. My city-folk family was packed into my mother's celery-colored, finned Mercedes Benz and it was aimed straight for Badger, California.

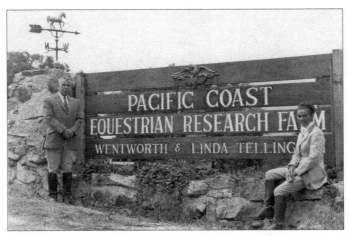

Went and Linda Tellington flank the welcoming sign at Pacific Coast Equestrian Research Farm at Badger, California where they relocated in 1965.

The countryside altered from rolling foothills to more curvaceous and demanding mountainous terrain. Finally we approached something resembling a settlement. The sign read "Badger, CA Elevation 1,950', Population 13." As per our instructions, we continued for several more winding miles and, okay, there's the landmark M Bar J Guest Ranch on the right. The trip was longer than expected but finally we pulled up to a large gate with an eagle-adorned sign that grandly stated "Pacific Coast Equestrian Research Farm – Wentworth and Linda Tellington."

My brother Taylor was enthralled with the Great Dane puppies at the Research Farm during our inaugural visit.

We clambered out of the car and unfolded when suddenly Wentworth Tellington himself, who seemed to appear from nowhere, greeted us. By his side were two huge, brindle-colored, tail-wagging Great Danes. Went introduced us to Tiger and Hara and their giant-pawed litter of puppies, with whom I fell in love instantly. A stocky, broad-shouldered muscular man who stood about 5'8" and in his late 40's, Went sported short graying hair, wire-rimmed glasses perched in front of steel gray eyes, and a big wide toothy smile that made his dimpled cheeks billow. His razor had not yet been engaged with his face on that particular day. He possessed charm and undeniable confidence; we liked him immediately. We noticed several unfinished projects and Went quickly pointed out that "around here, we do everything at a snail's pace," evidenced by the half-finished rock wall surrounding the base of the regal PCERF sign.

The Main Building included the office, store, living room, dining room and kitchen. A large bell hung outside the kitchen door.

The required level of skill to compete at Ram Tap far outweighed my ability at that time.

New England accent, Went explained to us that Linda and students Linda ▄▄▄▄▄er and Anne Greer had taken several horses to a show at Ram Tap in Fresno and so we wouldn't meet them that day. However, Went was eager to show us the farm and seemed to enjoy the opportunity of getting to know the Yewell family.

At once I knew I was standing precisely on the earthly spot where I needed to be for a long time. Mrs. Chadwick had just been promoted to sainthood based on her epiphany for my future.

A torrent of information flowed from Wentworth as my family scrambled to keep up with his tour. Eager to fit in, I bobble-headed in agreement throughout our brief visit. Details of the upcoming School of Horsemanship beginning in June, just a few weeks away, were firmed up. Although most students enrolled for the entire summer, I was just hoping that my parents could afford to launch me into the four-week session. Whatever it took, somehow I knew I was going to be there. I couldn't wait to rub this dirt into my hair.

The facility was simple but smacked of importance. In fact, it had been converted from an old 365-acre chicken ranch nestled in a long narrow valley. The expansiveness of PCERF was sprawled in a linear fashion over about one mile as the road wound around numerous curves. Some of the structures were old but they were in solid condition and the paint was fresh. The main building served as the headquarters and in front stood a very tall flagpole with Old Glory handsomely waving over an expansive parking area.

The library alcove is where Linda registered new students or had a respite moment with one of the Great Danes.

At the west end of the main building sat the office, the engine room where the daily PCERF operations, memberships and mail order business took place. On the approach to the office entrance was a corner library alcove with a large table and benches for reading. On the other side of the office was a small store where students could purchase snacks, sodas, school supplies, books, and a few incidental sundry items. The interior walls proudly showcased impressive paintings and photographs of horses and riders sailing over massive obstacles or crossing rugged terrain. None of it made sense to me yet, but I would learn. To me, this was the perfect school and it wasn't in Switzerland.

Another wall separated the office and store area with a large rock hearth and fireplace that served as the backdrop for the living room area. A beautiful black grand piano, couches and comfortable chairs divided the living area and dining room. The floors were hardy linoleum that could stand up to ranch life.

An enormous kitchen anchored the east end of the building. It was equipped with an ample walk-in refrigerator and all the cooking implements needed to accommodate large groups of people. A swinging door and Formica service counter divided the space from the dining area. Adjacent to the kitchen were the laundry facilities. A long porch protected the building from the southern exposure, sheltering it from either the hot summer sun or inclement winter weather. Benches were scattered along the way where people could rest or read. Outside near the kitchen door hung a massive bell that sent a resounding tone beckoning everyone to meals.

A brick floor graced the Lower Barn, which housed four stalls, a tack room and a feed room.

Across the large parking area sat a small corral and the Lower Barn, one of the original old ranch barns, with white paint barely clinging to the wood. It was my favorite barn; a comforting feeling came from the four stalls, brick floor, small haystack, and a feed and a tack room that had obviously fought off years of dust. Kitty-corner from it was a huge pole barn for hay storage that was bulging with oat hay. An old rickety shop filled with fascinating objects and tools hunkered across from the hay barn. Stashed under some nearby enormous shade trees were several guest cottages and a modest house where Linda and Went lived.

The Winter 1968 Class started a tradition by signing our names in wet concrete that began as a walkway from the Dormitory to the Main Building. (front row: l to r) Bruce Scott, Shannon Yewell, Sharon Kuntz, Pam Cameron, Crystal Sandberg, Carol Cook, Linda Day (middle row: l to r) Beth Preuss, Roberta Wiebe, Diane Woodard (back row: l to r) Sylvia Jordan, Linda Tellington

Above the main building was the recently-built dormitory that also had a covered porch. The exterior was rough-hewn pecky-cedar wood that gave it a rustic feel. It had four large rooms, each with its own bathroom and bunk beds for eight students. The first room held the most prestige, as it was for the long-term students and office staff. At maximum capacity, the dormitory housed about 28 people. The upper barn had an apartment reserved for the guys who attended the school.

Just beyond the dormitory and up a hill was a large pond that Wentworth built as a summer swimming hole. Across the dam was a steep hill; at the top stood a round pen. Directly up the hill sat a small house for special visitors. Adjacent to the round pen was the Upper Barn and nearby was the open-aired Compound that included about 40 stalls.

The land that the Research Farm sat on was blessed with an artesian well that supplied plenty of cold clear water to the ranch. The unique advantage of an artesian well is that the water has traveled through porous rock from a higher elevation and then rises to the surface. It does not require a pump because the pressure builds up from between the layers of rock and as water always does, finds the path of least resistance to the surface.

The winding Dry Creek Drive that accessed the farm split the property down the middle. On the west side was a huge pasture for the horses that sloped upwards. At 1,950 feet elevation the terrain hosted a variety of California Oaks and a mix of pine and fir trees that textured the panorama. The green grasses of spring would soon be turning golden brown, typical of the California summer landscape. Large granite rock outcroppings held the land together as if they were bones.

My mother paid the tuition deposit for the Pacific Coast School of Horsemanship. We said goodbye to Wentworth and I was set. After returning home to Altadena I began preparations for my adventure. A few short weeks later, I hugged my father, sister and brother and friends farewell and my mother and I drove the Mercedes back to Badger. I was delivered to what would become my home for the next year and more importantly, become the springboard of my life. We arrived after the four-and-a-half hour drive to a bustling parking lot and dozens of people.

On that day I met Linda Tellington for the first time. We waited our turn to register and finally were called to join Linda at the library alcove table where she interviewed each new student and collected pertinent information. My mother and I sat across from her as she filled out the paperwork. At that moment, little did I know she was not only enrolling me into the School of Horsemanship program, but into the rest of her life!

At this confluence I felt blessed to be in the presence of this dynamic woman and I knew it was a pivotal moment in my life. Her brown hair was pulled back into a knot at the back of her head, showing off her clean open face. She had a quick wide smile and big soft eyes; hers was a magnetic persona that drew both my mother and me into her. There was nothing pretentious about Linda. She wore simple reserved clothing and no make-up. Her perfectly-shaped hands pushed the pen across the paper with ease. I was a beaming 19-year-old girl; Linda was 29 and Wentworth was 20 years her senior.

Dormitory Room 4 was my new address. Mother and I gathered my suitcase bulging with hunt boots, riding breeches and other summer attire and trundled down to the last room on the block. Just inside the door stood a familiar face from Altadena. Carolyn Woltjes and I were elated to see each other. It turned out her older sister, Eleanor Woltjes, was on the staff as Linda's Assistant Instructor and held the distinguished honor of having been awarded the Gold Medal from the Pacific Coast School of Horsemanship. Eleanor had just arrived from Scottsdale, Arizona where she taught horsemanship and riding at the Searles Ranch.

The throng of giddy girls bid goodbye to their parents. My mother, certain that she had finally found the right tonic for me, breathed a sigh of relief as she returned to Southern California. The 1967 Pacific Coast School of Horsemanship was open for business and ready to launch.

Life turned into a bowl of cherries with Carolyn as my bunkmate as we merrily began decorating our bunk area. We had a lot in common and she was a phenomenal artist. Our roommates were Lucy Diehl from Bisbee, Arizona and Kathy Young from Coos Bay, Oregon. In Room 3, our neighbors were Silver Brandon of San Leandro, California, Pam Parker of Bellevue, Washington, and Nancy Maddock of Tiburon, California. About 20 girls were lucky enough to belong to this summer session. Martha Merriam of Rolling Hills, California joined the group a few weeks later. All our lives were about to change forever.

Aside from Went, there were only a few other men on the Farm. Bruce Scott, who wore Buddy-Holly-type eyeglasses and had close-cropped hair and a wiry-framed body, was the farm farrier. Hailing from Pottstown, Pennsylvania, he was a freshly-minted horseshoer from the nearby Porterville Horseshoeing School. Then there was an older ranch hand, Jim, who was made from the stuff of cowboys. He lived with his schoolteacher wife Marilyn in a trailer near the Upper Barn. We were fortunate to have a wonderful woman named Dottie who prepared most of the meals, assisted by Peggy Wherry who lived nearby (she brought her Arabian horse Apache along too). Doris Churchill had rolled up her life into a new pickup truck, camper and horse trailer, loaded her horse and made her way to Badger from Illinois to work as the office manager. And there was Diane Woodard of Oakland, California, who after a call from Linda, said, "I quit" to her last job and came to the Research Farm to assist Doris in the office.

I wondered how the Tellingtons originally developed the Pacific Coast Equestrian Research Farm and how on earth did they land in this remote location called

Badger. Even more challenging was the question of who are the Tellingtons? So I took it upon myself to learn more about Linda and Went, who both fascinated me immensely. From June of 1967, I spent the following 12 months at the Research Farm saturating myself in the horsemanship program and the philosophies of these two brilliant people.

I, along with several other students, friends and associates, herein on these pages jubilantly share our unique stories from those extraordinary years of Linda's life. We soaked ourselves in Linda's vast knowledge and watched her change the lives of countless people and just as many horses. It was that unique PCERF education that, for all intents and purposes, became the springboard of my life.

CHAPTER 2

THE ALCHEMY OF A STAR:
RISING TO THE TOP WITH A SMILE

*Linda's propensity for animals began at a young age when she trustingly
touched a bear cub while the cub relaxed in her Aunt Helen's lap.*

Shannon Yewell Weil

I was wide-eyed when Linda started telling stories of her early childhood, particularly when she started talking about her animal-loving family. "Our home was filled with a stream of furry and feathered visitors," she began. "Once when my Dad was out cutting hay, the mower ran over a nest of duck eggs," smiles Linda. "Knowing that the hen wouldn't return to the nest, Dad very gently picked up the eggs and brought them into the kitchen. He put the eggs in the box where a mama cat had just given birth to a litter of kittens. The cat accepted the eggs and kept them warm until they hatched. Then the mama cat raised the ducklings. That was my Dad — he was so gentle."

Harold Hood, known simply as "Hoodie," and his wife Marion were hardworking people of Edmonton, Alberta, Canada. They began building their family on June 30, 1937, the day their first daughter Linda was born. Soon thereafter came five more siblings — John, Gerry, Susan, Robyn and baby brother, Randy.

Still carrying a Canadian accent in 1967, those of us from the U.S. were intrigued by Linda's pronunciation of 'out and about' as 'oot and aboot.' Linda continued her animal tales with, "I remember when my Grandfather brought in a runt piglet, and we kept it warm in the oven until it was strong enough to go back *oot* with the sow." If that wasn't enough, we all laughed as she dug up another story for her animal-loving students: "Then there was also a little bunny that would come in the house, hop up the stairs, and find my Grandfather in bed. The rabbit would jump up onto the bed and rustle around in my Grandfather's beard to wake him up." Now I was hooked; I was completely fascinated by this woman.

"That was how my parents and grandparents raised the Hood children — with lots of care and warmth," Linda said, remembering the years that nourished her natural brilliance with all animals. Many years later — after Linda's *'oot'* and *'aboot'* faded to 'out' and 'about,' I furthered my sojourn into learning more about her early life.

When Hoodie first lifted his petite six-year-old daughter Linda onto the back of a reluctant mare named Trixie, little did he know that moment would become the cornerstone of her life, setting the stage for her ability decades later to revolutionize how humans relate to animals.

Now that Linda was of school age, the tightly-bonded father and daughter team paid a visit to an old rough-hewn wooden barn where Trixie was for sale. Ambling buttermilk clouds were strewn across the late afternoon sky as Hoodie led the mare outside for a "test drive" with Linda perched on her back. When Trixie decided that they had seen enough, she turned around and walked straight back inside the red barn. Knowing full well how to find her way home, Trixie proved to Hoodie that he had found the suitable horse.

"Dad knew this horse would take care of me," smiles Linda. "She always knew the way home." For several years Linda rode Trixie across the flat farmlands east of Gibbons, Alberta, back and forth to school, regardless of the harsh weather conditions that Canada could serve up, freezing a lumberjack's plaid flannel shirt in minutes.

Linda would throw a leg over anything, including her dad's dairy calves.

When Linda spoke of Hoodie's ambitions, it was apparent that he had set a sterling example in her life. "After several years of manually operating milking machines for thirty cows every day," Linda said, "My Dad decided that having a dairy farm was a good way to kill yourself. So he decided to go into business for himself, even though he only had an eleventh-grade education. He was an amazing man," Linda said of her father. "I remember when he took the train to Kansas where he borrowed money to buy a huge piece of equipment for dehydrating alfalfa. When it arrived at our farm he started buying alfalfa from other farmers and drying it. That worked out well except for when it rained and hampered production."

Hoodie kept mulling over how he could beat the weather issues, which prompted him to purchase a peat moss bog. "He enlisted my brothers to drive the trucks carrying the peat over the sixty miles to the dehydrating plant," Linda remembered. This turned out to be a very successful business, Alberta Rose Peat Moss, with customers all over the world. "Dad gave all six kids shares in the company and made my Mom the president. I had so much respect for how my parents conducted themselves and how they treated each other. Mother always kept a photo on the fireplace mantle of Dad milking a cow just to remind him that he should never get too big for his britches!

A big-boned broad-backed babysitter of a horse hauled Linda and brother Gerry all over the Hood family farm.

"I also have wonderful memories of our family going to church together. I'm grateful that they took me to a church where the minister came from a place of love rather than hell and damnation. That message has stayed with me to this day," said Linda. She added that, "On Sundays our busy house was full of friends who would come for dinner.

"My Mum kept a neat and tidy house on the farm," continues Linda. "She always had help in the house, usually a young and oftentimes pregnant girl who was in need of support. It was a huge old farmhouse, and Dad would get up during the winter at 4:00 a.m. to start the huge furnace in the basement. It was hard to warm up the whole house; there was often ice on the inside of the windows. I'd run downstairs and get dressed over the heat register that was blasting out hot air. One funny story about my Mum was when a wintery day forced all of us to stay inside, and my brother Gerry was running around like crazy. Mum hobbled him with my Father's necktie to keep him relatively quiet. Today Mum would probably be turned in to the authorities!

"Mum really believed in honoring the human spirit, regardless of who it was. The railroad tracks ran past the farm about an eighth of a mile away. One day a hobo came to the door asking for food, and Mother gave him a job in return for the food. I remember her telling me that she wanted to make him feel useful, instead of just giving him a handout. That's the way both of my parents were," says Linda. "They believed in the Golden Rule. Mother never said anything bad about anyone. Where I grew up there was a lot of prejudice against the Indians, but my parents were not that way at all.

"My maternal grandfather George lived with us," Linda remembers fondly. "Actually, he was my grandfather Will Caywood's brother. Will loved the racetrack so much, but didn't want his wife to have to live the racetrack life. So he divorced his wife and had his brother George look after her. Will came to Edmonton, bought a house for her, and then had his brother George marry her," reports Linda. "George was also wonderful with horses. I remember him putting his hands on the horses; he was very quiet with them. George was just as big of an influence on me and my relationship with horses as my grandfather Will was.

"Our house on 118th Avenue was white, with a huge U-shaped barn with thirty stanchions that I converted into box stalls. Somebody must have helped me I'm sure," laughs Linda. "When I was eleven, Dad had me raking hay and paid me the same wage that he paid his hired hands. He felt that I did a man's work so I should get a man's wage," stated Linda. "I remember taking that money to the bank with my grandfather to open my first bank account. That taught me responsibility and respect. My parents saw each of us children as special human beings, which certainly influenced us and gave us a strong foundation."

Linda continued to share some of the dozens of memories of her family and their love for animals. "When I was three years old my parents had moved to the 'tent town' of Yellowknife in the Northwest Territories of Canada, to help my Grandfather George with his goldmine. One day after she took lunch to my grandfather and Dad and was returning home, a three mile hike from the mine, she saw bear tracks following her home. It didn't bother her; she knew about bears. She wasn't afraid because her father had brought home a baby bear to raise after someone had shot and killed its mother," recollects Linda. "Mother also told another story about a wonderful cat that would follow her everywhere. There was a time when we were out in a canoe and the cat jumped in the lake to swim out and greet us. I also remember a time when a mouse fell into an open jar of molasses that was sitting in the huge pantry. Mum picked out the mouse, washed it off, and turned it loose outside."

Briarcrest Stables

"I was nine-years old on the day we were moving from my Grandpa Jim Hood's farm that was in Gibbons, thirty miles north of Edmonton. It was that day that we passed by a place called Briarcrest Stables. In the arena there were about thirty riders practicing a drill team performance. Right there on the spot I told my Father that Briarcrest was where I wanted to take riding lessons. He said fine, but that I should make arrangements to trade lessons for work at the stables," remembers Linda.

The following Saturday, Hoodie dropped his daughter off at the entrance to Briarcrest Stables. Linda walked in to find Alice Greaves-Metheral, a famous riding instructor. "I asked her if I could trade cleaning stalls for riding lessons. The no-nonsense woman stood back, sizing me up and replied with, 'How much riding have you done?' I answered in earnest, 'I've ridden every day to school since the first grade.'

"Pleased with my response, she put me on a horse to see how well I rode," Linda said. In that moment Alice's eyes widened as she saw for herself the natural talent and ability that Linda possessed. Linda said of her good fortune, "After that first Saturday I never once had to clean stalls; I just had to ride the horses."

A young, dark-haired, horse-crazy girl named Diane Wiebe (Hemstock), whose father was a hockey player and mother a homemaker, became Linda's best friend. "Linda and I were inseparable and the closest of friends. We met when we were eleven just before the seventh grade," remembers Diane.

Diane, who stood a few inches taller than Linda, went on to describe their years at Briarcrest. "There were about four or five girls who loved working in the barn. We all worked hard cleaning the stalls, the barn and the tack. But by far, Linda was the best rider of us all — we called her Linda the Queen" – because she didn't have to clean stalls.

After a siren of telephone calls to Diane's slower-paced home every weekend from Linda, it wasn't long before Diane's mother bestowed her with another well-earned nickname of "Alarm Clock Hood." By 8 o'clock on Saturday and

Sunday mornings the ringing telephone announced that Linda Hood was ready for action. "It's *Alarm Clock Hood!* became the joke in my family," Diane said.

Diane said of Alice Greaves, "She was a pretty crabby lady to us but not to Linda. Of our little group of girls, none of us could ride like Linda. We just didn't have near the ability that 'Linda the Queen' had. Alice would put Linda on the most difficult horses and she would ride and jump them beautifully. Alice would yell and carry on while the rest of us were busy cleaning saddles and stalls and taking horses to the water trough. But Linda never had to do any of that because she was too busy riding. Alice definitely treated Linda nicer because she had a magic about her that none of the rest of us had. But we had a lot of fun just the same."

"From the time I was ten years old until I was fifteen, after school I went directly to Briarcrest Stables. Mrs. Greaves had a stable full of excellent school and show horses. Most days I rode three horses come rain, shine or snow," Linda recalled.

Alice was renowned for training top show hunter and hunter-hacks in addition to running a profitable rent string. "Because I had so many hours of riding under my belt," continues Linda, "I was the kid who rode the young horses after Alice bucked them out in the round pen. I also got to ride the show horses being prepared for competition in hunter and hunter-hack classes. And it was my job each Friday to get on each of the rent string horses one after the other and whack them around with a rubber bat to prepare them for riders taking them out on trail rides. Back then the common thinking about horses was very rudimentary compared to what we know today.

"We didn't have indoor arenas in those days, but we had lights outside so we could ride at night. I showed a lot of hunters, jumpers, Western pleasure and English pleasure and did a lot of 'catch riding' at the shows. My main interest was being with a horse — not necessarily to win — but to have the very best time that the horse and I could have. I wanted the horse to enjoy the process, the experience, as much as I did," Linda said. "I was honoring the horse, its very being, and I was very successful in winning a lot more than my share because of that. It was an incredible experience. Something happens when you have a heart connection with the horse."

Linda's successes were accompanied by dedicated education. "During the cold Canadian winter months, each Tuesday evening Alice gave us a lecture that covered all aspects of horsemanship including feeding, stable management, horse anatomy, breeds and judging conformation. She used the same training methods and criteria used in the U.S. Cavalry officers' training.

"When I was twelve years old," remembers Linda, "an elderly Canadian Cavalry

Shannon Yewell Weil

officer who served during the Spanish-American War had been watching me ride for quite awhile. One day he gave me a well-worn book written by a U.S. Cavalry officer on a method of starting young horses without bucking. After reading the book, I started a two-year-old Thoroughbred mare who was boarded at our farm. By following the book with its step-by-step instructions for ground driving, I rode her for the first time with no trauma and no bucking." This officer and his gift of that book had a profound affect on Linda for the rest of her life.

Even at a very young age Linda amassed numerous trophies, including retiring the coveted Calgary Herald Equitation Trophy after winning it three times.

Linda won more than her fair share of trophies and ribbons and became the 'go-to' rider for 'catch rides,' which meant a rider would be asked at the show to compete on other people's horses. Unmistakably, even at this tender young age, Linda was a first-class horsewoman. Diane says of Linda's talent, "I've seen

Linda walk over to a horse that people were fighting with and the horse settles the minute Linda is in its presence. I've never understood it, but there is something magical inside her soul that horses instantly recognize."

A nine-day, prestigious horse show was held nearby every spring. "About thirty of us would ride the horses down the road past the airport to the fairgrounds," Linda remembered. Nobody had a trailer in those days, so if you were showing your horses you rode them to the arena. We must have been at least twenty miles away. Alice would round up everyone who could swing a leg over a horse. It didn't matter how good a rider they were, she just needed riders to get the horses to the show." They rode in huge groups and when they arrived the real work began. "We had to braid and groom the horses, and clean the saddles," Diane reminded Linda. "I hate to say this, but I didn't have to do that," Linda admitted, who was always spared the heavy workload. "But I do have wonderful memories of riding those beautiful Thoroughbreds through Edmonton. We always wore a carnation in our lapels when we showed. There was a live organist at the horse show who played music for the classes — I always had a sense that the horses loved the music."

Where did Linda learn her unique and winning ways? "At an early age I remember my grandfather George coming in a stall with me. I watched as he gently put his hands on a horse, then run them softly all over the horse's body." Linda flushed with emotion as she reflected on the pivotal moment that unlocked her profound relationship with horses. "He said to me, 'When you put your hands on a horse you are listening to who they are; you're making a connection beyond any words.' I also remember my Mother standing next to the arena rail and every time I would ride by she would say, 'Smile, dear.' Today I know that when you smile it affects your hormones and state of mind, and the horse senses that too. When I smile, it affects me and everyone and everything around me."

Diane vividly remembers the hunter/jumper classes and ladies classes. "Linda was always sought after to ride in the Ladies Classes by gentlemen who wanted their horses ridden in competition. Everyone wanted Linda to ride their horses. I remember she was so busy that one time she pawned a horse onto me. I was scared out of my mind! Linda said, 'Oh, you can do it — you can do it.' And I said, 'I'm not *you!* I rode, but I don't know how I did it without falling on my head."

"When we went to Calgary a couple hundred miles south of Edmonton, there must have been a huge truck to get the horses down there," Linda said. "I remember going down to a ranch outside of Calgary a week ahead of the show. They bred and raised Thoroughbred hunters and jumpers. I spent a week riding their horses then I showed them. Even for our equitation classes, the horses were all new to me. I won many equitation classes on horses I had ridden maybe ten minutes."

"The judges put all the horses and kids through their paces. Then they would bring back the top riders, and of course you were one of them," Diane said to Linda. "I remember watching that judge put you through paces that none of the rest of us knew how to do. Then they made you change horses. And you changed horses with one of the Brand boys who was riding a little Appaloosa/ Quarter Horse. He couldn't handle the horse you were on and you rode his horse like a trooper," Diane boasted of her friend. "I was so proud of you. I remember sitting in the stands thinking this is so awesome because I knew you could ride a strange horse far better than any of the rest of them." In 1953, Linda won the coveted Calgary Herald Equitation Cup for junior riders for the third consecutive year and retired the trophy.

Linda followed with, "Afterwards at the exhibitor party I was offered a job in a big hunter/jumper stable in British Columbia. I was only fifteen at the time so I asked the judge, Mrs. Hall-Holland, about the offer and she said, 'Do not go the professional route; get an education first,' which Linda took as good advice.

Linda and brother Gerry are both using double bridles to ride in the Hunter Hack class they entered together at the Edmonton Spring Horse Show, which lasted nine days.

"One of my favorite memories is prompted by a photograph of my brother Gerry and me at a show all duded up with double bridles. We always rode in the pairs class because Gerry wanted me to ride with him. He'd say, 'You have to be nice to me.' In this particular class his horse was acting up, so in the middle of the class — when the judge's back was turned — we jumped off and exchanged horses," Linda said with a hearty laugh.

The impressive Riding Hoods swept the family class at every horse show, with mom Marion, dad Hoodie and five of their six children. Randy, not pictured, was not yet two-years-old.

"The only time Mum would ride horses was in the Family Class once a year during the nine-day Edmonton Horse Show," remembers Linda. "She'd get on, and then warm up at the walk, trot and canter. She would do that only two times before the class. However, we won the Family Class for four years in a row."

Diane remembers the Family Class with great fondness. "So here's this family, the Riding Hoods, with five kids and two parents. At the most the other families had three members riding. And then came the Riding Hoods. They always won this class – side by side, riding abreast at the walk, trot and canter. Some of the families led the little ones on a lead line, but not the Hoods — they all rode."

"At the Edmonton Spring Horse Show, " Linda recalls, "it was not uncommon for a pleasure class to have sixty riders in it. In the Junior Equitation class, in both Calgary and Edmonton, the top ten riders would be required to change horses. They were often mixed western and English riders and hunter hacks and three-gaited horses. One year when I won I traded with a rider who had a three-gaited Saddlebred mare. That was a bit of a challenge but much fun."

Linda recounts one of her major achievements, "When I retired the Calgary Herald Equitation Trophy after winning it three years in a row, there was a huge celebration. I was supposed to ride in on a horse, with 5,000 people watching in the arena." She was apologetic for the way it turned out, though. "There was a long break before my next class and I walked into the arena wearing a tweed skirt and a conservative jacket, which was far less impressive than being on a horse in riding attire. It was still a great honor to receive this trophy."

And so it began — from clinging to recalcitrant mare Trixie to retiring highly sought-after equitation trophies. Linda's extraordinary life was being carved out in equine form.

CHAPTER 3

WENTWORTH TELLINGTON:
THE MAN BEHIND A GREAT RIDER

While Linda was bringing home armloads of trophies and ribbons from horse shows, also living in Canada at the time was an adventurous native of New Hampshire — Wentworth Jordan Tellington. He was a brilliant student and fortunate enough to attend good schools such as Andover, Harvard University and Norwich University, eventually earning degrees in English Literature and American History as well as a commission in the U.S. Cavalry.

While attending Harvard, Went boxed, played football and was a member of the Reserve Officers' Training Corp (ROTC). The ROTC field artillery unit appealed to him and he found himself riding horses again. In 1935 he discovered polo and played this rousing and demanding sport for two winters.

Went then transferred to Norwich University in Vermont, the official military school of the New England states where young men and horses were trained in a highly-disciplined United States Cavalry horsemanship program. In 1937 — the year Linda was born — he graduated from Norwich and had earned sufficient credentials to become a staff officer at West Point where he taught mechanical engineering and polo. He was the first non-West Point graduate to ever teach as a regular officer there.

Brimming with patriotic pride, Wentworth was perfectly happy to fight for his country but not necessarily as a big risk taker. The Cavalry was the most elite arm of the Army and the ambitious Wentworth strived for placement at the top of the heap. In the fall of 1937, Cavalry school training exercises included riding over various obstacles, as well as jumping over stone walls that dotted the rolling hills of Vermont. Burlap sacks filled with sand and other items were hidden in those walls and part of the exercise was to stab those sacks with a saber as the rider and steed jumped over the walls.

In the evenings Went and fellow students would watch "March of Time" newsreels that depicted Hitler's tanks rolling through the Sudetenland of Czechoslovakia.

Shannon Yewell Weil

The footage showed images of soldiers staring down the barrel of a 90-mm cannon. Went sat in his seat thinking, "Do they really expect me to use my saber against those cannons?" He was considered a rebel when he thought about becoming a tank person, a position that wouldn't afford him a promotion. The men who could promote you were older officers who were also great horsemen, such as General George S. Patton. So Went decided to become the very best horseman he could in order to be recognized for a promotion. When promoted to Major, he had distanced himself even farther away from tanks.

Went reflects his intensive Cavalry background as he demonstrates the Balanced Seat position.

Wentworth became an aide to Colonel John F. Wall, head of the U.S. Cavalry Remount Service, president of the American Horse Racing Association, and author of the classic books, "Judging the Horse" and "Famous Running Horses – Their Forebears and Descendants." Wall was an extremely good judge of horses and was sought after by leading breeders in the Thoroughbred horse racing business in Kentucky, Maryland and Pennsylvania. While Colonel Wall delivered his advice in a low-key manner, Went would stand back, observe and listen intently. After the discussion with the breeder ended, Colonel Wall and Went would continue the conversation wherein Wall would reveal what he really thought about the horse, which is how Went acquired a great deal of his equestrian knowledge. Went considered himself a privileged student.

In 1944 Wentworth co-authored his first book along with Armin Kohl Lobeck, "Military Maps and Air Photographs, Their Use and Interpretation," published by McGraw-Hill. It still comes up in bibliographies as a reference book for locating military sites. During this time Went also rode as a competing military officer at the prestige's horse show at Madison Square Garden in New York City. Somewhere along the way he debuted as a pianist at Carnegie Hall. Went Tellington was indeed the quintessential Renaissance man.

Went combined his knowledge as an engineer and geophysicist while providing the pack horses for exploring for oil in Alberta.

Later in his life, as a Registered Professional Engineer, Went was the Chief Geophysicist for a large consortium of American oil companies that explored the northern part of Canada. Coupled with his horse experience, Went partnered with another man and set up a pack horse outfit that catered to geologists, engineers, and explorers in the oil business. He also led mineral explorations in the rugged far reaches of Canada. They rented out 30 to 40 pack horses at a time and Went was constantly perfecting his eye regarding the finest qualities of horses. So how did this rugged Cavalry-officer-turned-engineer encounter young Linda Hood?

By winning the Knock-Down-and-Out Class on Bouncing Buster, Linda caught the eye of Wentworth Tellington at the Spring Horse Show in Edmonton.

In 1952, on the ninth and final day of the prestigious Spring Horse Show in Edmonton, Alberta, spectator Went Tellington found himself sitting next to Marion Hood, Linda's mum. He was astonished and commented aloud when young teenager Linda won the biggest jumping class of the show. Her precise equitation, matched with her bold and fearless style, smacked of star quality. Quite frankly, Wentworth was instantly smitten. "Oh, that's my daughter!" responded a smiling Mrs. Hood to Went's remarks. Went immediately wanted to meet Linda. Drawing on his U.S. Cavalry training and as a protégé of Colonel Wall, his eye missed nothing as he watched Linda ride. Went knew well the art of excellent horsemanship, which is exactly what he saw in Linda.

"When he first saw me I was catch-riding a horse named Bouncing Buster in a six-foot, 'knock-down-and-out' class," remembers Linda. "The horse's regular rider had broken his arm, so I picked up a ride on Buster and won the Cup that day. If you were a good rider you got lots of horses to ride. Went came to the exhibitors' party and wanted to buy the horse for me because Bouncing Buster was for sale. But I said no, they wanted too much money for him. He wasn't worth the high price so I simply refused to accept his offer."

Hoping to get to know Linda better, Went invited her and her parents for a visit to his home. "At that time, he lived in a beautiful house right along the Edmonton River," reports Linda. "During that visit the conversation turned to the subject of hiring me for the summer. My job would be to take care of the horses at his base camp operation where he led pack trips for oil explorers. He had already hired two Austrian engineers to operate the Magnetometer, a piece of equipment used for oil exploration that measured magnetic fields in the earth and showed where oil might be found in the earth's strata. The Austrians would be performing that job and making the necessary calculations to find the oil. I would simply be looking after the fifteen pack horses that particular summer."

Linda's thoughts drifted back to that visit. "As we sat there I remember shaking as if I knew that meeting Went would have a significant impact on my life's work, whatever that was going to be. I knew at that very moment that this man would change my entire life forever.

"I had a few boyfriends and was going steady at the age of fourteen when I was in the tenth grade. Went was twenty years my senior, so I certainly had no interest in him. That would have been the furthest thing from my mind," Linda laughed.

She had just turned 16 that June and Linda's parents' decision for her to take the job with Went came easily for one simple reason. "I had been at the Calgary Horse Show, another nine-day horse show, where I met a cowboy who was about thirty years old," says Linda. "I was casually watching him work a horse in the afternoon before the show began. After he finished he invited me to go out with him and so I did. Afterwards he wrote me a letter and much to my surprise he asked me to marry him. I had no interest in him whatsoever but my mother got a hold of the letter and read it. She jumped to conclusions and thought I must be secretly interested in this fellow. Suddenly she was very motivated to get me out of town. So by agreeing that I accept the job with Went, it became the perfect solution to get me out of the cowboy's sight for good.

"The base camp that Went had set up was in the Rocky Mountains north of Jasper in Alberta, Canada," remembers Linda. "The two Austrians turned out to be rather irresponsible 'would-be cowboys' and Went ultimately had to fire them. So their jobs fell to me and Went taught me how to work with the Magnetometer searching for oil anomalies." The lucrative operation concentrated on obtaining oil leases and then selling those leases to big oil companies.

Fresh off the racetrack in 1952, Moon King, a grandson of Man O' War, was shipped in a railroad boxcar from Lexington, Kentucky, arriving in Edmonton, much to Linda's delight.

At the end of the summer Linda returned to school and Went finally had an opportunity to purchase a fine horse for her. "In 1954 he had a friend on the east coast go to a Fasig-Tipton Thoroughbred sale in Lexington, Kentucky. The man bought a beautiful, big, six-year-old chestnut stallion named Moon King (1948, Hunters Moon x Somersault) who was a grandson on his dam's side of the great Man O' War. The horse was shipped to Edmonton on a railroad car and when Moon King arrived he had one half of a boxcar all to himself filled with thick bedding," reflects Linda. "His attendant even slept with him in the car while they traveled across the country. He was free to move around and when the door slid open and he was led down the ramp, his coat glistened in the sunshine. He had arrived in wonderful condition. Although Moon King had not been raced, he had already been bred to several mares.

"He took to the show ring brilliantly and turned out to be an amazing stallion. I remember riding him in the Edmonton Horse Show, his first class. He was a spectacular stallion with great conformation and very much resembled the conformation of his grandsire, Man O' War. He was such a gentleman; in our first show we lined up in a pleasure class next to a mare in heat and he just didn't even look at her. I did really well with that horse."

Linda continued to amaze horse show crowds while racking up more blue ribbons and trophies. By the time she was 17 years old, Linda had won the Hudson Bay Challenge Trophy, retired the Calgary Herald Trophy in equitation, and was presented with the award for the zone champion of Canada — among other winnings totaling several hundred. As an equestrian, her future was indeed bright.

Despite the fact that he was 20 years her senior, Went soon realized that he wanted to marry Linda. Her parents finally consented when Linda turned 18. The marriage of Linda Hood and Wentworth Tellington was a merger of two forces of extraordinary talent and knowledge that held great potential. Thinking back to their early meetings, Linda soon knew that Went would have a significant influence on her life. There's no question that he did.

Although lovely, the wedding of Linda Hood and Wentworth Tellington paled in comparison to their accomplishments and talents. Held in a small church on the outskirts of Reno, Nevada where their dear friends, renowned Arabian horse breeders Hadley and Mildred Beedle, were members. Linda's parents, Marion and Hoodie, were present for the ceremony and the Beedles stood up for the bride and groom. Linda said, "I felt beautiful in the most sophisticated dress I'd ever worn, complete with a hat and white gloves." While in Reno, Went mixed in a little business and brokered the sale of a mine. After they were married, the couple left Canada for good.

Shortly after their wedding, in 1956 Linda and Went escaped the harsh winters of Canada and moved to the warm climate of San Juan, Puerto Rico.

By the mid 1950s Linda and Went ventured even farther south to the warm climes of Puerto Rico. Went was drawn to the gentler weather that was kinder to his aching body. Between his athletic endeavors and an accident in Canada that left him with several broken bones, he carried constant pain. "We had a great time in Puerto Rico," Linda remembers. "We lived in San Juan and I worked in the Caribe Hilton Hotel art gallery. Went taught at a bi-lingual school and also worked on some engineering projects."

But while relaxing in the tropical splendor, it wasn't long before Went began reflecting on the outstanding education he had received. He felt a compelling responsibility to give back to a school with a reputation that matched that of Andover. A year later, Wentworth landed a teaching job at the renowned Chadwick School in Rolling Hills, California, and gladly accepted the position because it also was in a warm climate. He was hired to teach mathematics and English at the beautiful eucalyptus-tree-framed campus where the married Tellington couple lived in a whitewashed cottage.

After arriving at Chadwick School in Rolling Hills, California, it didn't take long for animal lovers Linda and Went to acquire Thor, their first Great Dane.

Colonel and Mrs. Chadwick, namesakes of the esteemed school, selected only the best teachers for their staff. "While Wentworth was teaching," Linda said, "I wanted to go to a nearby university after we got settled. That's what my plan was. However, upon our arrival Mrs. Chadwick promptly announced to me that I would be teaching the eighth grade Social Studies class. She also told me that I would be the Girls' Dormitory Mother." Just three years older than the senior students, Linda paid meticulous attention to maintaining respect from the students. She even became a student in several of Wentworth's classes including one on Creative Writing. "I diligently submitted every challenging assignment he asked of the rest of his class," Linda recollects.

Susan Mayo, who now owns Susar Arabians in Denton, Texas, was a young girl when she lived in Rolling Hills, California in 1958. She was not a student at Chadwick, but she rode out of their barn. Susan said, "Linda had several young injured or retired Thoroughbreds off the racetrack that she rehabbed and then sold. My parents purchased a Thoroughbred for me named Rip from Linda and Went. I became Linda's riding student and she taught me how to train Rip." Susan began helping Linda with the horses that came through the barn, and eventually became her assistant. Linda didn't have other students at that time and the only other people she trained for were the Fosters in Rolling Hills who had an Asil Arabian breeding program. "The horse stable soared with activity when the Tellingtons developed and laid the foundation for their horsemanship program," Susan remembers.

There was another student who regularly came to the stable and ultimately played a major role in Linda's life. Linda was impressed with the attractive and charming young man named Roland Kleger, and remembers, "Roland was in his senior year at Chadwick, and a student in Wentworth's English class. It was in this class that Went recommended a book for Roland called "Grass Beyond the Mountains" by Richmond P. Hobson, Jr. that would ultimately help shape his life and lead him to Canada where he wound up owning a ranch in northern British Columbia.

"Roland's interest in horses began because of a football injury," continues Linda. "Since he could no longer play on the Chadwick team he had a yearning to learn to ride. The father of a friend sent a horse for Roland to keep at the Chadwick stable and I became his riding teacher. I was careful not to spend much time with him to prevent talk among students, since there was an unspoken attraction between us that caused some of his classmates to speculate about his interest in riding.

"Looking back it seems strange that I gave Roland rather unorthodox and minimal instruction, starting him off bareback, and sending him out to practice on his own, telling him to let me know when he could stay on bareback at the trot and I would teach him more," smiles Linda. "That may have been an ingenious and intuitive way to teach a young athlete to ride and much to my surprise, in a relatively short time he mastered the art of staying on bareback in the steep landscape above the coast of Rolling Hills, California. He also had a special way with horses and wound up training horses on his ranch in Canada many years later." Little did Linda and Roland know at that time a bright future awaited them, but over four decades would pass until they married in 2000.

CHAPTER 4

THE LURE OF LONG DISTANCE RIDING
BINT GULIDA – "SHE WAS SOME HORSE!"

Long before endurance and competitive trail riding evolved to high-tech status, including cushioned saddles, biothane tack and helmeted, electrolyte-toting riders outfitted in comfortable attire, the fledgling sport witnessed a chestnut Arabian mare named Bint Gulida and world-class rider Linda Tellington traveling the trails in true style and grace.

Went was determined to make a name for *Linda Tellington* in California. His Cavalry-charged background that prepared riders to train and ride over long, rugged distances as swiftly as possible, funneled his team toward endurance riding. "He was the driving factor behind my competitive endurance career," Linda said of their partnership. "Went was a brilliant trainer and I was his rider."

Went's analytical mind was always searching for the very best ways to work with horses, and he transferred that fervor to long distance riding. Went coupled his Cavalry knowledge with experiences developed from the first competitive trail ride in America, pioneered in the 1930s by the Green Mountain Horse Association of South Woodstock, Vermont. That 100-mile ride, rooted in the Cavalry style of riding, took place over a period of three days: 40-, 40- and 20-mile days. Went gleaned every ounce of information he could from that ride, in addition to how the Cavalry managed horses over distance.

As of 1955 there was only a single organized endurance ride in the West, the Western States 100-Mile One-Day Trail Ride over the rugged Sierra Nevada mountains. This challenging event quickly caught the attention of the Tellingtons.

Went's expert U.S. Cavalry Horsemanship training methods — where the principle objective was to train riders and horses to travel great distances over difficult terrain for long periods of time — would certainly suit the sport of endurance riding. He was confident that training for and competing in endurance riding would be an ideal way for Linda to make a name for herself. So now the 100-mile ride from Tahoe City to Auburn, California was on their radar, viewed with full-on enthusiasm.

The story of how Linda and Went found the exceptional endurance mare Bint Gulida leads us on a journey of two 100-mile trails with the Tellingtons, one in California and one in Oklahoma.

In 1959, Linda already had several horses in her training program but none seemed capable of withstanding the rigors of serious long distance riding. Now all she needed was the right horse.

Pursuit was under way to find the ideal endurance horse. After poring over pedigrees and scouring advertisements in Arabian horse magazines, Went and Linda settled on bloodlines offered by one of America's original Arabian breeders, Dr. John L. and Ellen C. Doyle of Sigourney, Iowa. After an extensive exchange of letters and phone calls with the Doyles, the Tellingtons set out from California with horse trailer in tow for the long drive. When they finally arrived, they found a typical Midwestern breeding farm. "It was not a showy place," said Linda. "But the Doyles were very hospitable people. They brought out several three-year-old horses to show us, including a chestnut filly. She had a white blaze, white splashes on her legs, alert ears and a wide observant eye." This was the soon-to-become-famous Bint Gulida. "She had only been haltered once or twice," said Linda, remembering how closely they inspected the skittish filly.

"Well, she was some horse!" was the phrase Went used when describing the Arabian mare Bint Gulida.

When asked what made her pick Bint Gulida, Linda paused for a moment and said, "That's a good question." After another pause she continued, "Only Went could answer that question." Since Went passed away in 2000, we are fortunate that he left the details in an interview with *Anvil Magazine* editor Rob Edwards of Georgetown, California that described why the Tellingtons chose the skittish, unhandled chestnut filly with such a magnetic presence.

"Well, she was *some* horse!" Wentworth exclaimed.

He continued: "She was a very well-built animal. She had a fantastic barrel; her flank area measured 3" greater than the heart girth, gifting her with great lung capacity. She had, as Arabian horse authority W. R. Brown would say, 'a roomy middle,' and she was very well let down. Her knees and hocks were close to the ground, so she had short cannon bones and good, clean, long muscles in the forearms and in the gaskin area. She had a powerful body, and her forearms moved a very light load below the knees. And it was of good leverage because it was closer to the ground. With a horse whose knees are too high, you've got poor leverage and not as much muscle to move a lot more weight. So structurally that was a good thing about her. She was an extremely well-balanced horse fore and aft. She didn't have too long or too short a neck. She had one of the loosest gullets of any animal I've ever touched. You could manipulate her gullet even when she was nervous, and it was always a shakable gullet.

"She had a big spread between the jaws so she had no trouble breathing. And she had a well-set tail. A horse whose anus is too far forward is not a good prospect. It's more important even than a slope of the shoulder. The slope of the shoulder is a critical thing, however. The line of her shoulder was perpendicular to the slope of her ilium — just ideal. All those things were great physical attributes. She had only been handled enough to halter break her and have her feet taken care of."

Went elaborated on his research of Bint Gulida's bloodlines. "She was a W. R. Brown type that had been chosen by Carl Raswan who was the guru of Arabian horses for decades. W. R. Brown formed the Arabian Horse Registry in 1908 and had some wonderful horses. He did promotional racing with the United States Army from the Third Cavalry Regimental Headquarters outside of Burlington, Vermont, to the Washington Monument. W. R. Brown's good gelding, Crabbet, won this 300-mile race every time. Bint Gulida was the granddaughter of Gulastra, Brown's most famous stallion. I took all that into consideration, but I picked her as a specimen on her own. She was an Egyptian Arabian horse with the highest possible qualities." Went ended his comments by saying, "However, I wouldn't pick an Egyptian-Arabian just because it was an Egyptian-Arabian."

Bint Gulida was born 24 September 1956. Her sire was Ghadaf and she was out of the dam Gulida, who was by Gulastra of the Saklawi Jedran Ibn Sudan strain. Bint Gulida's pedigree traced back to excellent lineage. She had a straight Egyptian lineage from the Crabbet Stud in Sussex, England where in 1878 Wilfred and Lady Anne Blunt imported the first Arabian horses to England. Their daughter, Lady Wentworth, who carried forward the huge success of this magnificent breeding operation, continued the iconic history. Wilfred and Lady Anne Blunt founded the Sheykh Obeyd Stud, just outside of Cairo, Egypt, where half of the horses were kept. However, many of the best ones were shipped to the Crabbet Stud in England, a farm that had been in Wilfred Blunt's family for generations.

Bint Gulida's bloodlines are savored in Al Khamsa, Inc., an organization devoted to the preservation of the Bedouin Arabian horses bred by nomadic horse breeding tribes of the desert. Her pedigree is described by these terms as well: Asil (which means pure), Blue List (an 'A List' originally published in 1952 by Miss Jane Llewellyn Ott as a catalog of horses proven to trace in every line directly to the Bedouin-bred horses of the desert), Doyle (we've already met the Doyles), and Heirloom (Egyptian Arabian horses, which descend entirely from the Al Khamsa Foundation Horses and their predecessors exported from the ancient region known as Arabia Deserta before 1914 that figure in the pedigrees of the Root Mares and Root Stallions of the Royal Agricultural Society preservation breeding program).

It was apparent that Bint Gulida was definitely built for endurance and she was about to belong to Linda Tellington.

The young filly had never been in a horse trailer and much to Linda's dismay was tranquilized in order to load her. When she and Went reached a gas station to give the filly her first rest, Gulida stepped out of the trailer, staggered and fell down. Linda recalled, "The effects of the tranquilizer had caused such an adverse effect on the horse that she overheated and had a temperature of 108 degrees," Linda said. "While she laid on the ground in distress, we hosed her off for more than an hour until she was ready to get up. After she recovered, we put her back in into the trailer and continued on our drive.

"We brought her back to Chadwick and just observed her for a few weeks. Despite her feisty behavior, I was determined to ride her but Went doubted that I would ever be able to get on her back because she was so reactive," Linda says. "So I just started ground driving her a little more every day, then slowly I started getting on her bareback." Linda remembers from over four decades ago, "I had read that American Indians would break their horses at night in the moonlight, so I waited until after sundown to ride her and soon I was riding her bareback in the dark. I truly believe Gulida tuned into me quickly because of the night riding." And that's how the duo ultimately solidified their bond.

Susan Mayo has fond memories of this pair. "What I remember most about Linda and Gulida is how much alike they were. Gulida was a powerhouse with huge quarters and incredible drive." Although only measuring 5'4", "Linda was equally powerful."

Bint Gulida, who stood 14.3 hands tall, continued to challenge Linda — who had trained and ridden hundreds of horses by this time. "If anything was out of sorts, Gulida would pick up on it immediately; I really had to pay attention to her and keep my own emotions in check. She didn't miss a thing. Any horse will mirror you and reflect how you are feeling, so I paid close attention to how I felt while around her."

Linda spoke about an age-old wisdom about training. "I was once told that if you lose your temper with a horse, put the horse back in the barn and return to it when you have calmed down." As Linda cultivated her own methods, she moved past that approach. "That seemed like sensible advice at the time, but thanks to the method I've had the good fortune to develop over the past 50 years, there is never a reason to lose my temper. If I had lost my temper with Bint Gulida she would have been a basket case of uncontrolled nerves. When I think back, I believe she was responsible for me learning to control my emotions," Linda admitted.

"One moonlit night while at Chadwick School, at 2 a.m. I was awakened by a neighbor calling to let us know that four or five horses had escaped from their pasture and had gone on walk-about," Linda smiled. "Fortunately for me, Bint Gulida was stabled that night so I went to get her to round up the horses. I was half asleep and without thinking I hopped on her bareback and headed down the road to find the fugitives." Linda had only been riding the mare for less than a month at that time and had forgotten that Gulida had never been ridden bareback outside of the paddock. "As I headed out I was not in a good mood, slightly ticked off that I had to leave my cozy bed. But it only took me a couple of minutes to realize Gulida was upset by my attitude," Linda said. "I got it! Then I realized I'd better calm down and tune into her. I did this by quieting my breathing and totally changing my mind to one of gratitude for being out on this magical moonlit night on my sweet horse. It worked. She calmed down in a minute or less and we had a great time. That was a turn-around moment in my relationship with her."

*Linda riding her champion mare, Bint Gulida, striking a long trot
over the terrain of Rolling Hills.*

Once Linda began riding Bint Gulida regularly around the knolls of Rolling
Hills, Went implemented his regimented interval-training program of five days
a week with two days off. He was always testing endurance horses to see if they
were worthy of Cavalry standards. One day would be spent cantering for 10
miles, the next trotting for 20 miles. Observant of the tiniest bits of minutiae,
Went noted, "We believe sweat should be watery and not sticky. It should be
clear and not white or lathery looking."

"You know, she never had an unsound day; she was amazing," Linda remembers
of Bint Gulida. While conditioning Gulida on Went's aggressive training
program, "It was very difficult to tire her out," Susan Mayo remembered. "We
used to work her in plowed fields up above the Chadwick School." Everyone
agreed that Bint Gulida was a strong horse, not very friendly towards people and

preferred to be left out in the elements year round. However, she did have many equine friends over the years. "She adored a mare named Urdaneta and the two were inseparable," said Susan.

As with all her horses, Linda liked to have other people ride them to broaden their experience. Another lucky Pony Club student, and ultimately a Tevis Cup Ride finisher, Martha Merriam of Loomis, California said, "I remember Bint Gulida very well and what a blast she was to ride. Riding her was like riding a small locomotive with lots of thick Arabian mane to hold onto. She was very round, and very responsive. To me she was the epitome of an Arabian mare." Rho Bailey, who now lives in Cool, California and was one of Linda's early riding students, added that it was simply an honor to have known Bint Gulida.

"Gulida was charged with energy," Linda smiles, and in thinking about grooming her, "she had some challenging habits. One was her resistance to having the whiskers around her mouth trimmed. She acted as thought she got a shock every time a whisker was cut. She loved being outside, no matter what — storms and everything else." Linda continued to herald this special horse's greatness by stating, "She was one of the smartest horses I've ever had and certainly the most responsive."

Linda's reputation as a successful horse trainer grew widespread and she began attracting the attention of prominent Arabian horse breeders of the caliber of Patricia "Tish" Hewitt of Friendship Farms in Illinois and John Rogers of Walnut Creek, California, who in 1954 imported the great stallion *Serafix from the Crabbet Stud in England. Mrs. John Ekern Ott also sent her Al Khamsa Arabian stallion Lothar to Linda's stable for training and breeding. Bazy Tankersley sent them Al-Marah Rainbow, a six-year-old mare that had been sent back to the pasture after she reacted poorly to any training at their farm.

"I have found that some of the hardest horses to initially connect with turn out to be the best ones in the end," Linda points out, reflecting on the difficulties she encountered with some of these horses.

Linda and Bint Gulida progressed rapidly and the memory evoked an image of their bond: "Riding Gulida I sometimes felt like a Centaur." Of all the exceptional horses Linda has ridden none of them compare to Bint Gulida. "She really took care of me. I never questioned her judgment; we had a very special trust and she was so much more than a horse," Linda professed. "I loved her intense curiosity and she always wanted to know what's over the next hill. It was a great feeling to always be in tune with her."

CHAPTER 5

A TEACHING JOURNEY
THAT BEGAN AT CHADWICK SCHOOL

"During the years that I taught at Chadwick, in 1960 I also became an instructor in the U.S. Pony Club," Linda started out. "It's a voluntary position within an international organization founded in England to prepare young riders to become Olympic riders. My District Commissioner was a man named Colonel W. R. 'Pinky' Brown who was instrumental in bringing this horsemanship program to America."

Soon Colonel Brown recognized the gifted and bright young woman he oversaw in his district. "After about a year as a Pony Club instructor," comments Linda, "I was rewarded for the job I was doing and received a very honorable recommendation from Colonel Brown. It was an invitation to a 10-day training with the renowned Captain Marsden at Camp Teela-Wooket for the U.S. Pony Club's Certification Riding Instructors Program in Jefferson, Vermont." Not only was Linda the only instructor in the class selected from the West Coast, she was also given a scholarship to attend the program.

The Tellingtons' trip to the training in Vermont had multiple purposes. After she returned home to Rolling Hills, Linda typed a single-spaced letter to her family telling them about the journey.

Their brand new custom four-horse trailer stood up to the Tellingtons' rigorous standards as they hauled horses to the east coast and back to California.

Shannon Yewell Weil

Excerpts from that September 23, 1960 letter read...

Dear Mum, Dad, Gerry, Susan, John, Robyn and Randy,

"We had a beautiful four-horse trailer made to haul horses. It had 7-foot ceilings, a dressing room and all the conveniences possible. We got a very good deal on it and this is the first 4-horse trailer this trailer company had made. So we got it at cost with the understanding that they could examine it and make any changes they wanted to and then we would make another trip with it. It was guaranteed trouble free for 10,000 miles; we've now been 24,000 miles. The manufacturer rode along with us to Colorado Springs on our first trip to check it out but we didn't have one bit of trouble even though it had not been road tested. They painted it until 3:00 a.m. and we left at 4:00 a.m. Monday.

"We hauled four horses east on that trip. We took Betsy, our Thoroughbred mare to be bred, and left her in Colorado Springs on a ranch. Rip, Susan Mayo's horse, was to go to Washington, D.C. where they had moved, and we hauled a yearling Arab to be delivered to Ohio. We also hauled a horse to Portland, Maine for Bette Davis, the movie star. The horse actually belonged to her daughter, Barbara, who was one of my riding students at Chadwick. We drove straight through to Colorado Springs and lay over at the ranch for a day and then we left there at noon and arrived in Ohio at 4:00 p.m. to leave the Arabian.

"And then we drove through the night and arrived in Washington D.C. the following morning. We left Rip and headed for northern Vermont where the Pony Club Instructors School started on Monday morning. We had car trouble on the through-way and had to stop at a motel and leave Sally, Bette Davis's horse, in the trailer. I unloaded her and exercised her while Went had the car fixed. We were on our way by noon.

"We drove through Sunday night and arrived by Monday afternoon. The course was marvelous. I was on a scholarship and the only one from the West. There were 30 instructors in all; our teachers were all very well known. They did a very good job. I wish someone in Edmonton would start a Pony Club.

"We left the camp Sunday afternoon and drove over to Went's father's house in New Hampshire. We stayed overnight there and after visiting with him until the following afternoon we drove on to Portland to deliver Sally. We arrived after dark and then stopped at a motel and spent the night there. Then we spent the next day on the back roads through New Hampshire and stopped at nearly every antique shop we saw. We found a lovely little copper Arab for $3, an old sidesaddle, which is terribly uncomfortable, for $10, and an old spinning wheel, which was exactly what I wanted.

"We headed down to Virginia to get five Welsh ponies for someone in California. It took us a whole day to get them, as they were at three different farms about 50 miles apart. At the last farm we stayed overnight. They had 200 ponies and a gorgeous old house with all the original furniture from the 19th century. Half their children and sons- and daughters-in-law lived with them. We had a very nice visit there.

"We then headed west and had our first stop at Sigourney, Iowa where we had an Arabian horse lined up to look at. We were crazy about one four-year-old mare but Mrs. Doyle (she and her husband had sold us Bint Gulida), who owned the mare and about 16 other horses, had been widowed for three years and she and her husband had never sold any of their foundation stock. There wasn't much chance of getting the mare. The price was $4,000 but she had sold this mare once before and when the people came to get her, Mrs. Doyle had given back their cheque. We didn't have much hope and didn't get her.

"We drove to Des Moines that afternoon and found a yearling filly that we bought for ourselves for $800. We were just crazy about this filly and felt very lucky. The average price for this filly out here would be from $1,500 to $2,500. We squashed her in with the other five ponies in the trailer and were on our way. Actually they weren't crowded as each stall is 101 inches long, longer than the average, so we opened the doors between the front and the back and put three horses on a side with partitions between them. There was enough room so that the ponies could even lie down.

"Then we drove through Estes Park, Colorado and let the horses rest there while we watched a day of the International Arabian Horse Show. We arrived when they were judging for the champion mare and stallion of the country. Each class had almost 20 horses, each of which had qualified to compete, and each class took almost four hours to judge. There were three judges; each one judged separately then all the scores were added and averaged and the horse with the highest score won.

"We had planned to head straight west from Estes Park over Highway 40 but were warned against it since we were pulling four tons with the Chevy Nomad. We almost didn't make it up to Estes Park and there were steeper grades ahead. At one point on the road to the Park we were going 10 mph and were heating up. So we turned around and came west through Cheyenne, Wyoming, which is Highway 30.

"We drove through Reno and stayed with Hadley and Mildred Beedle overnight and got to Donner Pass at 4:00 p.m. and had to pull over because the car was functioning so poorly and boiling over continuously. We dropped the ponies off at 1:00 p.m. (Friday) and headed home. The ponies were left at San Francisco and we drove the rest of the day and arrived home at 7:00 p.m. The car gave out at Redondo Beach but we stopped in a garage and got it going well enough to limp the few miles home."

Love, Linda & Went

P.S. When we were driving non-stop one of us slept while the other one drove. We did this all night.

Linda elaborated on the 10-day Pony Club training course she attended by saying, "We learned classical horsemanship and rode at least twice every day. We practiced our equitation in quadrille formation, which led to precision riding. There were ten or twelve horses in a class and we could easily be broken down into pairs or sets of three or four horses. We had to keep our horses one length apart at all times. The instructor would issue a command by saying 'Walk – HOooo!' It was difficult because all the horses were hard-mouthed and ridden in snaffle bits. Trying to keep your horse back off another horse's tail was so exhausting, and hard on both the horse and rider." Linda learned a good lesson from that experience and applied it to her own approach to teaching. She went on to say, "That made me realize at Chadwick that if I allowed a student to ride a horse that they didn't get along with, they had to fight with it. That's also why we used Pelham bits if a horse needed one. But the majority of my school horses were ridden in snaffle bits because they were light-mouthed."

Linda taught the Rolling Hills Pony Club after she had earned her Instructor's Certification.

Now equipped with her new Pony Club Instructor's credential, coupled with the knowledge she learned from her first riding instructor, Alice Greaves, Linda developed her own unique broad spectrum of horsemanship. The Pony Club at Chadwick School kicked into high gear, drawing on young Palos Verdes Peninsula area horses and riders, among them horse-crazy Martha Merriam.

In the back of her mind, Linda dreamed that one day she would have her own school of horsemanship and with Wentworth's help, she knew it was possible.

CHAPTER 6

ONWARD AND UPWARD:
THOROUGHBRED BREEDING FARM
AND GEMS OF GYPSY WISDOM

In 1960 the Tellingtons moved to the largely agricultural area of Hemet in the San Jacinto Valley in California's Riverside County. I knew about fragments of this part of Linda's life, but I wanted to fully understand why she and Went moved to the Hemet Thoroughbred Farm.

Students who came from affluent families surrounded the Tellingtons and one student's father, a Hollywood businessman, approached Linda and Went about forming a partnership in his aspiring Thoroughbred horseracing business. He yearned to have the horses he bred race under his name but he didn't know anything about them. "He would provide the financial backing to purchase a farm if we would manage it for him," Linda said. "We agreed and left Chadwick."

The Tellingtons moved to the Hemet Thoroughbred Farm on Esplanade Avenue where they oversaw 80 mares and two stallions. "We also had an Arabian horse operation called Banat Ar-Rih (Daughter of the Wind) Ranch with twenty Arabian mares and two stallions," Linda points out. "One Arabian stallion, Lothar, by *Fadl out of Habba, who belonged to Mrs. John Ekern Ott, also stood at this ranch."

Linda described the situation in Hemet by saying, "This agreement with the Hollywood businessman only lasted for a couple of years. Actually the rub came from the fact that he insisted on going to the Thoroughbred sales with us to buy horses. This was awkward for us because he lacked the knowledge about bloodlines and horses in general that was required to build a solid racing herd and business." However, the period of time spent in Hemet proved to be very productive for the Tellingtons.

Linda is obviously enjoying Arabian stallion Lothar while galloping across Hemet's sandy terrain.

Linda earned the reputation of being "tough as a boiled owl" when this Thoroughbred stallion, Fault Free, reared straight up in the air the first time she mounted him. In typical Linda Tellington style, the horse quickly learned to trust her.

"We bought a bay Thoroughbred horse named Fault Free as a breeding stallion," remembers Linda. When the horse was delivered Linda unloaded him from the trailer, saddled him up and climbed on. The horse proceeded to rear straight up but Linda stayed on him as if glued to the saddle. After quietly listening to the horse and putting a gentle hand on him, the stallion responded to her. He began to settle down and followed her commands, and soon Linda was riding him in a relaxed frame around the arena. Mrs. Jackson, a visiting Arabian horse breeder, commented after watching this dramatic display, "That Linda — she's as tough as a boiled owl!"

A Grandfather's Wisdom: Horseman Will Caywood

Until this time Linda had never met her maternal grandfather, Will Caywood, and yet he was to become a major influence on her life's work. Now that he was in his 80s and retired from his winning career as a Thoroughbred racehorse trainer, he contacted Linda and Went and they invited him to relocate from the Hialeah Race Track in Florida and to live with them in Hemet. It was here he shared his 50+ years of secret equine remedies and massage methods, which he had learned from Gypsies around the racetracks in Russia. He had also gleaned knowledge from the Gypsies about assessing a horse's personality according to swirls and the shape of the horse's ears, nostrils, and lips, among other physical attributes. He credited his success of 87 winning Thoroughbreds to these practices, and was crowned 1905 Trainer of the Year at the Hippodrome, Russia's largest racetrack in Moscow. Linda hung onto every word her grandfather imparted; in 1960 massage became a significant component of Linda's work with horses, the first of three steps which ultimately evolved into the internationally acclaimed Tellington TTouch® Training Method.

Will Caywood was a very small, yet bold, rider who possessed a natural talent with horses. He began riding racehorses in county fairs in Iowa as a teenager. It was at one such race that young Will's ability caught the eye of a wealthy man, who saw in him the making of a great rider. He convinced Will's parents that it would be a good idea to take the boy to Chicago, Illinois as his protégé, where he would have many more opportunities than in Iowa. The man said, "Will might even become famous!"

And indeed Will Caywood did become famous. He was a leading jockey in the U.S. for eight years in the golden era before World War I. Many of his greatest runs were at the glamorous turn-of-the-century City Park Race Track in New Orleans, Louisiana.

Linda's grandfather, Thoroughbred trainer Will Caywood, peeks under the horse's neck in the winning photo when his horse Night Tour won the one-mile race at Bay Meadows, California on December 6th, 1947.

Will was relatively unprepared to take on an assignment that kept him traveling for several years throughout Europe. He knew no foreign language and so little geography that he confessed years later that at the time he could not actually visualize in his mind where Russia was. Fortunately for him, he was provided with a Gypsy guide and interpreter who accompanied him everywhere. The Gypsy, "Orlo," was a big man, about 6'1" and weighing around 190 pounds. He could speak several languages fluently and was well acquainted with horses, having worked for many years around Russian racetracks.

Linda comments on this Russian connection in her family: "As a visiting American to Russia in the 1980s I was enthusiastically received by the directors of the Moscow Hippodrome and the racetrack in Krasnodor, where I gave several demonstrations of Tellington TTouch. It was interesting to discover that the most experienced and successful horse people were Gypsies. It's fascinating to consider the influence on my work of that original Gypsy equine massage and how it inspired me to conduct a study of the swirl patterns on the heads of 1,500 horses."

American jockey and trainer Will Caywood and the big Russian Gypsy Orlo, though incongruous in size, found working together very congenial — in fact, they became fast friends. Their friendship lasted right up to the time when Will had to flee Poland just before World War I rather than risk becoming a German prisoner of war or remaining in the Czar's sphere of activity just as the Red Russians were on the verge of wresting the reins of power from the aristocracy.

The parting was hurried; Will was concealed in a boxcar with some horses and shipped to France. Will was such a poor letter writer that he lost track of Gypsy Orlo, never learning whether or not he had lived through World War I. Recalling the many close scrapes his cohort had already encountered, Will said of him, "The Gypsy could probably survive anything but a direct hit." Now, however, the vicarious Orlo, source of much valued information, was long since gone. Only the magic of Will's fingers in appraising a horse's legs and the touch of his healing hand proved the value of the knowledge gleaned from the Gypsy culture that Will so admired.

Will Caywood was not just some old-time horseman who decided to tell the Tellingtons everything he knew. He would probably have taken his secrets to the grave except for the fact that he was the grandfather of Linda Tellington, whose early climb up the ladder of success with horses inspired him to pass on his knowledge. After all, this information was his granddaughter's rightful heritage.

As an interested horseman and a trained engineer, Went Tellington recognized the inspiring quality of Will Caywood's knowledge. Went was anxious to organize that information into a body of systematic material, study it in an efficient way, test it as thoroughly as possible and evolve it into a "discipline."

Went dropped everything when Will, then an old but very agile man of 80, was in the mood to talk or demonstrate how to do something. Will was very patient as Went honed in to be sure he understood certain details and then make copious notes. Went also had to be a patient listener — waiting for the gems of Will's wisdom, scantily interspersed through hours and hours of fascinating reminiscence. Eventually the full scope of the Gypsy teachings (including physical therapy for horses), as interpreted through Will's long years of experience, was chronicled.

Linda said, "We gratefully acknowledge the detailed, patient, guru-like influence of my grandfather Will Caywood, giving us the benefit of his uncommon skill with, and understanding of, horses." She well understood the importance of massage as her grandfather had passed down from the Gypsies; it developed into a significant component of Linda's work with horses and became the foundation for the Tellington book, "Physical Therapy for the Athletic Horse."

"Those were the days when nobody talked about their training secrets. Grandfather

Will kept his secrets to himself until he shared them with us — those secrets were critical to his livelihood. But Went made the decision to share them because Will was retiring and there was no need to protect those secrets anymore."

"When my grandfather revealed his racetrack secrets to us, Went made a commitment to share that knowledge. People commented that it was so wonderful that we shared our information — and why wouldn't we? That's how I was brought up," smiles Linda.

Another student of Tellington methods and philosophy was Roland Kleger, who also basked in the wisdom of Linda's grandfather. "After graduating from Chadwick in 1958, Roland attended the University of California at Pomona while studying agriculture," remembers Linda. "Now that we were living in Hemet, which was only about an hour away, Roland spent many weekends over the winter of 1960 at our ranch to learn more about horse management. Our Guardian Angels must have been planning for the future because Roland actually spent much time with my grandfather. Roland took the opportunity to soak up his wisdom, spending many hours in the stable with grandfather Will."

"He was such a gentle man around the horse," Roland recalls. "If a horse was afraid of him, he would just be quiet and take the necessary time to introduce the horse to a bridle or whatever training step he was working on. Or often he would sit and clean a bridle nearby without ever paying any attention to the horse. Ultimately the horse would demand his attention and the bond would be struck. He was so patient and it was always a pleasure to watch him around the horses."

Will Caywood attributed his success to two factors: First, every racehorse in his training stable was 'rubbed' with a Gypsy form of equine massage for 30 minutes a day. "We began using this form of massage for our competition horses in 1960," remembers Linda, "and I am certain this had a major influence on the performance of my mare, Bint Gulida, when we set an endurance world record that held for seven years in the Oklahoma 100 Miles-in-One-Day Jim Shoulders Endurance Ride in 1961. Bint Gulida won first place and Best Condition.

Second, "My grandfather also said he entered a horse in a race only when 'it told him it was feeling fit enough to win.' He clearly had a special connection with his horses," Linda said.

Fruit does not fall far from the tree in Linda's family. Will Caywood's gifts with horses were clearly passed on to his granddaughter. Linda's strong work ethic, coupled with her remarkable talent, swiftly bolstered her reputation throughout the equine community for successfully training difficult horses.

CHAPTER 7

Thousands of Miles in the Saddle:
Linda's Endurance Experiences

Went and Linda had dedicated months of training for endurance riding in the year 1961. Linda was aiming for her first attempt at the Western States 100-Mile One-Day Trail Ride – now known as the 'Tevis Cup Ride' or just the 'Tevis.' Whatever it is called, one thing is certain — its extraordinary reputation has never waned.

Linda spent hours riding Bint Gulida on the trails surrounding the Hemet area. I remember hearing a story at the Research Farm about Linda coming back from a long ride on Bint Gulida to find Wentworth lounging by the swimming pool. He checked the vital signs on their carefully-selected chestnut mare and noted that she wasn't even tired. Went would say, "Give her another ten miles or so," and off rode Linda again in the Southern California heat.

Long before the area around Hemet was developed Linda could ride out from the Hemet Thoroughbred Farm to train Bint Gulida.

Then the time arrived to drive north to Auburn, California for the final preparations before the Tevis, the grueling competition over the Sierra Nevada mountain range. The ride was founded in 1955 by modern-day pioneer Wendell T. Robie, who once declared, "The Tevis Cup is very slippery and hard to win."

Linda has fond memories of Wendell. "I remember him as a pioneer. He always looked very sporty, as if he were a horse — his ears would be pricked up and headed down the trail. He had a very balanced physique, rather a small stature but a huge presence. Very focused. I feel like he's here with us now. He was godfather of the Tevis Cup Ride, even though Lloyd Tevis' name is on the winning trophy. I think about all the time and effort he put into the Ride. And when I visit the Sierra Nevada foothills, it's a real pleasure to be close to the Tevis Trail again."

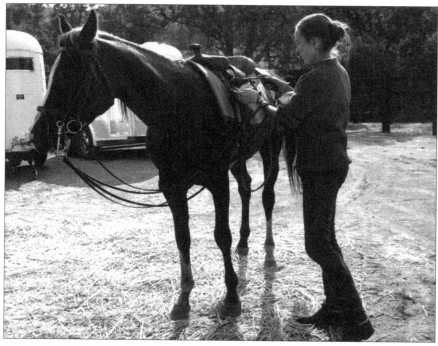

Linda and Bint Gulida spent a week in the Auburn area prior to her first Tevis Cup Ride to become familiar with the Western States Trail.

As with most riders in those days, Linda spent a week in the Auburn area prior to the ride. "While practicing for the Tevis, I slept on the ground in the paddock I'd created by my trailer. One night, Bint Gulida actually laid down beside me to sleep," Linda fondly remembers. "It seems like yesterday to me." Then on another morning while Linda was sleeping, Bint Gulida decided to take herself for a walk and ducked under the corral rope to investigate the area. Linda woke up, called the mare and she came right back to camp.

Other memories abound of Bint Gulida taking herself for a stroll. "On another afternoon we were camped near Foresthill on the Tevis Trail where I had parked our big five-horse van in a clearing. I started to walk to town to get some food. I glanced over my shoulder and Gulida had caught up with me. She just wanted to go along and be with me. Her intelligence was exceptional and she became very sociable. I never spoke loudly to her and wouldn't have dreamed of punishing her because she was so sensitive."

Prior to the start of the 1964 Tevis Cup Ride, at the original base camp at Tahoe City, Linda spent time chatting with Wendell Robie next to his horse Timour, a half-Arabian gelding.

Linda reflected fondly on the magical history of Wendell Robie and all the Tevis riders and horses that have crossed the Sierra Nevada range throughout the years. "Phil Gardner, Hal Hall, Kerry Ridgway DVM, Wingate "Winkie" Mackay-Smith, Matthew Mackay-Smith DVM, Julie and Bob Suhr, their daughter Barbara White, Ernie Sanchez, Ed Johnson, Pat and Donna Fitzgerald — all the riders who have been associated with the Tevis for years have life chapters carved on this trail. The Trail rings of memories of those who have developed the Ride; the history of this original Emigrant Trail; the spirits of the Native Americans, pioneers, gold miners, horses, mules, donkeys and riders who still linger out there on the trail; the gold hauled out of its mines, rivers, creeks and crevasses. The Trail tells of fortunes made and lost in the towns of Last Chance, Deadwood, Michigan Bluff and Foresthill — towns that are now silent. This is what makes the Western States 100-Mile One-Day Ride — the Tevis Cup Ride — so alluring, so provocative and today keeps calling people to test their own grit and put their toe on the starting line."

Arriving at Robinson Flat during the 1961 Tevis Cup Ride, Linda and Bint Gulida are looking fresh.

58

Robinson Flat – circa 1960s

In the serene mountain meadow known as Robinson Flat, Tevis riders take a respite at the mandatory one-hour vet check.

On July 29th, 1961, the Tevis Cup started 45 riders, 28 of whom crossed the finish line within 24 hours. It was the first 100-mile ride for both Linda (rider #26) and her five-year-old, 920-pound mare, Bint Gulida. They finished in 6th place. Drucilla Barner, first woman to win the Tevis Cup, captured the award on her 3/4 Arabian gelding Chagitai. There was no Haggin Cup for Best Condition; it was not awarded until 1964. Once forbidden to ride the 100 miles, women obviously perform well in endurance riding and now dominate the sport.

The Jim Shoulders 100 Mile Ride – September 9th, 1961

Student Susan Mayo joined the Tellingtons to help crew on Linda's next endurance ride. They loaded Bint Gulida in the trailer and headed to Moore, Oklahoma. They arrived about 10 days early to prepare for the 100-Miles in One Day Jim Shoulders Endurance Ride, named for the legendary cowboy who dominated the sport of rodeo during the 1950s and had won 16 world titles.

Even though it may sound like status quo to endurance riders today, in 1961 it was unheard of to put a horse through two 100-mile rides in a season, much less within two months of each other. Linda and Bint Gulida did it with grace and success. Yet again, Linda set a precedent in endurance riding.

"When we arrived in Oklahoma ten days prior to the Jim Shoulders Ride, I turned down numerous hospitable offers of stall accommodations for Bint Gulida," Linda remembers. She found the ideal place for her independent mare in a ten-acre pasture scattered with a few calves seven miles from the starting line. "Some of the local people were puzzled by this decision, but it was the best accommodation for Gulida who felt relaxed and happy with our choice," Linda recalled.

To get the lay of the land, Linda pre-rode much of the trail on Gulida. Linda and Went also drove the trail in a Jeep a few days before the ride. They made detailed notes on yellow 3x5 index cards that Linda carried with her on the ride to help stay on pace and to identify all the turns. Nothing was left to chance and the preparation proved beneficial.

The ride started at 2:00 p.m., theoretically to avoid the Oklahoma heat. With a hatless head, a white blouse and riding pants, Linda rode her mare in a McClellan saddle. PCERF student Susan Mayo vividly recalls, "I remember the pit stops and the fact that Linda and Gulida were in remarkable shape and not really showing the strain of the ride at all."

Linda and Bint Gulida finishing the 1961 100-mile Jim Shoulders Ride in Moore, Oklahoma, setting a record riding time of 13 hours 36 minutes as Went crews for her.

As evening fell, a critical factor loomed over ride management: The date had been chosen based on the thought that it was on the night of the full moon, but the date actually was on the dark of the moon. Many riders were at the mercy of a pitch-black night and got lost on the trail. The index cards tucked in Linda's pocket kept her locked into her riding plan. "By the time the morning light broke, I had ridden ninety-four miles. I was tired and sleepy and I knew we were far ahead of everyone else so I just walked Bint Gulida the last six miles to the finish line." Had they trotted they would have shaved even more time off their impressive record. Linda and Gulida cleaved a five-and-a-half-hour gap before the second place horse and rider crossed the finish line. The total elapsed time for the winning pair was 16 hours and 36 minutes; riding time was 13:36. Bint Gulida was declared to be in better condition than any other horse in the contest, "ready to go on," and captured the Best Condition award.

In the Tellingtons' 1967 book, "Endurance and Competitive Trail Riding Manual," the first on long distance trail riding, it reads: "Finishing in good form, Linda's position on Bint Gulida is erect. Bint Gulida's stride is smooth, long and efficient as she takes the final step crossing the finish line in a winning time and winning the best condition award too. The second place horse arrived five-and-one-half hours behind Bint Gulida. This horse and rider, although not as well prepared, finished on sheer courage."

"I remember the finish and that both Linda and Gulida seemed like they could continue on with no effort," Susan reminisces. Linda modestly insists, "I won by so many hours because the other riders got lost." However, conventional wisdom dictates that she was simply riding the most superior horse that day and that her strategic planning, aptly headed by former Cavalry officer Went Tellington, had paid off.

Linda's record time of winning both first place and best condition on the Jim Shoulders Ride stood until seven years later when the legendary Pat Fitzgerald of Reno, Nevada set a new record.

In her 1969 revered book, "The Arabian War Horse to Show Horse," noted Arabian horse expert Gladys Brown Edwards cites Bint Gulida as an outstanding example of the endurance qualities possessed by this breed. She points out that this mare was inbred to Gulnare and consequently also to *Rodan and *Ghazala with nine fairly close-up lines to Mesaoud, and also linebred to Ribal. With this fine breeding, it's no wonder that the Doyles were reluctant to sell her to the Tellingtons.

CHAPTER 8

THE DAWNING OF THE
PACIFIC COAST EQUESTRIAN RESEARCH FARM
AND SCHOOL OF HORSEMANSHIP

In 1962 the Tellingtons had their sights set on a new plan. They left Hemet and the breeding farm and headed for the California coast where they could leverage Linda's fast-rising notoriety. "While we were in Hemet I also acquired a lot of riding students, many who drove all the way from Los Angeles. After all, I was a riding teacher and since we truly weren't interested in the breeding business, it gave us the idea to start our own place," Linda reflected.

"A friend of ours owned several hundred acres of property on the California coastline west of San Luis Obispo, near Los Osos in Hazard Canyon. It was about halfway between Los Angeles and San Francisco. Because they weren't doing anything with the land, they offered it to us to set up a horse facility on the bluff above the ocean.

"Went was always developing new ideas and concepts. He was all about moving forward and that's when he came up with the idea to form the Pacific Coast Equestrian Research Farm and a School of Horsemanship," Linda remembers. "At the time the only literature available about horses came from the Department of Agriculture and focused on horses as working animals. Went's interest was to develop information that related to the growing population of backyard horse owners. He wanted to teach them about proper feeding, training, trailering and general horsemanship."

The Tellingtons set up a summer horse camp for young students at Hazard Canyon. The Pacific Coast Equestrian Research Farm's title was derived from three simple sources: It was located on the Pacific Coast, its focus was all about horses, and Wentworth wanted to conduct research. PCERF would become the foundation for Linda's own school of horsemanship, which was based on the piles of information accumulated from Alice Greaves' Tuesday evening lectures, the structure of Went's Cavalry background, and her grandfather's wisdom, coupled with knowledge from the highly-regarded Pony Club Instructor Certification program.

In the November 1962 issue of the Arabian Horse World magazine, the Tellingtons began running advertisements for Linda's summer Pacific Coast School of Horsemanship in Los Osos near Hazard Canyon, California.

64

Sometimes aloof to people, Bint Gulida performed exceptionally well in Linda's capable hands as she effortlessly climbs a sand dune near Los Osos at Hazard Canyon, California.

Linda and Bint Gulida enjoy the surf of the Pacific Ocean.

In 1962 the Tellingtons opened their Pacific Coast Equestrian Research Farm at Hazard Canyon, California, which was the base for Linda's Pacific Coast School of Horsemanship.

The plan was to continue promoting Linda. Advertisements touted the new school in the *Arabian Horse World* and *Western Horseman* magazines, billing Linda Tellington as the Director of the Pacific Coast School of Horsemanship. The target market was the greater Los Angeles area where the Tellingtons had built a reputation from both Pony Club and Chadwick School experiences.

"As a ten-year-old girl," Paula Stockebrand said, "I was an absolute horse nut. I whinnied and ran around acting like a horse. I had stacks of *Arabian Horse World* magazines and I wallpapered my entire bedroom with horse pictures." It was in those magazines that she read the first advertisements for Linda Tellington's School of Horsemanship near San Luis Obispo in California. "I dreamed about going there some day," Paula remembers.

"Gwen, my younger sister by about four years, grew up in the wake of my love for horses. I remember at my aunt's place in Texas I would pull her up behind me on the old ranch horse and we'd ride around together." Gwen's special gift with horses was apparent back then; they adored being near her.

Living in Virginia at the time, the Stockebrand family would soon move west to the golden state where her father would be stationed at the Naval Air Station at Point Mugu near Ventura. "I kept reading the advertisements for Linda's school," reflects Paula, "and after we moved from Virginia to California I drove my parents crazy until we went to visit her place at Hazard Canyon," now called Montaña de Oro State Park.

"I was fourteen when I was finally a summer student there in 1963. The Tellingtons hired my parents, Archie and Bunny Stockebrand, to operate heavy equipment, help build the facilities and fix old Army surplus trucks and tractors.

Students were in charge of caring for their own horses.

"At Hazard Canyon the horses lived in pens out under the eucalyptus trees. We had to clean the stalls, and then drag heavy canvas tarps full of manure down the aisles to dump them. It was very heavy work for young teenagers but it taught us the responsibilities that come with horses.

"The Tellingtons were the reason that we got our first horse, a wonderful Quarter Horse named Ginger," continues Paula. "They told us that we would get more out of the summer camp if we had our own horse. That's how my younger sister, Gwen, began her true connection with horses — it was because of the Tellingtons."

Linda's summer School of Horsemanship was born out of rustic beginnings. The students slept in tents and camped near an open kitchen but the conditions didn't deter assistant instructor, Susan Mayo, from living in style.

Linda pours hot chocolate at the outdoor dining area.

The young campers lived in sandy conditions for the summer while they bettered their horsemanship skills. Martha Merriam, an original Pony Club member at Chadwick, went on to spend many summers with the Tellingtons and knew every facility well. "We slept in tents and had an outdoor kitchen and dining area," Martha fondly reminisces about the rough camp life. "There were nearly ten thousand acres in a state park to ride on, plus the thrill of riding down to the beach was always fun." Susan Mayo remembers laughingly, "We only had a shower once a week when they hauled us in to a local motel!"

That December the Tellingtons received a telephone call from a woman in Pasadena, California who asked if they offered riding classes for adults. She lamented that the only place she could get lessons was at the nearby prestigious Flintridge Riding Club but the classes were all filled with kids and she was looking for a program for adults. The woman came to visit the Tellingtons over Christmas, which became the flashpoint moment for their full-fledged riding program for adults.

Susan Mayo stands at the head of the horse while Linda describes the anatomy.

Disassembling and cleaning tack taught students how bridles fit together.

Riding with outstretched arms, a rider's balance is tested.

Without the benefit of a conventional arena, riders still learned fundamental techniques while riding without stirrups.

Jumping in pairs with arms spread wide was a favorite exercise.

Riding with saddles but without stirrups, students are gathered on a bluff above the surf.

Linda demonstrates riding into a tide pool on Arabian stallion Skowreym, owned by Tish Hewitt of Friendship Farms, Illinois. As an endurance horse he was best at 50-mile distances. Later Skowreym spent two seasons breeding the mares on Chincoteague Island off the coast of Virginia.

This illustration identifies the proper angles for jumping up a bank.

High above the sand dunes the posse of students overlooked the Pacific Ocean.

Riding down the sand dunes was great fun according to student Martha Merriam.
Above the Pacific Ocean Linda fearlessly takes a horse down the steep sandy slope.

Endurance Advice in *Western Horseman*

In May of 1963 the Tellingtons' popularity had grown so much that *Western Horseman* magazine launched the first of ongoing monthly articles called "Let's Go" by Linda and Went Tellington. The following is the opening paragraph of that original article:

"THE DEVELOPMENT of endurance riding as a constructive sport on the broad panorama of American horsemanship is loaded with potential trouble and fraught with certain inherent difficulties. Nevertheless, the sport is growing and maturing. It offers many horse owners a good challenge, a pleasant outing in the open country, and an opportunity for congenial get-togethers where the most common report you ever get is 'a good time was had by all.'"

No doubt about it — readers were learning more about the fledgling sport of endurance riding. Went and Linda were drawing more interest to long distance riding, a direct influence from their knowledge of U.S. Cavalry training.

The focus of their training centered on the Tevis Cup Ride. In their "Let's Go" article they reported on the August 3rd, 1963 Tevis Cup Ride that bolstered the Tellingtons' position in the endurance world. Linda and Al-Marah Rainbow were among the 52 horses and Tevis riders gathered in the coolness of the morning just before daybreak in front of the U.S. Post Office at Tahoe City, California. Feeling small next to the towering forest of Ponderosa pine trees and the looming Sierra Nevada mountains they were about to face, Linda took on an awesome task. In an extraordinary attempt, along with Linda were four of her young students also representing the Pacific Coast Equestrian Research Farm. Linda was about to become the first person to lead a group of junior riders over the grueling 100 miles of trail.

A First for the Tevis Cup Ride

Stirring the first and most vivid images of the Tevis Cup Ride for me was the photograph taken in 1963 of Linda riding Al-Marah Rainbow and leading a group of four of her students. Photographer Charlie Barieau captured the Tellington group in a dramatic photograph as they neared the top of Emigrant Pass marked by the famous Watson's Monument, resplendent with an American flag. After I learned the story captured by this photo, it was all beginning to make sense to me. The seed was now firmly planted in my enthusiastic mind, and in 1977 and 1979 I, too, captured my own Tevis buckles.

During the 1963 Tevis Cup Ride, Linda, riding Al-Marah Rainbow, leads her group of students, Dana Kirst, Patty Edwards, Cherie Miller and Linda Erkkila, up to Emigrant Pass (elevation 8,750') on the Western States Trail.

Recognized internationally, this is the sterling silver version of the Western States Trail Ride (Tevis Cup Ride) buckle awarded to everyone who finishes the 100 miles in 24 hours.

The story of Al-Marah Rainbow depicts the origins of Linda's work today. "Our preference for choosing an endurance horse was one said to be challenging and difficult to train because they made the best endurance horses," Linda stated. "That's why we picked Al-Marah Rainbow out of Bazy Tankersley's herd of three hundred horses. We went back to Maryland, where she was based at the time, and picked a gray mare that we felt we could campaign. This was a mare that Harold Black, who was Bazy's top trainer at the time, returned to the herd because he felt she was untrainable. So we took her as a six- year-old." (Author's note: In my curious way, I had to do a little research and discovered that Rainbow shared some of the same bloodlines as Bint Gulida did. They both had Gulastra as their grandsire.)

Linda continues, "When we brought her back to Hazard Canyon, we kept her in a big paddock on her own instead of turning her out with our other horses," Linda remembers specifically. "I personally went out and fed her and spent time with her every day. I got her to the point where she would come and take hay from me — this of course was long before TTouch. I would just sit there while she ate.

"I was very careful when I brushed her the first time because she was really flinchy and reactive. I took a very soft brush and gently brushed only her neck daily for an entire week. At the end of three weeks, I could easily catch her so I brought her in and tied her up to feed her. But without thinking I ran the brush quickly down her neck. She had a terrified reaction and let out a loud squeal as she instantly turned and bit me right in the stomach. Then she jumped back and shook, anticipating punishment. But I knew she didn't mean to bite me. I stood there holding my throbbing abdomen; it hurt so much. To counter the pain I began counting and taking long deep breaths. After I gathered my wits, I reached out and quietly put my hand on her neck to let her know I knew she didn't mean to bite me. Rainbow took a deep breath and that was the beginning of our friendship. In that one experience, she changed her attitude and absolutely trusted me afterwards. Then I was able to start preparing to ride her. When I look back on those days, all those experiences laid the foundation for the Tellington Method as we know it today."

PCERF Students Conquer the Sierra Nevada Mountains

Linda prepared Rainbow, along with four young students and their horses, and headed for the Tevis Cup Ride in 1963. Martha Merriam recalls camping on a warm summer night in Auburn before the Tevis. "I went along as part of the crew for Linda and the other four students. There were about ten of us in the Tellington group and we were all camped at the Gold Country Fairgrounds in Auburn the week before the Ride. Tucked in our sleeping bags on the ground, it was a big slumber party right next to the horse corrals. Late one night we were awakened by the sounds of a loose horse. I peeked my head out and there was Linda — stark naked — running after the loose horse," Martha laughed. "She brought him back to his pen and peace was restored."

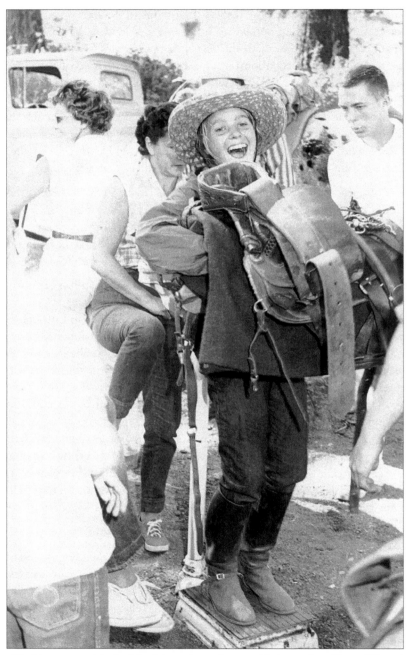

All riders are weighed with their tack at the pre-ride inspection. Dana Kirst, in typical Tellington fashion, is complete with her tall black hunt boots.

At the Ride check-in at Tahoe City, Linda is excited about taking Al-Marah Rainbow over the 100 miles of the 1963 Tevis Cup Ride.

Ride Day approached and Linda was aboard the seven-year-old gray Arabian mare Al-Marah Rainbow alongside her students Linda Erkkila on El Rahysan, Patty Edwards on Feral, Cherie Miller on Al-Marah Bathsheba and Dana Kirst, who was only 13 years old, on Dolly, a black half-Welsh mare. The five riders decided to start as one rider on a "Three Musketeers" basis. All for one, and one for all. If any trouble happened to anyone, they would all pull from the ride. This mindset gave them total dedication to each other and helped sustain them through the tight spots.

While the riders head west and climb up the Western States Trail to Emigrant Pass,
Squaw (Olympic) Valley sits peacefully in the morning mist behind them.

At 5:00 a.m. sharp, the group of riders left from Tahoe City, riding the seven miles from the start along the Truckee River. Arriving at the floor of Squaw Valley, now they were warmed up and ready for the five-mile climb up the ski runs and over the summit of Emigrant Pass. Their ride went extremely well and regardless of the long, hot and arduous day, their tenacious preparation under Went's guidance paid off. Each girl knew how many swallows her horse required to consume enough water. They rode the last 18 miles through the darkness and over the Mountain Quarries Railroad Bridge, which in those days had no side rails, that stands high above the American River. Late that night the 'Tellington Five' came into Auburn's Gold Country Fairgrounds happily singing "California, Here I Come." All together at a trot, they crossed the finish line only 16 minutes behind their original planned schedule.

Linda on Al-Marah Rainbow finished in 14th place, Cherie Miller on Al Marah Bathsheba was 15th place, Patty Edwards on Feral was 16th place, Dana Kirst on Dolly was 17th place and Linda Erkkila on El Rahysan 18th place. They were all riding Arabians with the exception of Dana Kirst who was riding a Welsh pony cross. They were hailed as a huge success.

Pat Fitzgerald won the Tevis Cup that year, riding his seven-year old Arabian (Rushcreek) "Ken."

The day following the 1963 Tevis Cup 100-mile Ride, a sit down Awards Banquet was held to celebrate the victorious riders who successfully crossed the Sierra Nevada mountains. Linda is seated on the left with the entire Tellington Team. Among them are starting on the left, Linda Tellington, Dana Kirst, Linda Erkkila, (third from right) Eleanor Woltjes, Martha Merriam, and Went Tellington are hidden. Wendell Robie (white shirt) is seated at the Head Table.

*In the follow-up 1963 Arabian Horse World article, "When You Wish Upon a Star,"
Wentworth said about Dana Kirst, "You feel ten feet tall with a Tevis Cup buckle on your
belt — even if you're only thirteen years old."*

Linda and Al-Marah Rainbow stand with the hardware they won, including a Tevis Cup buckle, over three weekends at endurance rides.

The following year, 1964, Linda rode a horse on Tevis for Tish Hewitt of Friendship Farms in Illinois. Skowreym, an 850-pound, 11-year-old gray stallion, was excellent at 50 miles but simply wasn't a 100-mile horse. "I was down near the river in El Dorado Canyon when friend, veterinarian Matthew Mackay-Smith, came along, riding one of the Moyles' horses. He saw what bad shape I was in and threw a wet towel over me. He recognized that I was suffering from heat stroke," reports Linda. "There wasn't much consideration for the rider in those early years, only for the horses. We were riding in tall black hunt boots, in McClellan saddles and running down the hills."

Even though Linda didn't finish that year, she ultimately finished five out of six Tevis Rides, giving her an admirable 83% completion rate.

CHAPTER 9

THE GLORIOUS HUNGARIAN HORSES

Articles in the 1961 *Western Horseman* and *Arabian Horse World* magazines raved about the young California horsewoman named Linda Tellington and her brilliant Arabian mare, Bint Gulida. The stories hailed Linda's two remarkable rides that year, the second one on the Jim Shoulders 100-Mile Ride in Oklahoma where she won by five-and-a-half hours over second place and captured the Best Condition award. Having notched a 6th place finish on Bint Gulida at the 100-mile Tevis Cup Ride just six weeks before, Linda was indeed earning a big name in the new sport of endurance riding.

Impressed by Linda's outstanding accomplishments, one woman was prompted to make a telephone call to the PCERF's Hazard Canyon encampment. The curious caller sported an interesting accent and wanted to make arrangements for a visit. From reading the Tellingtons' monthly magazine articles, the caller was intrigued by their philosophy and was keen on examining this place called the Pacific Coast Equestrian Research Farm.

Her name was Countess Margit Bessenyey of the Bitter Root Stock Farm in Hamilton, Montana. She announced to the Tellingtons that, "I will be arriving with several horses, a few dogs and a couple of people," she said, "and we'll be staying for a month." The Countess never traveled anywhere without cases of the best champagne and all the accoutrements that surround that elegant lifestyle. For Linda, this fortuitous visit would become the beginning of a long and close relationship with one of Montana's most beloved women.

"The first time I saw Margit I was struck by her natural beauty," Linda said speaking of Margit's deep auburn hair and gentle smile that highlighted her wide face, all of which was framed by prominent aristocratic cheekbones and a well-defined jaw. "And the horses!" Linda exclaimed. "When her Hungarian horses came out of the trailer I was very impressed. They were as classically conformed individuals as I had ever seen." Linda remembers that significant day, reflecting, "I felt like a member of my own family had just arrived; that's how easy it was to welcome Margit."

*A fetching woman, Hungarian Countess Margit Sigray Bessenyey was an excellent horsewoman who possessed beauty and a great panache for life. She is seen here at the Bitter Root Stock Farm with a son of *Honpolgar IV.*

The Countess possessed an unflappable demeanor that surrounded this wealthy and elegant woman. Margit was just as comfortable wearing denim jeans in the saddle or swinging a leg over a fence while checking livestock as she was dining at the Waldorf-Astoria Hotel in New York. She was quite at home in the rustic camp setting the Pacific Coast Equestrian Research Farm offered. Every evening at dinner she uncorked several bottles of her excellent champagne and shared it freely, which consistently led to lively conversations. The Tellingtons soon learned the incredible story that drove the Countess to them and they became fast friends, which opened remarkable opportunities for Linda.

Although she had spent most of her youth in Hungary, Margit knew the United States well from childhood visits to relatives in New York and Montana. Now she alternated staying between the two states, spending May through October in Montana. In 1958 Margit married fellow Hungarian refugee and retired diplomat Baron George B. Bessenyey; technically Margit was both a Countess and a Baroness. Baron George and Baroness Margit planned to raise horses together.

Countess Margit Sigray Bessenyey in traditional Hungarian dress posing with her beloved Hungarian Furioso horse, Brownie.

As the champagne flowed, the Tellingtons learned more about Margit's extraordinary life and that of her close Hungarian friend, Countess Judith Barczy Gyurky, another aficionada of the Hungarian horse. Margit told of the unbelievable journey and sacrifices they had made for the sake of their beloved horses. Since her 1946 arrival in this country, she and Judith had been on a mission to establish the breed in the United States. It was Judith Gyurky who ultimately produced one of Linda's all time favorite Hungarian horses, a stunning, bold stallion named Magyar Brado.

Magyar Brado well represented the excellent qualities of the Hungarian horses, shown here with Linda riding him bridleless.

The Magyars and Their Horses

The Hungarian people, known as Magyars, were a horse-loving nation and each family sought to surpass the other in breeding a superior line of animals. For the Magyars, the horse was the most important animal in their culture.

A PCERF sepia-toned brochure, printed a few years after the breed captured the attention of the Tellingtons, regaled:

> *Dear Fellow Horseman,*
>
> *We at the Pacific Coast Equestrian Research Farm have been privileged for several years to work with a breed of horses little known to most Americans.*
>
> *Since 800 AD when Hungarian horsemen struck fear into the hearts of all who crossed their paths as they rode through the Carpathian Mountains on raids into Western Europe, Hungarians have been recognized for their excellence in horsemanship. Perhaps the most significant product of these many centuries of excellence is the Hungarian horse itself.*

Margit was the granddaughter of Marcus Daly, one of Montana's Copper Kings during the 1880s. The Dalys were also a well-established family on the east coast, so it was to be that a New York newspaper's society column announced the news of Hungarian Count Anton Sigray von Febre's marriage to American-born Miss Harriot Daly of New York, the Dalys' youngest daughter. The Count was the head of his family and had large estates in Sabutkan in Upper Hungary. He was a Member of the House of Magnates of Hungary and of substantial wealth stemming from his birthright in Hungarian aristocracy. The Count was absolutely fearless at whatever he undertook and was an excellent and avid polo player. Margit, their only daughter, enjoyed growing up on the family's vast estates in the Hungarian countryside where she and her father shared a deep love of horses.

Countess Judith Gyurky standing next to a grand hearth with her hunting hounds.

Two distinguished young women born into Hungary's Magyar aristocracy, Margit Sigray and Judith Barczy Gyurky, became well-acquainted with one another in the early 1900s. The equally vibrant and strong-willed Countesses loved the refined horses raised by their families. Judith grew up in a similar setting to Margit, basking in the luxurious lifestyles enjoyed only by the highly privileged, a stark contrast to peasant life in Hungary. Yet, as fate would have it, they would both be flung into an extraordinary and harrowing journey, testing the very depths of their souls. These traumatic travails centered on their love of the Hungarian horse.

As presented in the book, "The Heavenly Horses," author Virginia Johnson details why the history of the Hungarian horses reflects the reverence held by those who know them well. Aficionados of the breed have practically memorized her book, but for the sake of those unfamiliar with their story and fascinating past, here is a summarized version of their incredible history.

Dating back to the sturdy, small, fast and athletic horses ridden by Genghis Khan, by crossing those mares with high quality Thoroughbred foundation sires, the Magyars produced what became the Hungarian horses. They were strong, handsome horses of good bone, standing between 15.3 and 16.2 hands high, that exhibited bravery, versatility, intelligence and endurance, blended with excellent temperaments. Many bore the deep reddish bay color of the stallion Furioso.

An important and unique trait of the Furioso line was that, as warhorses, they could be trained to bond solely with their assigned mounted military officers. If captured by the enemy, the horses reverted to being unridable. These horses were also very adaptable. Officers could easily ride into a situation, dismount and hitch up their Furioso saddle horses to pull a tender hauling a cannon. This is the strain of horses that Margit's father, Count Sigray, favored.

Countess Judith Barczy Gyurky and the Mark of Clover

Countess Judith Gyurky spent much of her youth on a magnificent estate belonging to her grandmother in a small town in Hungary called Rozsyno. She often referred to going "back to the castle" where she relied on many maids and servants.

Her grandmother's oldest groom, whom they called Uncle Pista, taught Judith and her sister the significance of a revered type of Hungarian horse. It was the horses with a "Mark of Clover" on its nose that Judith would ultimately pursue.

Folklore about these horses may actually have a foothold in truth, according to an excerpt from Judith's book, "Mark of Clover:"

> The legend of the Clover, it is a strange thing and originated in Pagan times before the birth of Christ. As far back as the ninth century when carefully selected horses were bred that bore an unusual sign upon the tips of their muzzles. It was a slate blue mark in the shape of a four-leaf clover and was vivid against the pink of the nose. It was rumored among the Magyars that it was the mark of the Gods; as long as the Gods favored the clan, no one could hope to breed a better horse. When it came to endurance and speed tests against others, the Magyar animals always won. Additionally the Magyars were among the earliest to geld their horses.

According to the centuries-old story, the family that owned a horse with the Mark of Clover on its muzzle would prosper and the nation in which the horse lived would exist in peace, but if the Clovers disappeared, the family would be ruined and the nation destroyed.

Uncle Pista was exceptionally proud of one special little Clover horse named Sarga that Judith rode as a child. Both Judith and her sister would laugh at Sarga's marking and called it a mushroom. It wasn't until some years later when Judith truly discovered the significance of the Mark of Clover.

Judith was just 13 when World War I broke out in 1914. Unfortunately, one day a military mountain regiment came by their estate and drafted Sarga, along with some of the family's other horses, for military duty. The special Clover Horse was gone. Sadly, the young Countess was certain that she would never see her little horse again.

A Mare Named Igézo - *The Charmer*

World War I finally ended and it was the summer of 1919 when 18-year-old Judith married a dashing young man named Paul. They moved to Vienna where they lived a joyful and rich lifestyle. One evening they were out with a group of elegantly-dressed friends at the amusement park "Wurstl-Prater" to ride the rollercoaster and merry-go-round. Late that night Judith noticed some horses for rent at the park. The grizzled horse owner kept a leather muzzle strapped to the head of an ugly small dun mare and when she refused to move he beat her with a large whip. Incensed, Judith told the snarling man to stop whipping the horse, which led to a heated argument. To spare the horse from its terrible life, she insisted on buying it. Her interest alone spiked a demanding price, even though the owner called the little mare a *devil* horse. Judith bought the mare on the spot for a ridiculously high sum.

Judith's friends laughed as the ensemble parted company. The friends drove over the mountain to their favorite early morning breakfast spot, leaving Judith and Paul behind with their newly-purchased horse. In her evening dress and fur wrap, Judith and husband Paul accompanied a man who led the mare home to her stables where her coachman scoffed at the scruffy animal. When Judith removed the mare's muzzle, she stood in shock as she stared at the Mark of Clover on the mare. Judith was elated as she recognized the funny mushroom shape on the horse's nose. She had just rescued her very own Sarga with the Mark of Clover, and undoubtedly her own life and that of her husband. As fate would have it, the next morning Judith received word that her friends had been in a car accident the night before on their way home over the mountain and all had been killed. Perhaps the Mark of Clover had protected not only Sarga, but also Judith and her husband.

Now that Judith was living in Vienna, she had nowhere suitable to keep Sarga, so she sent her to a cousin's stud farm where she was bred and produced several foals. She then lost track of Sarga.

Years later, Judith, who was a well-known rider in the region, was looking for a new competition jumping horse. She heard about a prospect that had just come into the nearby Cavalry regiment as a remount horse, an unattractive but talented mare that would jump out of a six-foot-high enclosure. But she had a vicious temperament towards people. She was called a four-legged demon by the men who knew her because she was so nasty and would bite and kick to avoid being caught.

For a small sum Judith bought the gray horse that no one else wanted. It was Judith's instincts about using gentleness instead of the rough treatment the horse had received that would change the mare's disposition. They named her Igézo, which meant *"the charmer"* in Hungarian.

Curiosity led Judith to investigate Igézo's breeding; the results revealed an astonishing outcome. After some sleuthing that took her to the village of her cousin's farm, she learned that Igézo was out of a mare named Vérces who was Sarga's last foal. Judith was shocked that she had bought a horse that no one else wanted and it turned out to be Sarga's granddaughter. Now the Clover Horses were back in Judith's life again.

Judith was admired and even idolized for her independence, as a woman boldly competing throughout Europe. She showed her horses in Switzerland and Italy, earning many accolades for her jumping accomplishments. She thrilled audiences with her spectacular sidesaddle skills by jumping over huge fences, Judith's specialty.

Countess Judith Gyurky jumping Igézo sidesaddle and winning the 1936 Olympic Trials in Berlin. She was not allowed to compete in the actual Olympics because…she was a woman.

Together Judith and Igézo competed against the official Hungarian military team and won the tryouts at the 1936 Olympics held in Berlin — while riding sidesaddle. Judith, however, was denied the privilege of competing in the Olympic competitions because she was a *woman*. After her retirement, Igézo was bred many times and the colts were purchased as studs for the government remount. She kept the fillies for herself and thus began the foundation band of Judith's best mares.

World War II Tramples Hungary

Triggered by the German invasion of Poland in 1939, World War II broke out and all of Europe lapsed into upheaval. The conflict soon advanced into Hungary, a German ally, and Count Sigray found himself in the role of reserve officer. Widespread fear and hostility erupted and the magnitude of the conflict struck when he was suddenly imprisoned for being an outspoken anti-Nazi activist and for his pro-American political beliefs.

It fell to Margit to defend their home when the invading Russian Army began plundering all the grand estates that lay across Hungary. As she held her ground at the entrance to their estate, the soldiers respected the courage of beautiful young Margit. But her heart was broken as she watched the Russians take away the Sigrays' beloved horses. These fine horses were swiftly relegated to the duties of warhorses pulling wagons or artillery, or used as officers' mounts, signaling the destruction of the magnificent breed.

Horses were valued as a prized commodity for the armies of that era. The Russian soldiers swept across Hungary and Poland while confiscating the best ones from stud farms throughout the lands, including the Janow Podlaski Stud, home to Polish Arabian stallions Ofir and Witez II. No good horse was safe. Word of the capture spread fast through the villages as people whisked their precious and disguised stock to the safety of Czechoslovakia before the marauding Russian soldiers could confiscate them.

Finally in 1946 Margit and her mother fled to the United States where they were soon reunited with her father, who had been rescued by the American Occupation Forces from a concentration camp in Europe. Sadly, he died shortly after being reunited with his family. Margit's mother passed away a few years later, leaving the Countess with a fortune that had increased substantially from the initial $2,500,000 her mother inherited upon her father Marcus Daly's death in 1900. Margit bought out her cousins and gained full ownership of the Bitter Root Stock Farm in Montana in 1950. Alas, Margit's husband Baron George B. Bessenyey died within a year of their 1958 marriage. Margit never remarried. Now on her own, she had a sizeable ranch in her possession. The property was perfect for raising horses — but the only ones she wanted were the Hungarians that had been scattered by the winds of World War II.

Before the war ended, with Russian invaders in pursuit, Judith Gyurky had fled Hungary with 64 horses and survived only by barely escaping in a nail-biting saga that ultimately left her with a dozen horses. After a harrowing journey through Europe worthy of a Hollywood film, she finally settled near Charlottesville, Virginia, determined to rebuild her herd of Hungarian horses again.

A Perspective On Life

While Europe was enveloped in the turmoil of World War II, halfway around the globe Linda Hood was dutifully riding to school across the serene Canadian landscape while perfecting her horsemanship. Linda was eight years old when the war ended in 1945. It would be another 16 years until she learned of the traumatic wartime sagas endured by Countess Bessenyey and Countess Gyurky and their horses. When their paths ultimately crossed, Linda would join these two women to introduce the Hungarian horses to America. It was an undertaking that consumed both Margit and Judith for the rest of their lives. It also changed Linda's life forever.

U.S. Army to the Rescue – Margit Bessenyey Builds Her Herd

In Europe, at the end of World War II, General George S. Patton ordered Colonel Fred L. Hamilton, Chief of the Remount Service, to round up the treasured horses of several breeds that were confiscated by the Nazis. Not only was it the honorable thing to do, it was necessary to keep the lineage of these breeds intact. A team of six officers that included two veterinarians and one well-seasoned horse trader accompanied Hamilton to Hostoun, Czechoslovakia. Of course the Germans intended to keep the best horses for themselves and tried to mask the identity of the horses under a mud-smeared façade of unkempt manes and knotted tails. However, the savvy U.S. officers knew how to find the best horses and flushed them out.

The Americans took a pass on the well-groomed, second-best horses the Germans gladly presented along with their papers. The U.S. officers insisted on checking into the dark dilapidated quarters concealed out of sight behind the respectable stables, sensing that it was there the best horses were sequestered. Colonel Hamilton was one of the few Americans who could recognize the Hungarians of the Furioso lines, as well as those of Fenek, Shagya and Nonius lines. They rounded up the horses and drove them to Austria and finally to the German Remount Station in Bavaria. Hamilton then selected 150 of the Hungarian Halfbreds to ship to the United States.

What could possibly go wrong after the countless traumatic episodes of just getting the horses to the ship? In what seemed to be a routine maneuver, the worst appeared to be behind them, but not so. After a hair-raising voyage across the Atlantic Ocean on the Stephen F. Austin, a Liberty ship classified for Army Transportation Service, the horses were hurled about in the dark hold during a horrendously rough storm that nearly sank the ship. Veterinarians were on hand to patch up the injured mares and stallions that fought with each other after their stalls were broken apart. Finally the battered equine cargo arrived on United States soil. Among the horses onboard was a grey stallion named *Honpolgar IV.

Both Judith and Margit had every reason to believe in this type of Hungarian horse. In 1911, Dr. Van Slatin, the Master of Imperial Horses in Austria, said, "We believe the horses bred in Hungary are the best Cavalry mounts in the world. They are not too large and have a great proportion of Arab blood in them." To substantiate that claim, an article in the November/December 1946 issue of *Remount Magazine* reported, "Perhaps the most valuable horses that were imported, however, if we take a long-range point of view, were the Hungarian Halfbreds... In a matter of size, they breed far more truly than do most breeds. Almost every Halfbred stands between 15 hands and 15.3 and most of them will weigh very close to 1100 pounds. In conformation, they are big horses on short legs, deep through the heart, broad of shoulder, with great bone... short cannon bone and good feet. They are fine, yet powerful."

Meanwhile a Manhattan, Montana rancher named Jim Edwards wrote a friend at the Remount Service in Fort Robinson, located in the Pine Ridge region of northwest Nebraska, requesting that he be sent a "pretty" stallion that he could use as a stock horse. His request was fulfilled when a handsome grey horse was shipped to him for his inspection. The horse wore Adolf Hitler's brand of an eagle above a Swastika indicating that the Germans had confiscated the horse. Recovered by the Americans, his name was *Honpolgar IV, soon nicknamed 'Humphrey.' Born in 1943 and standing 15.2 hands, his sire was a Thoroughbred (Honpolgar by Duncan Gray [Thoroughbred] out of Short Holiday [Thoroughbred]) and his dam was a Furioso mare (182 Furioso VII by Furiosos VII [Furioso] out of Ibolya [Hungarian]) from the Kisbir (pronounced *kish-ber*) Stud Farm, which meant that *Honpolgar IV was a true Halfbred.

Humphrey lived up to everything Edwards wanted in an excellent horse — intelligence, good bone, well-muscled, willing and sure-footed. Jim, who knew nothing about Hungarian horses, was delighted with the stallion and leased him immediately. Humphrey soon became a family member and claimed his favorite grazing spot on the front lawn next to the house. His only fault was he didn't like water; perhaps he related it to the horrible Atlantic crossing.

The Remount Service was discontinued in 1949, which prompted a letter to Jim Edwards stating that all the horses would be sold at auction and he was to return Honpolgar to Fort Robinson at once. Jim's return letter made it clear that if they came looking for the horse that neither he nor the horse would be found. Basically the Remount Service wasn't getting their horse back. So to simplify matters, they sold the horse to Jim for a small sum.

Margit's love of her father's refined Hungarian horses would not leave her mind. She missed the nobility, grace, speed and stamina of these horses and wanted to begin breeding the native Hungarian Furioso horses in Montana. They were now threatened with disappearing completely; she knew she had to help save them, if only she could find some mares.

Word reached Margit that some Hungarian mares were to be auctioned at Fort Robinson, and she commissioned a veterinarian and fellow countryman to buy nine mares for her and ship them to Montana. These horses had the exact bloodlines Margit wanted and thus she began building her foundation breeding stock. They were proven Cavalry mount producers as well as polo ponies, racing stock, hunters and pleasure horses. But now she needed a stallion. When she heard about Jim Edwards and Honpolgar, she immediately paid him a visit. He wouldn't sell the horse but agreed to lease Humphrey to her, so the stallion came to live at the Bitter Root Stock Farm where he covered Margit's few mares.

At that time the only other people in the United States who were breeding Hungarian horses were Steve and Wanda Cooksley in Anselmo, Nebraska, a relatively short four-hour drive from Fort Robinson. According to their account, they raised this remarkable breed for their cattle operation and "were attracted to the Hungarians for their stamina, good sense and especially their long, ground-covering stride." *Honpolgar IV was used for breeding at their ranch as well.

In 1954 Margit bought a beautiful 510-acre estate called Mount Aventine Manor House in Indian Head, Maryland along the Potomac River with the idea of having an Eastern base for her horses in addition to her Montana operation. Margit teamed up with Countess Judith Gyurky to promote the Hungarians as an all-around horse. They agreed on a strategy to build a breeding program that would equal that of the already-established Swedish Warmbloods, Hanoverians, and Trakehners. The Hungarians were just as good, and now with Countess Gyurky and her horses in the heart of Virginia's fox hunting and steeplechase country, she could promote the horses by jumping and showing them. Margit wanted to concentrate on long distance riding to promote the excellent endurance qualities of these horses. And that's why one evening she called the Tellingtons.

CHAPTER 10

TRANSFORMING A CHICKEN RANCH TO A
WORLD CLASS EQUESTRIAN CENTER

The Pacific Coast Equestrian Research Farm was growing and needed a larger facility to further its programs. In 1964, the Tellingtons, along with partner Jack Miller, father of student and 1963 Tevis Cup rider Cherie Miller, found a more substantial location and left the San Luis Obispo coast and moved inland. Their new address would simply be:

Went and Linda Tellington
PCERF
Badger, California

Along Dry Drive, the Research Farm lay in a valley nestled in the Sierra Nevada mountain range.

Badger is a tiny town in the oak-studded hills of the lower Sierra Nevada mountains in Central California. The Tellingtons found a suitable ranch in the foothills northeast of Visalia and southeast of Fresno. This was an ideal setting in which to expand and integrate horsemanship, engineering, history and art as well as Went's continued desire to pass along his plentiful knowledge. Now all they had to do was transform an old rundown chicken ranch into a facility that could serve as their international school of horsemanship. Soon a new dormitory, barns and corrals were built.

The PCERF Fall 1965 Newsletter reported:

THE BIG MOVE

For ten months we have been occupied with the major move from San Luis Obispo to the new location at Badger, California. Miles of fences, several riding rings, barns, a cross-country course, quarters for guests, a big dining room for 100 people, new office and shipping rooms, VYM manufacturing facility, storage areas, etc. etc. have been built and are now functioning. The experimental garden now has Comfrey plants almost two feet tall.

We can now devote more attention to correspondence with the hundreds of enthusiastic horsemen who have manifested interest in our work and particularly to the members who have "been with us" since the beginning.

Our motto is: "Better Horsemanship Through Clinical Inquiry"

The mission of PCERF was to explore the area between technology and tradition. The subjects of their experimentations included equine transportation, leather care, equipment, feeds, supplements such as VYM (a potent molasses and sea kelp vitamin mixture, a creation that Went brewed in 50-gallon steel barrels), specialized techniques for wound care, training, detecting physical ailments, and training for competitions – especially endurance riding and specifically the Tevis Cup Ride.

*Designed by the Tellingtons, this is the exterior view of the X-2 Trail-Van.
It was 8 feet wide, 27½ feet long, with headroom of 7 feet, 8 inches. It could haul five horses and the unit weighed only 5,000 pounds and could easily be pulled by a ½ ton truck. The horses traveled backwards allowing, among other benefits, their hindquarters to balance on turns and to also absorb the impact of sudden stops.*

The X-2 Trail-Van had a 6' x 8' tack and dressing room, three horses across with canvas mangers, a service aisle and spaces for two horses in the rear. Both ramp and step-up entries were included plus ample storage to stow a spare tire, extra gas, water, grain and tools. Hay bales were carried on the roof.

The Tellingtons' very popular "Let's Go" column in *Western Horseman* carried monthly news about endurance riding: "The Western States Trail Ride began about 10 years ago with less than 10 riders. Now in 1965 it is an internationally recognized event with over 50 riders annually." Slowly other endurance rides were beginning to crop up across the nation. Of note: Today the Tevis is limited to 250 applicants.

Readers learned of the activities that frequently centered on endurance or competitive trail riding and a favorite topic was how to best prepare for the Tevis Cup Ride. The Tellingtons wrote a plethora of articles for *Western Horseman* and *Arabian Horse World* magazines and whatever they wrote, people loved to read. Auburn, California's veteran endurance rider Phil Gardner, who was new to horses at the time, said, "Every month I couldn't wait for the day when the *Western Horseman* would come out. I would go to the local Woolworths store and buy a copy and the first thing I'd do was turn to the Tellingtons' 'Let's Go' article."

Symposiums at the Research Farm

Education was always foremost with Wentworth and Linda and the Badger facility became an ideal setting for their well-attended forums. Continuing with a practice they started at Hazard Canyon, the Tellingtons hosted the "First National Endurance Ride Conference for Riders, Judges and Organizers." It was a big event, drawing many enthusiasts to the sport, the same way Tevis founder, Wendell Robie drew new riders to the Tevis Cup Ride. There was no other institution like PCERF and it became the hub for learning cutting edge information about distance horses. Many leading riders in the sport participated, including riders Phil Gardner and Ed Johnson, Arabian horse breeder Sheila Varian, and veterinarians Matthew Mackay-Smith, Richard Barsaleau, Jim Steere and Murray Fowler. The conferences covered an array of topics appealing to riders, veterinarians and judges alike on the subjects of conditioning, feeding, caring for horses and long distance trail riding. It was a wonderful way to share information about the up-and-coming sports of North American Trail Ride Conference (NATRC) competitive trail rides and endurance rides.

Welcome to the Research Farm! Nothing made Wentworth happier than cooking for a crowd of people in his great big skillet converted from a huge gold mining pan.

Members of the Research Farm could read about the symposiums in the monthly PCERF newsletters or magazine articles. The Tellingtons always shared what they learned.

Linda concentrated on building her Pacific Coast School of Horsemanship, which ultimately attracted students from 36 states and nine countries. The robust curriculum was assembled from a combination of the coveted notes saved from Alice Greaves' classes, and the standard U.S. Pony Club training guidelines seasoned with Went's own Cavalry training. All of these components contributed to the lessons and tests that formulated the Tellingtons' own unique agenda. Wentworth wrote the exams, which today are still quite formidable.

In this 1965 photo, Linda, on Hungarian Pallo, and Went were already well-regarded as experts in the horse world.

The Brilliant Horse Brado – the Star of the Horse Herd

It was during this era that Margit suggested to Linda that she might look at another horse that Countess Judith Gyurky had bred. He was a big burly horse and Judith's hopes for him were so high that she offered him to the U.S. Olympic Team, thinking it would be an ideal way to promote her Hungarian horses. However, while in the hands of Olympic contenders the horse flatly refused to jump ditches. It was for that reason that he was was eliminated from contention and, much to her dismay, returned to Judith. Margit thought perhaps Linda could make something out of the sizeable yet problematic stallion.

Upon arriving at Judith's Port-A-Ferry Farm in Virginia, Went and Linda were introduced to the horse. He was a beautiful six-year old dark bay stallion named Magyar Brado – all of Judith's horses were prefixed by the word Magyar. When she met the reputedly obstinate horse, Linda liked him immediately.

A week after Brado arrived in California in the spring of 1965, Linda took him to the horse show at Pebble Beach. It was there Linda used her gentle touch and visualization techniques to teach him to cross ditches. Later Lynn Blades rode Brado at Pebble Beach as seen here.

"Brado was another difficult horse that we wanted," Linda recounted. "Judith told me he refused to jump ditches, so they just rejected him," Linda recounted. "Brado had an enormous heart girth that contributed to his daunting size. The barn hands were intimidated by him and they gave him the unflattering nickname of 'Pipsqueak,'" Linda said with a hint of disgust. "It was so disrespectful and as you know, we really paid a lot of attention to the names of the horses when they come to us. Because what you call a horse is how other people see them and treat them."

Once a U.S. Equestrian Team reject, Brado excelled under Linda's care. Linda, riding sidesaddle, is receiving the first place trophy and ribbon won at the 1968 Hunter Hack Championship at Oakland, California.

"Brado was so courageous and willing and we had a really special relationship. I have ridden other stallions but I just didn't have that same connection that I had with Brado," Linda mused over the magnificent bay horse. "He had such a courageous heart. Brado turned out to be one of my all-time favorite horses," Linda admitted. Indeed, he turned out to be a favorite of many riders.

Linda remembered when she brought Brado home from Virginia in April of 1966. "I brought him to California as a six-year-old. He was a fabulous horse but I only had a few days to get him ready before we had to leave for a major horse show at Pebble Beach. We arrived a few days ahead of the competition so I had time to work with him. I rode him at a walk out on the course to practice," Linda remembered as she discovered his problem. "There was a ditch about 100 feet in front of us and he stopped dead in his tracks. You know how stallions can be. When a stallion stops dead in his tracks with head up and back rigid, there's no moving him forward."

Linda reveals one of her most effective training methods by saying, "When Brado stopped I didn't urge him forward. I simply sat very still, quieting my mind and holding the intention that he would to go over the ditch in his own time, without fear. I just visualized that possibility for him but put no pressure on him whatsoever. I didn't let him go to the left or right or back. I just kept holding the potential of him crossing the ditch, seeing him on the other side. I have no idea how long it took, but he pricked up his ears, walked forward and jumped the ditch and he never hesitated at a ditch again. I believe this experience is what took us through tough places on the trail too. We had a special connection and he understood the respect I had for him."

With the Pacific Ocean is in the background, this is an example of a ditch at Pebble Beach where Brado overcame his fears. This is the amazing 14.2 hands high horse, Rebel, being ridden by a PCERF student.

The fact of the matter is that Linda instilled Brado with a level of confidence that he showed with everyone who ever rode him. Together Linda and Brado were an impressive team that went on to capture many victories.

The School Horses of PCERF

Along with the horses the Tellingtons brought from Hazard Canyon, the herd numbers increased when Margit sent down several Hungarian horses: Pallo, Taszilo, Graflo, Witch and another stallion Niscak.

A student confidently rides the grulla mare Dakota down a bank.

Carolyn Woltjes takes Red Fox over a jump while riding bareback.

The fearless Welsh pony Rebel shows his courage when faced with a large obstacle at Ram Tap.

In the fall of 1967, students practiced Roman riding. (l to r) Roberta Wiebe and Silver Brandon on Red Fox, Diane Woodard on Dakota, Jamie Pardee and Carol Cook on Rebel.

By now champion mare Bint Gulida had become a broodmare as seen here with her foal, Jacpot.

Linda starts Hungarian Graflo by line driving him over pasture obstacles such as this ditch. Linda learned the value of ground driving at the age of 12 from a tattered blue book given to her by a Canadian Cavalry officer who served during the Spanish-American War. He had been watching her dealing with young bucking horses and knew that the secret of line driving would overcome that behavior.

When he was ready to carry her weight, Linda carefully mounts Graflo.

Always involved with her horses, Margit Bessenyey documents Graflo's initial training while Great Dane Hara spectates. The main building and horse vans are in the background.

Linda allows Graflo to examine the ditch while he is adjusting to carrying her weight for the first time.

Graflo confidently crosses the ditch.

Graflo was the most difficult Hungarian horse that Linda trained. This moment revealed that she had finally gained his trust.

The Compound served well as a structure to teach students how to clean and care for their horses.

*The Compound could hold 40 horses. The road to the right went down to
a creek that ran year round.*

Both Linda and Went had keen eyes for selecting horses, and they carefully assembled a suitable herd for their program. An honest Quarter Horse named Red Fox, a Grulla mare tagged Dakota, the stately seal-brown Thoroughbred Resolute, a stout caregiver Thoroughbred bay mare named Earthaquake, a big black Thoroughbred named Rip Van Winkle, a chestnut Arabian gelding named Apache, another very small gray Arabian gelding named Huffy, a strong sorrel Appaloosa gelding named Chuckwagon Son, Zenith, a racy chestnut great-grandson of Man O' War, a sturdy gray Welsh pony named Rebel and Ringo, a small but tough-as-nails buckskin Mustang type — these were just some of the horses we would soon know well.

All of them were honest and wonderful horses for us to trust, love and adore and more importantly, create bonds with. With the help of these horses, we would learn to become better riders. During the week most of the horses stayed in what was called the Compound, a recently built, wooden, open-aired square structure that housed about 40 horses. Over the weekends they were turned out into large pastures.

Linda says that the reason the horses were so good is because of the respect they were shown. Each student was also respected; they were never expected to ride a horse they did not like. To further that philosophy, horses were not subjected to students who did not like and respect them.

"We had a rule that nobody rode a horse unless they really liked him or her," states Linda. "That's why we had such good school horses because they were never ridden by students that didn't enjoy and respect them." Matching the horse and rider was important for building confidence. Thinking back she said, "It must have come from when I was at the Pony Club training in Vermont. I was expected to ride a hard-mouth Thoroughbred in a snaffle bit while trying to keep that horse a length behind the next horse — it was really challenging because he did not respond well to the rein aids. That made a big impression on me and I never wanted my students to have to go through that."

I was assigned to a very sweet but green, lumbering, four-year-old chestnut half-Thoroughbred gelding named Sierra Spy who I nicknamed "Speed the Wonder Horse." A year or so later Sierra Spy became the favorite of student Val Pruitt. Val called him "Spartan" and together they excelled in Combined Training competitions and even completed the Tevis Cup Ride.

Sierra Spy was somewhat gawky as a four-year-old. Like most of the herd, when he was not in the Compound, he lived in the pasture across Dry Creek Drive from the main buildings of PCERF.

Never underestimate the possibilities for a horse. Several years later Sierra Spy became an excellent three-day eventer and went on to complete the Tevis Cup Ride.

Linda Remembers PCERF horses.

"Hungarian Tundra – Witch – but she was a white witch – seemed to be waiting in the wings while she learned her job. She came from Montana to PCERF with a broodmare belly but ended up being one of the top competitive three-day horses." Linda recalled riding her at Pebble Beach on a long drop jump that landed in the water – she was fearless and couldn't have been over 15 hands tall. "She carried many riders and was at least twelve years old when she came to PCERF. She had the heart the size of a lion, was very level headed and nothing bothered her.

"Rebel, a 14'2"-hand Quarter Horse/Welsh Pony was one of the few horses' names that I didn't change when we bought him. His reputation was that of a rebel, but I discovered that when a compatible person rode him he was happy, willing and courageous," remembers Linda. "He was a wonderful jumper and did well over big fences when he competed on our three-day event team at Pebble Beach. However, I learned very soon after buying him that if a rider did not respect him and thought of him as a pony, he was very uncooperative. He had a most unusual habit of defending his space in a pasture. If he didn't like a pasture mate he would literally walk backwards for up to twenty feet just to take aim and kick the horse.

"Red Fox, a lovely chestnut Quarter Horse, was another horse I bought for an extraordinarily reasonable price in Rolling Hills because he was said to be a runaway and very difficult. I was certain it was because he was kept in a stable without enough exercise and was ridden by a girl who did not like him because she was afraid of him. He turned out to be one of our very best, honest and most popular school horses ever.

"I normally paid a lot of attention to horses' names because riders would be influenced by the name. At an auction, I paid very little for a horse that couldn't run at the racetrack. He was potbellied and dull-coated and his registered name was Old Dobbins. From the time we changed his name to Bay Rum, he began to shine and became one of our best show hunters and a favorite in the school string.

"Years later I bought, again for very little money, a marvelous junior jumper Thoroughbred/Saddlebred gelding named Fighting Mad. He was said to be far too dangerous for a junior rider because he bit and kicked. Again, as soon as he came into our barn that horse was a treasure. He never once displayed those traits and I'm convinced it was because he responded to our respect and appreciation of him. We gave him the new name of Jumping Jack."

Students were assigned to a stall or paddock to manage in either one of the two barns or the Compound. On the perimeter were individual 10'x10' paddocks that surrounded a large open space. Our tools included four-pronged pitchforks, rakes and manure shovels. We loaded up burlap muck sacks and dragged them off to a designated manure pile. Students were responsible for twice-daily feedings, keeping fresh water available and cleaning the stall. Several students brought their own horses, but most were issued PCERF mounts.

Saddles and bridles were fitted to each person and their horse, reminiscent of how a remount station operated. Everyone had a go at riding in a U.S. Cavalry McClellan saddle. This was perhaps a bit of a shock to those who wanted to ride in the finer English or German jumping saddles, but it was soon discovered that there were no better saddles that demanded proper equitation than a McClellan. Rider positions benefited, despite the groans about the hard seat. Some students actually loved riding in a McClellan saddle. All the horses were ridden in loose ring or egg butt snaffle bits.

The majority of a special group of horses were stabled in the Upper Barn. Most of them were bay in color and had noble names like the magnificent stallion Magyar Brado. Hungarian Pallo and Hungarian Taszilo were both elegant geldings, as was a younger gelding named Hungarian Graflo. Another stallion, Hungarian Niscak, lived in the Lower Barn. These were the Hungarian Furioso horses sent to the Tellingtons by Countess Bessenyey to train for competition.

Several other young horses lived in a 40-acre field where the arenas were located. Two of those youngsters, Jacpot and Kaweah, were foals out of Bint Gulida by the famed two-time Tevis Cup winner, Arabian stallion Bezatal.

This horse population hovered around 30 head and was the heart of the Pacific Coast School of Horsemanship program. The horses facilitated students in performing to their best ability, ultimately transforming them into knowledgeable and confident riders.

CHAPTER 11

PACIFIC COAST SCHOOL OF HORSEMANSHIP: DISCIPLINE, REGIMEN, CAMARADERIE, SUCCESS

Linda's entire life pointed toward having her own first-rate horsemanship school; now her dream was flourishing. The dream began with Briarcrest Stable, Pony Club and Los Osos – Hazard Canyon, where the school's curriculum started taking shape. Wentworth infused his wisdom and education to validate their credentials. Now at the remote location of Badger, the residential horsemanship program was enhanced even more.

Paula Stockebrand (Fabionar) described the environment at PCERF best when she said, "The world with the Tellingtons was complex." Thoughtfully linking her insights, she continued, "Both Linda and Wentworth were excellent teachers. There was an omnipresent expectation to strive for excellence that was fostered by these two superior educators. Their influence was like two very nurturing parental figures combined with a dash of your favorite aunt and uncle who raised you during the summer. All of that was rolled up into a strict and disciplined environment that resembled a mini West Point." Paula paused for a moment and then added, "It was sink or swim and no one wanted to sink. In the end, countless numbers of students found their confidence through the Tellingtons."

"Went was the kind of teacher that would listen to you even if you were a young kid," recalled Martha Merriam. "He wanted to know what you had to say; it mattered to him."

"Although Linda and her assistants managed the daily routine of the school, Wentworth always had his eye on everyone. He had a real talent for pushing people when they needed to be pushed to bring out the best in them," said Michele Pouliot.

Alexis Flippen (von Zimmer) validated her time spent at Linda's school by saying, "It was a very transitional time in our young lives and Went and Linda were very influential figures. To this day when I talk about horses and explain a significant detail people say to me, 'How did you know that?' and I tell them that I learned it at PCERF."

Daily Routine

Everyone, including the Great Danes, pitched in when there was work to be done around the Research Farm.

By adhering to a tight schedule the residential students enthusiastically contributed to the cadence of the Research Farm. As a student, I fell easily into the daily rhythm, which reinforced a sense of purpose. I felt as though I belonged at the school. From my many conversations with other students who were lucky enough to attend PCERF, the same holds true for them as well. I consider it a nourishing environment that held us accountable for our actions.

By being part of something bigger than ourselves (a perspective that horses naturally bring to people) the school amplified that feeling and we became emotionally and energetically vested in PCERF. In return we gave 100% towards the program's success and took pride in ourselves. It was an enormous responsibility for Linda and Went to run the daily operations, but they empowered all of us to feel as though we *owned* PCERF while we were there.

Students were not forced to participate in any exercise beyond their level of safety. However, they were always encouraged to push beyond their comfort zone. What had been merely dreams with horses turned into daily realities at PCERF. I believe I can speak fairly for others by saying this experience left a lasting impression, reinforcing the belief that we could accomplish anything we set our minds to.

On the whole, the Tellingtons did everything on a large scale; they had big plans and goals and knew how to accomplish them. Just being around Went and Linda every day whisked us into their stream of life through horsemanship. They taught us how to dream, prepare, and manifest our goals and adventures. However, all of their teachings started with the basics as simple as learning to tie knots with a rope.

*Great Dane Hara watches over the students as they care for their horses
in the Compound twice daily.*

In the morning's coolness, Linda encouraged us to accomplish our chores before the 90°-heat scorched the day. We rose at the crack of dawn, threw on mucking clothes and hurried off to feed and water the horses. While they were eating, we cleaned stalls and paddocks. Then it was back to our rooms to change into our required riding attire of breeches or jodhpurs, a belt and a rat-catcher shirt and temporarily, sneakers. At the sound of the bell, the dormitory doors flew open and everyone obediently flocked to the dining room for breakfast. Rotating teams were assigned to responsibilities such as kitchen patrol, making the operations run smoothly. When chores were completed, we returned to our rooms to complete our uniforms by pulling on shiny black hunt boots and grabbing our black velvet hunt caps. Creaky screen doors slammed shut as the echo of leather-soled boots scuffling along the concrete porch signaled the exodus to the horses for another exciting day of riding with Linda.

Shannon Yewell Weil

Morning Mounted Sessions

We used our grooming tools to thoroughly clean our horses from head to hoof. Then we'd saddle up and carefully place the bridle on our steed's head. No other pieces of equipment were used with the exception of an occasional crop. Often we rode horses other than those we cared for every day. After mounting we'd head to the upper field arenas. For riders unaccustomed to steep hills and mountainous trails, it was alarming at first. Diane Woodard (Scott) remembers the first day she left the Compound and rode down a steep dirt trail that nearly scared her to death — her fears soon vanished as she became confident. A quarter-mile dirt road followed the flowing contours of the land until we again met the winding Dry Creek Drive. Crossing the macadam, always with feet out of the stirrups for safety in case our horses slipped on the pavement, we went through a gate into the 40-acre field. It was a good warm-up ride for the horses and gave the riders time to settle into their saddles. The faithful Great Danes, Tiger and Hara, always accompanied us.

The first arena was set up with jumps.

The first arena was set up for stadium jumping. A little farther up the hill was a second arena used for flat equitation, quadrille and cavaletti training. This arena was carved out of a lazy slope in the pasture and provided a perfect corner to practice riding up and down banks and slides. At the far end of the field was the dressage arena.

Large groups were split between Linda and her Assistant Instructor.

Rebel takes a young student around the jump course.

All it takes is a rope with a saddle blanket to make a jump.

Susan Reilly (California) on Red Cloud winning the Outside Hunter Class,
Summer Show, 1968.

Susan Reilly riding her Mustang, Red Cloud, over the Dragon Jump.
Susan and her parents, John and Helen Reilly were active with Wild
Horse Annie in Nevada to save the Mustangs and Burros.

Encircling all of the arenas was an impressive half-mile cross-country course consisting of a variety of jumps, drops and obstacles created to present varying degrees of difficulty. The unique course had downed trees, brush fences, jumps with drops or slides, rail fences and one jump was even painted with a huge, colorful dragon (courtesy of Carolyn Woltjes and yours truly) staring at the approaching horse and rider.

Viewing a rider from two different angles provides an excellent perspective of the Balanced Seat position. (See Appendix A for the 33 points of the Balanced Seat position.)

Rider training began with common horse sense and confidence, starting with the basic procedures of safely mounting and dismounting. While Linda instructed us she constantly reinforced the Balanced Seat position, which is described like this:

Upper Body: All parts of the body from the hips up: Eyes forward, back straight, hands over in front of horse's withers; knuckles thirty degrees inside the vertical; hands two inches apart and making a straight line from horse's mouth to rider's elbow.

Base of Support: All parts of the body in contact with the horse or saddle:

Crotch deep in the saddle; inner bones of the knees and calves against the horse's sides. Toes out about fifteen degrees, according to rider's conformation; ankles flexed in; heels down, calf of leg in contact with horse and slightly behind girth.

Subtleties reminded us how to best perfect the balanced seat position. While in the saddle a mere glance down at our knee, for example, would indicate if your foot was in the proper position. If the boot toe was visible ahead of the knee, the feet were too far forward and easily remedied by moving the feet slightly back behind the knee.

The proper position would be behind the knee, creating a plumb line from your shoulder through the hip and down through your ankle under your hip. Another alarm went off if your elbows passed behind your hip signaling that your reins were too long. A quick adjustment with the reins brought the hands back over the withers where they can proficiently send communication to the horse's head.

Linda checks her position in a large mirror situated next to an arena.
It seems the horse is enjoying his reflection as well.

The exercise is explained in detail and then executed by the group.

Students were repeatedly drilled on maintaining the proper Balanced Seat position. By posting without stirrups in this exercise the rider can concentrate on balance and building strength in the thighs and buttocks.

Cavaletti exercises were practiced nearly daily to learn balance in the Two-Point Position or Field Seat.

We learned how to judge speed and pacing in order to rate our horses. It was an excellent training ground for other competitive venues and an ideal environment for becoming an accomplished rider. Hours of concentrated equitation drills, coupled with studying proper techniques, soon developed competent riders in the Balanced Seat position, the Two-Point Position and the Field Seat.

The format taught by Captain Marsden at the U.S. Pony Club Instructors' Training at Camp Teela-Wooket in Vermont was duplicated in Linda's Pacific Coast School of Horsemanship riding lessons. Each command was issued in the same fashion. For example, in a commanding voice Linda would say "Trot!" which would be the cue to gather the reins and collect the horses. Now with everyone prepared for the next cue, she would say "HOooo" in a long bold voice and the riders would commence trotting. When she spoke the gait command, it was an alert to be prepared and the "HOooo" meant to execute the command. It was really helpful and kept the group in unison.

"Trot, HOooo! Walk, HOooo!" was commonly heard coming from the arenas.

"That, probably without me realizing it, is so useful when we are leading a horse in hand," comments Linda. "You can use your voice commands so that the horse can understand what you want under saddle. When we are leading a horse we say, 'And HOooo.' So the AND is a really important preparation like the Cavalry command. It wasn't just a 'HO' it was a 'HOooo' that kept the group together. That's what we practiced a lot while coming up into pairs and threes or following one after another. We did a lot of drills like that, which has really been helpful to me over the years in my classes."

The pair Quadrille work instills confidence especially when riding around other horses. "One of the exercises I still teach when instructing groups, is that the riders go single file and then number off 1-2-3-4 so even numbers come up in pairs and then one will go forward then drop back. It's such a great exercise for riders and it's one reason that I enjoy teaching a class of at least four people rather than individually because the students learn so much more and become efficient riders."

Slides and Banks

Linda demonstrates on Hungarian Taszilo how to approach a steep downward slide.

Linda coaches a horse and rider as they leap up a large drop jump.

The drills covered changing gaits smoothly, maneuvering over cavaletti poles, and negotiating slides and banks, while always maintaining the proper position. Riding in pairs while holding the hand of a partner expanded the rider's awareness. Adjusting stirrups at both the walk and the trot was also part of the exercises.

Bad habits were quickly replaced by the proper and effective techniques of mastering the Balanced Seat position. Everyone practiced and soon found they could ride up and down steep embankments with ease and confidence. Pride prevailed.

Students were repeatedly drilled on maneuvers until the extremely difficult became comfortable and easy. Riding in pairs required thinking not only of yourself but of the horse and rider next to you.

The riders steadily build confidence for cross-country jumping courses.

Attempting these maneuvers was not always graceful in the beginning.

Students progressively improved to attempt bolder passes.

Precision jumping reaches a level where Linda trusts her students enough to stand in the middle as they sail past her.

Linda taught students to ride the terrain, not just the trail. Here Shannon is jumping Rip over a downed tree.

On Thursdays we rode bareback in jeans and tennis shoes. However, students were still expected to perform the same drills, including jumping fences and perfecting steep banks and slides. It helped to be dressed in the "Thursday" relaxed attire while learning how to vault on and off the horse from the ground. Confidence levels soared as the class became stronger and more courageous.

To challenge our riding skills we would take long trail rides and whenever there was a log to jump, an embankment to go up, a slide to come down, or a water crossing, we would all eagerly line up for the test. "We had treasure hunts on horseback and great trail rides," PCERF student Laurie Jurs reminisces, "where we would go swooping through the forests."

Aside from being a spectacular rider, Linda was also an excellent mentor and teacher. One of her charming characteristics is that every time she mounts a horse, Linda smiles. As a young girl, Linda's mother would stand ringside and in a motherly way whisper, "Smile dear!" as Linda rode past. "She would always say it with a smile in her voice and a message from her heart," Linda recalls. Not only does smiling reflect Linda's love for being on a horse but also it's impossible for your body to be stiff when you are smiling.

Tirelessly, Linda exemplified living and riding with purposeful intention. Both Linda and her assistant Eleanor Woltjes were patient and excelled at supporting student confidence while challenging their abilities.

Long before it was popular among athletes, Linda applied the intuitive skill of visualization while working with a horse's energy. We practiced her method with a horse that balked at crossing water or a ditch. Linda would show us how to sit quietly and imagine the possibility of the horse calmly crossing to the opposite side. She instructed riders to follow her example by pausing for a moment and visualizing the end result without conflict. All the while she made the horse think it was their idea. This is a simple and yet effective technique that was virtually unheard of at the time, but is relatively commonplace today.

Linda describes a key element to her teaching process by saying, "Visualization was incorporated in our training as early as 1964 for students competing in hunter and jumper classes. Students would stand outside the ring with their horses, and imagine cantering around the course, flying cleanly over every jump with perfect style. This exercise varied from the normal sports visualization, in that the riders would also imagine that their horses could see the same crystal-clear, successful images that they were visualizing. I believe the key to success is including your horse in the picture. Not just you alone. It's the team of you and the horse."

Linda demonstrates how to jump a downed tree while riding out on the trail.

Belinda Bowden and Mary Pruitt McBride on a trail ride. The Anglo Arab, Strider, on the right became a favorite horse of the students.

Trail Riding

"Mother Nature set up the optimum cross-country courses which made trail riding thrilling with Linda," student Martha Merriam remembered. "I loved riding down the sand dunes at Hazard Canyon. My favorite was jumping over weather-worn fallen trees." Linda would have everyone survey a natural obstacle, size it up and then the class would line up to jump it. The obstacle didn't matter — trees, ditches, creeks, rivers, sand dunes, brush. It was all there for the adventure of crossing.

A rider takes her horse through the year-round creek on the property.

The uneven topography at Badger offered trails with loose rock or large granite boulders; both required alert navigation. Martha went on to say, "A sharp smack in the face from prickly leaves of low-hanging oak tree branches served up a lesson in self-preservation. All of these elements taught students to duck for protection while still maintaining a balanced seat. Even today, every downed tree I pass is considered a prospective jump," she said. "With Linda by our side, we were fearless. By breaking everything down into procedures, Linda explained how the horse was reacting to a situation so that the rider could understand the scenario," Martha said.

Everyone had their share of spills and "unscheduled dismounts" but at the end of the day, students achieved far more than they thought possible while facing their own fears. "By blending the expectation to improve, coupled with the herd of smart, brave and trustworthy school horses, the riders were easily encouraged beyond their comfort zone," Linda said.

After a two-hour mounted morning session, we returned our well-worked horses to their respective quarters, untacked, bathed, fed and put them away. We hurried back to our rooms where the famished gang cleaned up for lunch.

Classroom Lectures

The dining room was converted into a classroom for the afternoon lectures conducted by Linda or her assistant. One of the primary textbooks used was "Horsemanship" by Gordon Wright and the United States Equestrian Team, masterfully illustrated by artist Sam Savitt. It was designed and written to produce the finest horsemen possible. The book's dedication indicated its level of standards:

> "THIS BOOK IS RESPECTFULLY DEDICATED TO THE MEMORY OF A GREAT MAN AND GOOD FRIEND WHO WAS EQUALLY DEDICATED TO THE CAUSE OF HORSEMANSHIP: GEORGE S. PATTON, JR. GENERAL, UNITED STATES ARMY."

Everything at the school was broken down into a series of procedures to master the finer points of equitation and horsemanship. Later classes used a book called, "The Cavalry Manual of Horsemanship & Horsemastership," also by Gordon Wright.

The School of Horsemanship program had four levels of achievement: Rosette, Bronze, Silver and Gold. The Gold Medal was earned after a Silver Medal graduate had established an equestrian business. Eleanor Woltjes and Lynn Blades were among the few who achieved this honor.

Three Program Categories: Riding, Theory and Stable Management

Hippology, the study of horses, was thoroughly explored through hours of lectures identifying breeds, basic anatomy, colors, markings, how to determine the age of a horse by their teeth, points of the horse's body, and every part of the hoof. We spent weeks studying conformation and with our new knowledge no horse escaped our scrutiny. Body types and how a breed best served various disciplines were studied. We learned about the mind of the horse, how they found their place in a herd, and why they responded to their environment with certain behaviors.

Gracefully clearing a log jump, Linda's Assistant Instructor, Eleanor Woltjes, was a PCERF Gold Medal recipient, which meant she achieved the Silver Medal in addition to establishing herself in the equestrian business.

Students are taught how to identify parasites while analyzing fecal samples in the microscope.

Health and disease were fascinating topics. We were taught methods of diagnosis, how to take the horse's temperature, pulse and respiration and how to analyze fecal samples while searching for parasites. We learned how to bandage the horse's legs and how to identify blemishes and unsoundnesses. And of course a favorite pastime was watching the horses be shod and learning from the farrier. Just as Linda had learned from her teacher Alice Greaves, we were fortifying ourselves with knowledge to be passed on to others.

Dressed in her usual skirt and clogs, Linda demonstrates how to properly measure a horse's body to meet the ideal conformation set by Thoroughbred industry standards.

Rider training began with common horse sense and confidence, starting with the basic procedures of safely mounting and dismounting.

The horse care routine was straightforward: water before feeding, feed hay before grain, and feed in small quantities and often. Do not work a horse hard after a full feeding.

Stable management was broken down into procedures that emphasized safety. Each person was armed with a bucket of grooming tools. We were taught the proper way to lead a horse and to never wrap a lead line around your hand. The Tellingtons taught us to always give warning when approaching the horse and to keep a hand on the horse's body while near them. A word of wisdom: "Attendants should not be loud or rowdy about horses," suggesting that horses mirror the energy that surrounds them.

The art of properly grooming a horse started with using a currycomb in a light circular motion to loosen mud, dried sweat and matted hair — never using it below the knee or hocks. We'd start at the head, working in a small circular motion all over the body, ending at the tail. A stiff body brush is used in an upwards-flicking stroke that removes the debris, followed by a soft body brush in the same flicking motion, bringing a shine to the horse's coat. Then it's on to the feet, safely picking up and cleaning the feet. We spent time learning how to tie a variety of knots, including a safety knot and a bowline. Bridle and saddle fitting were important lessons to insure the comfort of the horse.

It was our job to keep equipment and tools in an orderly fashion; Linda, Went and Eleanor kept a constant eye on our work. We soon found out that beneath Eleanor's pleasant appearance was a will of steel. A beautiful rider herself, she duplicated the strong work ethic that Linda possessed.

We were taught to identify the parts of a saddle and bridle and the proper techniques of tack cleaning. Not only is well-maintained tack attractive but it's also good for the health of the horse. Dirty saddles and girths are often the cause of many irritations and sores. Disassembling, cleaning and reassembling a saddle and bridle were commonplace tasks at the school.

Every few weeks the group would gather in a cool spot surrounded with boots, saddles and bridles. Chattering like magpies, the students scrubbed and cleaned headstalls, cavessons, cheek pieces, brow bands, reins, stirrup leathers, and girths piled in discombobulated heaps. Last we applied Wentworth's special aromatic Carnauba wax formula to condition and supple the leather. By the end of the session each bridle was carefully reassembled and hung correctly with the reins crisscrossed and the throatlatch fastened. Between these thorough cleaning sessions, bits and bridles were sponged off after each use and hung properly in the tack rooms.

We learned how to mindfully haul a horse trailer with consideration for cornering and the horse's well-being. On Friday there was always a written test that covered the subjects studied that week.

Responsibility was heaped on everyone. Especially in the fall, winter and spring sessions when the student population was lower than in the summer, students held positions as barn or pasture managers, looking after the kitchen chores and other incidental tasks. I immediately gravitated to the Great Danes, Tiger and Hara, whose house was near the kitchen. I felt it an honor to take care of them. They were definitely a part of the PCERF social strata. Linda gave me one of their puppies a year after I left the Research Farm. I named her Tara.

Watching Linda work with the horses, or any animal for that matter, was a magnificent sight. Her confidence and intention radiated — and they knew it.

By the end of the first week, we got the hang of our new and very different life. The new regime exposed our strengths and weaknesses, which helped direct our progress over the sessions. Linda was the ideal champion for her students who, like a brood of ducklings, followed her everywhere.

For me, some of the major benefits of living with Linda came from observing her subtle nuances. Fascinated, I studied the slightest traces of her personality that drew me in even closer to her. Often while she was walking or consumed in explaining a subject, it was not uncommon to see Linda unconsciously flicking her fingers. She was intensely energetic; I assumed it was a way of ridding herself of the excessive life force that sprinted through her body.

Even during random moments, her gift was shared whether she knew it or not. I recall an occasion at a show at Ram Tap when several of us were having a conversation. Linda was holding the young stallion Hungarian Niscak by the reins when he started testing his studly parts. Without missing a beat Linda countered him with one compact voice command, epitomizing her confidence, experience and knowledge. Without any physical contact from her, Niscak's shenanigans quickly ceased. In that split second she asserted her energy infused with intention and the *expectation* for him to embrace his manners at once. It was so fast that when it was all over, those standing nearby didn't know what just happened. But I got it and the horse got it!

The respect Linda gave each horse was reflected in its willingness to perform for her. Her body size and type are perfectly suited for equestrian sports, and coupled with her innate horse savoir-faire, strong competitive drive and natural talent, watching her compete was absolutely blissful — a vision of beauty. I think Linda Tellington is truly the best rider I have ever seen.

Stories of Went's and Linda's pasts were endless. One evening a classic Linda story was told at dinner. The previous year the Tellingtons had made a trip to a Three-Day Combined Training Event in Arizona. Linda said, "Several students and I were competing when I had a horrible crash on a big ditch and the horse fell with me. He got up but my ribs were in terrible pain. It really hurt but I quickly regrouped and climbed back on the horse and we finished the ride." Linda went on, "The next day, Sunday, I was still very sore and it hurt to breathe. There was a team event coming up on the schedule and we were down three riders. In order for us to win I had to ride in the jumping event or else our team wouldn't have had a chance."

Even Linda, who has a high pain threshold, grimaced at the memory. "The excruciating pain meant cracked ribs, so Went wrapped my chest with a horse's leg wrap and trussed me up. After I finished my round the judge, Herman Friedlander, who really liked me and heard that I had been badly hurt thought I was okay after seeing me ride. He came running over and gave me a huge bear hug. It almost killed me, for God's sake. It was very painful but what could I do? It was too late to warn him not to hug me because of my cracked ribs. I soon recovered and in retrospect, it was funny. I was pretty tough," Linda affirmed.

I must confess, my eyes were the size of saucers after hearing that story and I hoped that I never had to match her grit. Over the years I witnessed time and time again exactly how tough Linda really was when it came to digging deep and withstanding extreme conditions.

Went always noticed the slightest minutiae, especially when it concerned safety. One day he came into the lower barn while I was working on a horse and he said to me, "If that horse flips its head he will knock you over because of the way you are standing." I turned towards him with a questioning glance. "You're standing back on your heels," he went on to say. "When you stand that way, you are like a post and cannot move out of the way fast enough. But if you are on the balls of your feet you can actually move away from a situation very quickly." I duly noted his wisdom and thereafter was conscious of my stance.

Through his keen awareness, Went could test students without them realizing it. His strategy often began after a significant accomplishment by saying, "I didn't think you could do that," leaving the residual effect of, "Oh yeah? Well, let me show you what else I can do too!"

Rattlesnake Stew Becomes Metaphor for Life

Wentworth brought everyone together in many ways, and his acclaimed Rattlesnake Stew also served as a metaphor for life. He said, "Life is exactly like making a stew in the kitchen. Try anything once, but don't try everything at once because you will never know what made the stew a great success or a failure."

After the long days of riding and studying, some of my favorite hours at PCERF were spent in the kitchen with Wentworth. I never knew what to expect from him and I learned so much by working with him or just hanging around with him. I listened as he taught us to think by using facts, to keep a firm grip on our emotions, and to avoid simple opinions. Be patient and diplomatic, listen carefully and watch to see who responds to what in a discussion. Stay quiet. Just like with a good stew, take your time, and see how it turns out when it has cooled off and then after it's been heated up again. Let tempers settle down, laugh at your mistakes, but move on...

"Eating alone was bad news while eating together with a diverse group was stimulating," Went professed. "The best possible foods in taste and goodness are generally the least expensive." His solid advice was to, "take time to prepare, time to cook, time to digest, time to talk, time to think and time to mull it over."

As for the horses, he was as adamant about good nutrition for them as he was for people. He instructed us to feed hay to the horses first. Let them begin by adding a layer of roughage to their stomachs. Then as they are eating the hay, let them watch while their grain mix is prepared. Again it would get their digestives juices flowing and stimulate their appetite. So much of what he professed in the kitchen carried over to the barn.

Wentworth was adamant that dinner be enjoyed by candlelight because it creates a more relaxed atmosphere.

Tellington Field Trips

On weekends we all piled into vehicles and took the long drive down to the town of Visalia. But hold it! Whenever we left the Farm, we had to wear skirts or dresses... always ladies, no pants or shorts allowed away from the Research Farm. After all, we were Tellington Girls.

One destination led us to the Porterville Horseshoeing School 30 miles southeast of Visalia, located on the flat farmlands of the San Joaquin Valley floor, a stark contrast to the mountainous terrain of Badger.

The horseshoeing school drew students from across the United States for the

16-week session. We watched apprentices practicing the art of hot horseshoeing, and outside were work areas where young men became skillful at their craft on frozen cadaver feet clamped upside down in vises. They practiced trimming a hoof, shaping a shoe and nailing it onto these frozen feet. It was imperative to learn the anatomical structure of the foot as well as foot diseases before the student could practice on live horses. The adage "no foot, no horse" was the school's motto that day and every day.

The air was permeated with the distinctive smell of the horseshoeing trade. The fellas, mostly cowboys, were clad in blue jeans, wrapped in leather shoeing aprons, and turned out in boots and sweat-drenched shirts, with a red bandana tossed in here and there. Some sported smudges of soot on their faces. With their new tools and high hopes, they aspired to a career with horses. Our small group (dressed in skirts) appreciated their craft, which flattered the farriers.

On another occasion we were fortunate to visit a cutting and reining ranch where the trainer exhibited the excellent traits of a seasoned working ranch horse. For some of us, it was the first time we'd seen a real working cow horse in action — the experience was exhilarating! Our next outing took us to Gem State Stables, a large and well-known Thoroughbred breeding farm of its day.

Livestock Auctions

The best way to learn about ailments, diseases and unsoundness problems was to go to an old-fashioned livestock auction. On this outing we arrived at a parking lot filled with old pickup trucks and horse trailers. The outside pens were stuffed with horses of all colors, sizes and breeds. There was a stiffness in the air that comes from animals who are in a state of uncertainty — a combination of fear and unknowing. We made our way through the smoke-filled auction arena to look at the horses. Our lesson was to identify injuries or ailments and we were not disappointed. Look! There's a fistula of the withers, a capped hock, a bowed tendon, a ewe-neck, a Roman nose, over at the knees, a swayed back. Look — that one is cribbing. From laminitis to complete neglect, we saw stunning examples of poor horsemanship and learned to identify things that one can only find in a place where the saddest of cases can be found: a livestock auction.

Swirl Study

The Tellingtons shared a wide array of information derived from many resources that formed endless layers of knowledge. Learning was fun and easy since we were submerged in our favorite topic: horses. Wentworth's philosophy was to share his wealth of information as opposed to keeping it secret as many horsemen still do today.

For example, the study of swirls on horses' faces, necks and bodies attracted particular interest during the PCERF years. In fact, a survey was sent out to all members to take photos of their horses' swirls and to describe their personality traits in order to compile case studies in which 1,500 horses were analyzed. Refining the data into orderly logic proved an epic task that spanned several years to evaluate. The results of this mass of data eventually became the foundation of Linda's book, "Getting in TTouch: Understand and Influence Your Horse's Personality."

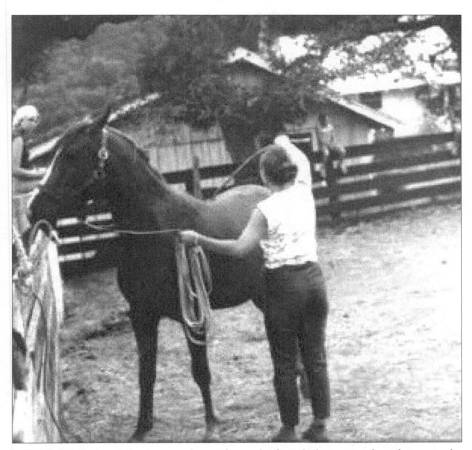

While Linda is starting a young horse, she randomly picked up a tree branch to extend her arm and bring awareness to the opposite side of his body. This photo reveals the early development of Tellington Wand that she uses today. Shannon is sitting on the fence observing.

Linda gave one demonstration on starting a young horse that truly illustrates the origins of her work today. While I was sitting on the fence watching her and Bint Gulida's colt Kaweah, she intuitively reached for a small tree branch and used it as an extension of her arm while running it over the horse's body. Unmistakably, this was a primitive predecessor to the now refined tool she calls a "Tellington Wand" – the 4-foot long, stiff dressage whip that plays a vital function in bringing awareness to the horse's body, used today with the Tellington Training Method.

Linda showed us how to work with problematic horses. She simply relaxes and they find their way to her. I watched her use energy as a means to connect with them long before it was an accepted concept. In fact, it was nearly 20 years before I actually heard people talk about working with energy as a means to convey their intentions to animals. Yet Linda did it naturally, although she didn't have the words to describe what she was doing. She showed me and I picked up what she was doing. The objective is to energetically convey an intention and expect a certain response or behavior in return. Today, of course, it is not at all unusual to consider working with the energy of any animal.

In fact, this practice is so natural to her that today Linda had to stop and reflect for a moment about how she relates to horses. I told her about the moment that she had taught me this lesson. Several of us girls were trying to catch some loose horses that were running free in the upper field by the arenas. As novices, we were basically just moving the horses around and they weren't taking us seriously. When Linda arrived to help us I was riveted by her focused intention. It was as if she intensely emitted a beam of energy aimed at the horses shoulder – spanning from head to tail. The first horse responded immediately and submitted to her as she walked up to him, the rest followed and all were caught.

"I love this reference of Shannon's about how she saw me matching energy with a horse," says Linda. "It brings up memories and feelings I have rarely considered. This focusing of energy was totally natural. I learned at a very young age that I could influence horses by calming myself and connecting with them by treating them as though they could understand what I was thinking. And they could!

"Shannon's comments reminded me of another time I had that same feeling. It was in the late 1980s and I was working with dressage rider Barbi Breen-Gurley for the first time at her Sea Horse Ranch in Los Osos, California. Barbi was riding a young mare that had a very nice working trot but had not yet developed an extended trot. I remember standing in the middle of the arena, consciously creating a connection with the breath of the earth, filling my body with each intake of air. Feeling completely grounded I directed a beam of light from my navel to the core of the mare and to Barbi's core. Instantly the mare shot forward with fabulous impulsion and extension in a spectacular flying trot. Barbi could hardly believe it and yet I remember it to this day.

"It started when my parents and grandparents treated animals as though they could understand humans so it was natural for me too and I never thought it was special. I was a voracious reader then, as I am today, and one of my favorite books was entitled, "Silver Snaffles" by Primrose Cumming. It was about a Welsh pony that talked to the other horses when the lights went out in the stable. This story had a big influence on me, and I began treating horses as though they could understand me at a rather young age.

"Thanks to quantum physics, it is no longer considered a mystery. It's now known that *every thought* is energy, and it was with clarity of thought that I knew I could connect with horses, as well as other animals."

PCERF summer horse shows were extremely popular among the students. It was an opportunity to test what they had learned while competing with peers as well as outside riders. Besides the Ram Tap Horse Trials in Fresno, students attended many other outside events too.

Shannon with Rip in a halter class at a PCERF horse show.

Shannon again with Rip, this time in the Ram Tap Combined Training Three Day Event.

Went takes footage of students competing at Ram Tap.

While Linda takes a respite moment between classes at Ram Tap, Went reties her stock tie.

PCERF Gold Medal recipient, Lynn Blades, on Hungarian Taszilo as they take the honors in both the 1st and 2nd Levels at the 1970 Valentine's Day Dressage held at PCERF.

Joan Turner riding Hungarian Taszilo demonstrates the versatility of the Hungarian horses.

Rattlesnake Charmer

Linda's sister Robyn Hood remembers the advice Went gave pertaining to country life. If we were bitten by a rattlesnake we should calmly say, "May I please have some help, I've just been bitten by a rattlesnake." This delivery would aid in *not* escalating our heart rate; an escalated pulse would allow the venom to course through our veins at a rapid rate.

On a hot afternoon up near the Upper Barn, the class was walking on the dusty road back to the dormitory. Stretched out to its full length of four feet was a rather ample rattlesnake basking in the hot day's sun. We all froze and immediately felt the rush of adrenalin that comes when confronting a poisonous snake. The brownish grey and black skin on the triangular-shaped head and diamond-patterned back was accentuated by a mature set of rattles. This snake had reason enough to be distrustful of the dozen or more people towering over him who could have killed him on the spot. Linda calmly walked up to the snake and began to honor it simply with her presence. Watching this serpent commune with Linda for at least ten minutes was extraordinary, and after they had their dialogue, it slithered away. It was obvious that Linda's magic with horses spread to all creatures. The magic lies in respect for the being.

CHAPTER 12

Tellington Girls at the Ready
for the Bitter Root Competitive Trail Ride

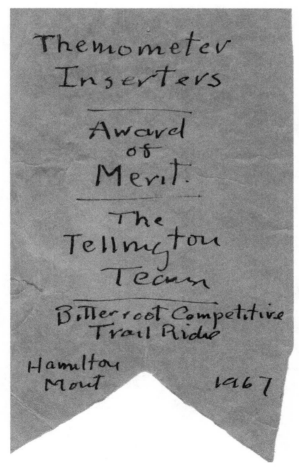

Created from a brown paper bag, this award was presented by Army General W. M. Johnson to the Tellington Girls for their outstanding service at the Bitter Root Competitive Trail Ride.

Unless we were at a competition, Saturdays at the school were saved for our weekly shopping trip to Visalia, a town tucked between Fresno and Bakersfield in Central California. On a warm late-July day, Linda asked me to hop in the grey pickup truck for the hour-long drive to town. Cruising along the rolling and winding valley floor, we heard the flump-flub sound of a flat tire and pulled over. Knowing that Bruce, the farrier, was not far behind us, we got out and waited for him to come along and fix the problem. Linda and I gravitated to some inviting river rocks next to a flowing stream. The ensuing conversation beside that refreshing water was a milestone for me.

Linda began with, "Margit Bessenyey has asked me to judge the NATRC (North American Trail Ride Conference) Bitter Root Trail Ride again in Hamilton, Montana on August 19th (1967). Went and I want to take five girls with us to assist in taking the horses' vital signs. Who do you think we should take?"

Carolyn Woltjes, Pam Parker and Nancy Maddock were three of the Tellington Girls who
ventured to the 1967 Bitter Root Competitive Trail Ride in Hamilton, Montana.

I thought for a moment about who had earned this privilege, and then suggested four girls who were interested in long distance riding: Pam, Laurie, Nancy, and Carolyn. Linda replied, "Those are the girls I had in mind, too." I fidgeted, knowing how desperately I wanted to go, and blurted out, "Would I be able to go too?" Linda quickly said, "Of course, silly!" While waiting for help for our crippled truck, I had learned how Linda felt about me.

In the cool of the evening a few days later the Montana-bound students assembled at the Upper Barn. Under Wentworth's tutelage, we began preparation for the NATRC ride. Dressed in his usual summer attire of a brown, short-sleeved, collared shirt, belted shorts, and durable leather sandals, Went was firmly planted in his teaching stance, his hand clasped around a highball glass of whiskey on the rocks.

The goal was for these five girls to become fast, confident and accurate at taking horses' temperatures, pulses and respirations (TPRs). We broke into teams; one person held the horse and counted out 15 seconds. The other team member inserted the stethoscope earpieces into their ears and pressed the flat stethoscope diaphragm against the horse's girth just behind the elbow. That person counted the lub-dub heart sound for 15 seconds, then multiplied that number by four to get the minute-long pulse rate.

Then we tracked the horse's respiration rate by watching the in-out movement of the horse's flank and learned that a normal respiration rate was 8 to 20 breaths per minute. Thermometers recorded a normal average of 99 to 101 degrees. Wentworth stood back, his keen eyes astutely tracking our progress. It was not unlike him to lob a few pointed barbs, should anyone drift from his focused instructions.

During our lesson, Went continuously told stories of Bint Gulida's excellent recovery rates at the mare's two successful 100-mile rides. He poured forth pointers about crewing at the Jim Shoulders Ride where Linda and Bint Gulida had won the ride as well as the best condition award, and about crewing at the granddaddy of endurance rides, the mighty Tevis Cup Ride, where Linda and Bint Gulida placed in Top Ten the first time she attempted this feat. He wanted to insure that we were familiar with every thump of a heartbeat, every heaving bellow of the lungs, the resting numbers for pulse and respiration, and normal temperature ranges.

It was 1967 and the Tellingtons had recently published a book called the "Endurance and Competitive Trail Riding Manual," produced and published by Pacific Coast Equestrian Research Farm, Badger, California U.S.A. It was a compilation of data accumulated while observing horses in the vigorous activity of long distance riding. Banged out on a manual typewriter, the pages were then copied on a *mimeograph* machine. The hand-assembled, soft-covered publication included details about conditioning, riding, managing and judging a ride. It also raved about the Tevis Cup Ride and contained material that still remains pertinent today.

An example of the detailed information in the book vividly explains the function of a horse's heart:

"The pulse is normally a solid sounding two-beat sequence with a second beat being somewhat louder than the first. There should be a neat space between the beats. A ka—plunk —— ka—plunk —— ka—plunk would be a phonetic description of the sound with the normal intervals for a healthy untrained horse. A poor heart sound would be a light heart going kaplunk —— kaplunk —— kaplunk. A well-trained horse heart sounds like this: ka—plunk—ka—plunk— ka—plunk. The overall pulse rate in an average healthy horse will probably range between 36 and 44, with 40 being close to an average. With training, the pulse tends to become a bit slower and may be as low as 24 or 26 in some great athletes. It is not uncommon for a trained horse to have an at-rest pulse of 32 to 34."

To obtain a resting respiration count, the book continues: "It is quite easy to spot respiration by standing more or less directly in front of the horse, cradling his nose in your hands while holding it close to your cheek. He may for a few moments hold his breath or sniff, but he will soon respond to the 'love-making position' and give you an accurate idea of his at-rest respiration when you feel his warm breath on your cheek. There should be no odor to his breath, by the way. Bad breath or bad-smelling sweat or bad-smelling droppings are all indications of maladjustment of the working mechanism of a horse."

The description goes on to say, "The ability to recover by relaxing and taking in one giant breath is characteristic of a well-conditioned horse." A useful technique taught in the School of Horsemanship program was about mirroring the horse to bring respiration down by breathing in exaggerated deep breaths. While slowing down your breath, the horse will soon begin to mirror you and begin breathing slower, too.

About gaits and speed, the manual continues with some Canadian influence, "To avoid boredom for both trainer and mount, you walk a mile or so and then where the going is good break into a good free, exuberant trot like a happy moose. It is highly important whenever you trot to post and change diagonals every mile or so."

Countess Bessenyey's Bitter Root Stock Farm

Margit knew the benefit of challenging horses over distance at speed. She felt the best way to test horses was to train them for long distance riding, so she wanted to put on a 50-mile ride and host clinics at her magnificent Bitter Root Stock Farm. That's where the Tellingtons and their experience in endurance riding was valuable so Margit enlisted their expertise to judge and put on clinics for the Montana area riders.

Linda has fond and poignant memories of the Bitter Root Stock Farm. "Over the years Margit organized a number of clinics and workshops where I presented comprehensive lectures," reflected Linda. "We would give workshops and then put on a ride so that people could apply what they learned. I remember those rides that wandered through the beautiful mountains around her ranch. Gosh, I wish I still had those notes from the lectures that I gave there!"

Margit Bessenyey riding one of her Hungarian horses.

Irish immigrants Marcus Daly, William Andrews Clark and F. Augustus Heinze were famously known as Montana's 'Copper Kings' of the late 1800s. According to the book, "Beyond Spirit Tailings: Montana's Mysteries, Ghosts and Haunted Places," Daly built an empire by seeking potentially profitable mines and convincing wealthy investors to provide financial assistance. In 1881, with the financial help of newspaper giant George Hearst and California land barons James Ben Ali Haggin and Lloyd Tevis, Daly was able to develop one of the world's most prosperous copper mines in Anaconda, Montana. He managed the Anaconda Copper Mining Company (ACMC) from 1881 to the late 1890s.

Shannon Yewell Weil

After the mining company was underway, Daly then turned his attention to the Bitter Root Valley where he scouted for limitless acres of timberlands. He purchased large tracts of forested land and built sawmills. He harvested the forests to supply the need for a whopping 40,000 board feet per day that was swallowed by the smelters of his enormous cooper operations in Anaconda. Daly ultimately founded a company town, naming it for one of his employees, James Hamilton.

His land eventually became a 22,000-acre farm known as the Bitter Root Stock Farm. Daly built a mansion called 'Riverside' that occupied a massive 24,000 square feet over three floors, adorned with 24 bedrooms, 15 bathrooms and seven fireplaces. This became the Daly family's summer home in the heart of the Bitter Root Valley. Mrs. Daly made certain that every room had a bowl of fresh roses that she raised in her abundant garden. The gentle rose scent lingered throughout the home, welcoming its many guests who typically stayed for several weeks.

In 1900, having achieved remarkable successes in his 58 years, Marcus Daly died on November 12th, leaving an enormous fortune to his wife and children. After Mrs. Daly's death in 1941, the mansion was closed until it was reopened in 1987 after it was purchased by the State of Montana in 1986 and is now operated by the Daly Mansion Preservation Trust.

The Tellington Girls: From Badger, California to Hamilton, Montana

With luggage strapped to the roof of the GMC Carryall, seven of us stuffed ourselves sardine-like into the passenger seats for the early morning drive to the airport. We said goodbye to instructor Eleanor Woltjes, who stayed behind to keep the school running, and waved to our fellow students as we departed Badger. Went, Linda, Pam, Laurie, Nancy, Carolyn and I headed down the winding Road.

Went, who was at the wheel, was under the impression that we had ample time to meet our flight. As he was about to make the turn into the Visalia Airport, Linda reminded him that our reservations were from the Fresno Airport. Went erupted, "FRESNO! We'll have to drive at high speeds to get to the airport on time!" With that declaration, he floored the gas pedal and we jetted north up Highway 99. Surrounded by a commotion of anxiousness the Tellingtons' traveling circus skidded into the terminal and made the northeast-bound airplane with only minutes to spare.

From the portals of the airplane we could see the breathtaking panoramas of the Bitter Root Mountain Range that divided southwestern Montana from Idaho. We landed in Missoula just 43 miles north of the Bitter Root Valley, collected the plethora of bags and headed straight away for the Bitter Root Stock Farm. Countess Bessenyey welcomed us warmly to her home where she spent May through October each year and showed us to the spacious and comfortable guesthouse. Linda and Went stayed with Margit in another house.

Several houses served as the manager's residence, bunkhouse, and more barns. From the corrals the view captured a mile-and-a-quarter racetrack edged with more sheds that housed horse vans and equipment.

Inside the barn was a room full of trophies and ribbons that dated back to when Marcus Daly's horse, Scottish Chieftain, won the 1897 Belmont Stakes in New York. Marcus was Countess Bessenyey's grandfather who established the Bitter Root Stock Farm where he raised horses for working, driving and racing.

We quickly settled in and the five Tellington Girls set off to visit with the beaming PCERF grad, Linda Harpster, who was lucky enough to have landed a position caring for the young Hungarian horses there. It suited her perfectly. From our guesthouse we crossed the lawn to where she gave us a tour of the exquisite large brick barn crowned with a cupola. Then we explored the elegantly furnished trophy room detailed with dark wood paneling that smacked of richness and reflected decades of success. Large glass cases displayed glorious silver trophies and ribbons, some hanging three deep. They dated back many years to when her grandfather, whom Margit had never met, raised and raced Thoroughbreds and Standardbreds, as well as breeding giant Percherons. The stalls within the stable were stately and immaculate. The sweet smell of native hay filled the barn – blue joint, Idaho fescue, wild oat, blue bunch and wheat grass – as the beautifully groomed horses munched in their stalls.

Laughter belonged to us as we took turns driving a pony cart up and down the lane in front of the barn. We barely comprehended the magnitude of our surroundings as we breathed in a glorious breeze that fluttered throughout the cottonwood trees. The sun filtered through leaf-patterned shadows onto the lane at our feet. We knew we were standing on hallowed ground that belonged to the brilliant Hungarian horses we so admired and respected.

Competitors had already arrived for the Bitter Root Competitive Trail Ride as trucks and trailers filled the parking area at the Ravalli County Fairgrounds. Horsemen and horsewomen came early to soak up the beautiful valley, study the terrain and rest their horses. The 40-mile trail ran across the rolling foothills up into the timberlands and climbed up to 6,000 feet elevation. Spectacular vistas appeared at every turn during the seven- to eight-hour competitive ride.

We met the hardworking ride managers, retired Army General W. M. Johnson and his wife Virginia of Missoula, Montana. We also met their daughter, Tex, who was a contestant in the ride. The Johnsons and Margit had spent weeks preparing for the ride to the extent that Margit had ordered her ranch hands off their horses and onto tractors to clear the trail of sagebrush and downed trees. Much of the trail blazed through virgin land that had never been disturbed. In her pragmatic way, Margit asked her ranch hands to simply drive the tractors across the hay fields to mow miles of trail for the ride.

Saturday's dawn welcomed us. Linda and Went marshaled us to the buzzing fairgrounds for a tempting breakfast. It was at the start of the trail where we were told at which checkpoints we would assist the veterinarians. Then we split up in various pickup trucks and reveled in the glorious scenery as we drove to the vet checks.

The Tellington Girls collected vital TPR statistics on each horse. Linda was a fair and objective judge and we were proud to watch her apply the riding and horsemanship principles she had taught us over the summer. When her keen eye noticed any anomalies, she pointed them out to us — she was always the quintessential teacher. At the 28-mile checkpoint, a chuck wagon luncheon was served for riders, crews and spectators who drove from town to enjoy the day's activities.

The Bitter Root Stock Farm sprawled over 22,000 acres surrounding Hamilton, Montana.

Wentworth kept up a flowing monologue about the farm. At that time, the Stock Farm was a world-class agricultural and horse breeding facility dedicated to raising beef and building the Hungarian Furioso breed. We were particularly impressed when he told us that the 40 miles of trail were entirely on the 22,000-acre Stock Farm land. He also thought it was useful for us to know that the beef raised on this ranch would ultimately be sold to the elegant Waldorf-Astoria Hotel in New York City. Impressed, we nodded with eyes wide.

At the awards banquet, guests indulged in a Big Sky Country barbeque. The sunny afternoon festivities were in full swing and, with the exception of the Tellington flock, the crowd of ranchers, cowboys, horsemen and horsewomen was crowned with cowboy hats. People were seated at calico-covered tables scattered under huge sprawling shade trees. Conversations abounded about horses, the trail and the ride, while guests happily feasted on steak, coleslaw and corn on the cob.

On the lawn stood one of the oldest living legends of the time, a cowboy small in stature with piercing blue eyes and a graying wispy mustache. He was decked out in the typical old West attire of striped pants, cowboy boots, white long-sleeved shirt and dark vest, with a red bandana circling his neck. The towering uncreased ten-gallon hat gave an illusion of height to his slight frame. It was Bob Brislawn, the Oshoto, Wyoming native. His son Emmett had won this ride the year before on his good Spanish Mustang stallion, Yellow Fox.

Amongst a wide range of publicity, Bob was once featured on a 1957 cover of *Life Magazine,* drawing notoriety as the founder of the Spanish Mustang Registry. His animated, weathered face was fully engaged in jawing with Wentworth, who stood with his arms folded across his broad chest. Bob was singing the praises of the superior traits possessed by Spanish Mustangs and was confident of their overwhelming dominance to other breeds. Bob compared them to Arabian horses and because Arabs had one less vertebra than other breeds, he admitted the Arab's excellent endurance features were on a par with a Mustang. "Yep, we'll just cut one open and I'll show ya!" he insisted. It wasn't necessary since we already studied that fact in our lectures. Mr. Brislawn seemed a bit discouraged that no one wanted to take him up on his idea.

In 1969, Shannon was thrilled to receive the coveted award presented by Countess Bessenyey, a sterling silver pin made by Tiffany & Co. in the shape of Montana.

As the horsemanship judge, Linda spoke at the awards presentation and commented on the overall condition of the horses and level of horsemanship. She and the veterinarian judge then announced the placing of riders and horses and handed out prizes. Margit presented what I consider to this day the classiest award ever given at any trail ride. It was a sterling silver pin custom-made by Tiffany & Co. in New York City. In the shape of the state of Montana, the pin's background was of the Bitter Root Mountain range and in the left corner were Bitter Root flowers, representing the valley where the ride took place. It simply read, "BITTER ROOT COMPETITIVE TRAIL RIDE." Countess Bessenyey had impeccable style and I was determined to return the next year to win one of those pins, which I did.

The morning before we were scheduled to leave Hamilton, Margit piled us all into vehicles and took us to see a crop of young Hungarian horses. She was a down-to-earth ranch woman and considering the fact that she could have anything she desired, the Countess still insisted on driving a vehicle with a standard transmission. She stated emphatically, "I don't know how to drive a car with an automatic transmission!" I was in awe of her and didn't want to leave Montana.

As we approached a large band of young horses, they galloped towards us, instantly recognizing Margit, but were a little shy of the rest of the group with the exception, of course, of 'animal magnet' Linda Tellington.

The Tellington Girls — Pam, Laurie, Nancy, Carolyn and I — were ever so grateful for this adventure. To have been invited to the Bitter Root Stock Farm and bask in its magnificence was a rare opportunity indeed.

More important, however, was the fact that Wentworth and Linda Tellington were sought by Countess Bessenyey to become the guardians of her beloved horses. She resonated with the Tellingtons' approach to horsemanship and to the inspired and unconventional PCERF programs. Margit had a deep history with the Furioso horses dating back to when they were warhorses in Hungary, even risking her own safety while bringing the horses to the United States after World War II. With her vast fortune, Countess Bessenyey could have chosen anyone in the world to train and showcase her Hungarian horses, but she chose Linda Tellington, reflecting the genius of Linda's talent.

CHAPTER 13

SOLID AS A ROCK, HEART OF GOLD:
MAGYAR BRADO

By the time we returned from Montana to California in late August 1967, the summer session was nearing its end. Final exams were over and we assembled in the school's living area for our graduation ceremony. Linda and Eleanor spoke about each person's achievements and the Pacific Coast School of Horsemanship Level One Bronze Medals were awarded. It was hard to say goodbye to friends; we had become the Tellington Tribe. But the regular school year beckoned.

Pam Parker and I were lucky to stay longer. Linda asked me if I would be willing to stay through September and join them in Colorado for the Peaceful Valley Two-Day 100-Mile Ride on Labor Day weekend. It was one of the few endurance rides in the country at the time. My *"never miss an opportunity"* mother said, "Of course you should go!"

Bruce Scott and Pam had been training the Hungarian horses for the upcoming 100-mile ride. Pam would ride Pallo, the tall, handsome eye-dazzler of a horse, and Bruce would be aboard Taszilo, a beautiful and smart bay gelding. He was a sensitive horse, noted by his "two interfering swirls on the forehead." Linda would ride her favorite champion, Brado. However, over the busy summer Linda spent most of her time with students and didn't ride very much. I was concerned whether she would be fit enough to ride 100 miles, but she thought nothing of it.

We packed the rig, loaded the horses — Brado, Pallo and Taszilo — into the five-horse grey van and headed out to Colorado. A 17-year-old girl named Simone Hamburger had just arrived from Quito, Ecuador and we folded her into the crew that consisted of Went and me. I drove the grey pickup behind the van.

Crossing the Sierra Nevada mountains on Interstate 80 heading towards Reno, Nevada, we made a fuel stop just before Donner Pass. While taking a stretch, Went waved his arm to the south, pointing towards the expansive, craggy and seriously-daunting landscape that made up the Sierra. He said, "Those are the mountains that the Tevis Cup Ride crosses!" A little stunned, I thought to myself,

"Holy cow!" While gazing at the humbling sight, I also thought, "People who enter the Tevis must be out of their minds!" My imagination went into overload while staring in awe at the majestic Sierra. The prospect of one day facing the challenge of riding 100 miles to earn a beautiful sterling silver Tevis buckle like Linda's had just gained more respect and appreciation. "I'll have to ponder this goal a little more…," I mused.

We enjoyed a couple of layovers to rest the horses on the nearly 1,200-mile drive. Crossing the Rocky Mountains, we headed north from Denver. As we began the 5,400' elevation climb, the GMC engine whined under the strain. After the long drive we arrived at the rustic Peaceful Valley Lodge in a stamp-sized town called Lyons. Went believed it was better to acclimate the horses by spending a week at high altitude before the competition.

Peaceful Valley Ranch continues to be a popular vacation retreat with a beautiful lodge and recreational facilities.

The hosts of the popular dude ranch were Carl Boehm and his family, known for their excellent hospitality and delicious meals. A huge horse barn stood across the little-traveled road that divided the facilities. Two Arabian stallions spent their days in nearby rail corrals at the front of the lodge.

There were only a handful of endurance rides in those days, so the dedicated few would drive all night to make the start. Phil Gardner, riding his Arab/Saddlebred-cross mare named Cricket, was one of them. He was accompanied by Wendell

Robie's granddaughter, Marion Robie, and her Arabian mare Hailla. Wendell loaned them "The Goose," his bright orange truck, and matching horse trailer to make the long trip.

Nevada resident Pat Fitzgerald, whose legendary reputation preceded him, brought his chestnut gelding Ken, the first Arabian horse sold for endurance riding by the Rush Creek Land and Livestock Co. in Lisco, Nebraska. Linda and Went regaled us with some of Pat's amusing pranks. Claiming he didn't have time before he left home, Pat was once seen shoeing his horse the day before a ride. Lacking a proper anvil, he used the trailer-hitch of his turquoise pickup truck, a Dodge power-wagon, to shape the shoes. Satisfied after several loud bangs with his hammer, he nailed the shoes on his horse's feet and declared him ready for the following day's 50-mile ride. Another time he backed his horse into a vet check and hollered out, "Well, ya gotta teach 'em sometime!" Pat, a colorful character, was a magnet for new endurance riders.

Pat's sidekick, Cliff Lewis, brought a flashy, nearly all black, short-backed, long-legged Arabian cross — a ground-covering machine named Black Jack. These were the die-hard endurance riders who could throw their horses in a truck or trailer and drive hundreds of miles just to get to a ride and usually win it or finish in the top ten. They were the pioneers of endurance riding. With the addition of a few local thrill seekers, the field reached about 20 riders.

The Head Veterinarian was Matthew Mackay-Smith, DVM of White Post, Virginia. While conducting the pre-ride veterinary check on Friday, it was clear to us that Matthew was some sort of character. *Fun* is the best word that describes being around Matthew. An avid endurance rider himself, he was one of the earliest veterinarians to get involved with the sport.

Linda had first met Matthew when he graduated from vet school, and they remain good friends to this today. He later became the Medical Editor of *Equus Magazine*.

At daybreak on Saturday morning the riders left the starting line. Our well-prepared team of three Hungarian Furioso horses ridden by Linda, Bruce and Pam took off without a hitch. Wentworth, Simone and I followed the veterinarians to the checkpoints and waited to help our riders. When they arrived we monitored the horses, counted swallows of water, and took pulse and respiration counts, as well as temperatures. Based on the theory that a horse will mirror you, Went taught us to stand next to the horse's head and take deep long breaths ourselves. We were looking for that one deep breath from the horses. As soon as they took that deep breath, their pulse and respiration rate would drop dramatically and their recovery would hasten.

The trail went though the scenic terrain of the Roosevelt National Forest tucked into the majestic Rocky Mountains. The stunning views were like a layered parfait sundae. Lush bright green grass strewn with granite rocks represented the bottom, followed by a band of the deeper green of conifers and Aspen trees. A jagged row of snow-capped mountains topped the parfait, crowned with whipped cream clouds. All this was smattered against deep blue skies, forming a breathtaking backdrop. The whitish-barked Aspen trees felt like the riders were in a Bev Doolittle painting. Columbines and the Mariposa Lily littered the trails, and the creeks rushed from snowmelt. Marmots scurried about the rocks and beaver lodges abounded while green meadows alluded to the promised land. It was a geologist's playground.

Linda and Pam arriving at the Gold Hill Vet Check.

Pam Parker taking Hungarian Pallo's temperature.

We reached Gold Hill, an old mining town about 30 miles south of Peaceful Valley and watched Linda's group of Hungarians trot past smartly. Went, clearly pleased with their progress, hollered out, "Those are some damn good horses!" For Brado's first 100-mile ride he, along with the other two horses, were exhibiting the unfaltering qualities of their Hungarian warhorse heritage. While I knew what to expect from Linda, Simone was awestruck by her performance. We caught up with the horses at the vet check situated near a lake. Pam took temperatures, a practice we were fervent about back then. Went reminded us to only put water on the horses' legs. He preached, "If the temperature outside isn't warm enough for you to put water on your own body, then don't put it on the horse." Linda's diminished physical training for herself that summer was beginning to show, but she drew upon her iron constitution and looked perfect in her McClellan saddle.

At the end of the ride, the miles had taken their toll. Holy smokes! I'd never seen Linda so exhausted. Simone and I took care of the three horses while Went kept his eye on all of us. His prize rider just had a very hard day. Sitting on a bale of hay in a fatigued heap, Linda welcomed a kind lady's offer to massage her cramping muscles. In that private moment it was difficult for me to see my *heroine* suffering in such pain and fatigue. Yet there was nothing I could do; I had to stay with the horses. But she was teaching me what it meant to dig deep into the depths of one's being in order to rise to the occasion.

Bruce and Pam and all the horses were fine. They were all a little tired but recovered quickly because they had logged so many training miles and were in great condition. Through it all Linda still smiled; she retired early in the evening to get some well-deserved rest.

The following morning we were up before the crack of dawn to prepare the horses for another 50-mile day. Linda mounted her loyal Brado and the pair repeated their performance. "For the last ten miles I was going to take it easy and just finish," Linda said. "I knew I couldn't catch Pat and Ken as they were a formidable pair with a good lead on me." Went always encouraged Linda to push harder and ride faster but she was comfortable with a pace that best suited the horse. "I just wanted Brado to have a great ride," Linda reflected.

"Up near Longs Peak I reached the elevation of 10,000 feet and I suddenly had the strangest experience," remembers Linda. "From out of the blue I felt the presence of my grandfather, Will Caywood. It was as if he was riding the horse with me and I heard him shout out, *'GO! You have plenty of horse left!'* I urged Brado, who was already trotting at a good clip, and he willingly broke into a fast gallop. I knew we couldn't overtake Pat (Fitzgerald) but we made up a lot of time. Never before had I felt my grandfather's presence in this way — and we flew."

Anticipating Linda's arrival, we waited at the ranch's lodge. Still smiling and tall in the saddle, Linda rode Brado across the finish line shortly after winner Pat Fitzgerald and his Rush Creek Arabian Ken. Even with galloping most of the last ten miles, Brado's recoveries were excellent. Now after completing the 100 miles, Linda was truly exhausted and reflected, "No wonder I was so beat, I galloped the last ten miles!" Bruce, Taszilo, Pam and Pallo arrived about an hour later.

Linda and Brado finished the two-day 100-mile ride in second place behind Pat Fitzgerald and Ken. But the real honor of the weekend was announced when veterinarian Matthew Mackay-Smith presented Brado with the Wadsworth Trophy for the horse in the best condition — the Top Ten horse in fittest condition to continue down the trail. This was a great feat for Brado, considering he had carried an unconditioned rider for 100 miles over rough, high altitude terrain. However, it wasn't just any rider…it was a beautiful rider. It was Linda Tellington.

Some of the other horses and riders didn't fare so well. One cowboy rode in a heavy western saddle and sat a jog the entire distance. Now paying the price, his willing horse was in the veterinarian's care. That night was the first time I'd ever seen a horse cry.

The Labor Day weekend was over and we headed back to California. After watching Linda's performance, I thought maybe that Tevis buckle was obtainable after all. The 'tough ol' boiled owl', as Linda had been deemed, impressed me again.

We made the long drive back to Badger and I reluctantly returned home to Altadena. After the first mopey week at home, my father asked me what I wanted to do next, to which I replied, "I just want to go back to Badger!" Three long and one short rings later, Linda answered the telephone and I cried, "I'm coming back!" My initial four-week session was about to evolve into 12 months at the Research Farm.

Linda and Brado in the Oakland National Horse Show

LTJ AND STUDENT ON HUNGARIAN
BRADO AND HUNGARIAN POLLO
WINNER OF THE HUNTER HACK
CHAMPIONSHIP
OAKLAND, CA   1968

Linda, on Brado, is holding her trophy from the 1968 Hunter Hack Championship, Oakland, California. Both she and her student on Hungarian Pallo, are riding sidesaddle.

I know I've said it before, but watching Linda ride a horse was the epitome of grace and beauty, which enhanced her exceptional teaching skills. The solid bond that Linda created with Brado was paying off in spades. Now she was taking the stallion into competition at the newly built Concord Mt. Diablo Trail Ride Association equestrian center in Concord, California, which hosted the fall Oakland National Horse Show and Combined Training Three-Day Event. Dressage tests were ridden on the first day and excitement grew on day two when the Cross Country events were held. Among her competitors were two highly-accomplished riders, Lyn McKillip and Donna Snyder-Smith, who both excelled at dressage, eventing, jumping and endurance riding.

Several students and I watched as Linda and Brado left the starting gate and disappeared into the lengthy and arduous cross-country course. We then moved closer where a crowd had gathered to watch the horses come down a narrow steep trail that hugged the side of a wooded ravine. At the bottom, the trail took a left-hand turn where it crossed a three-foot-wide reinforced ditch that allowed the creek water to flow through.

Spectators were assured of the trail's dangers after watching riders carefully cross the ditch at the bottom. Time passed and then we heard the signal of another horse and rider coming as someone hollered, "Stand back!" We instantly recognized the flash of Linda's pale yellow sweater against Brado's deep bay coloring. The pair, wasting no time, came flying down the trail at a full gallop. As if horse and rider were welded together, in one swoop they turned and sailed across the sizable ditch. Brado's long forelegs extended as he grabbed solid ground for his next stride, his hind legs thrusting his huge body through the air. They raced out of the woods and headed for the finish line. If only the U.S. Equestrian Team could see him now! Brado clearly loved every minute of this ride. No one would have ever believed that this horse once had confidence issues over ditches and had been rejected by the Olympic team! Now he was as solid as the Rock of Gibraltar. Linda and Brado won the Cross Country portion of the event.

The Stadium Jumping classes were held on the third day of the competition. A blue ribbon was waiting for the horse and rider who accumulated the highest score while covering as many jumps in the least amount of time. It was the Gamblers Choice class where exhibitors choose their own course with each fence cleared worth a given amount of points based on difficulty. The entry that accumulates the most points within a set time limit on course is the winner. Linda studied the course in advance and thought to herself, "Now, how would Went approach this?" His answer came to her when she realized that only the largest obstacles with the highest point values mattered. She now had a plan. The public address system announced, "Up next is Linda Tellington riding the Hungarian stallion, Brado." The duo electrified the stadium and Linda's eagle eye focused on their first obstacle.

A layer of spectators lined the rail watching Linda in her usual perfect riding form. In the chill of the late afternoon and tingling with excitement, we PCERF students were perched at a good vantage point above the arena to watch the last class of the day. Again the impeccable alliance between Brado and Linda would be challenged and a victory meant certain high point champions. Was he willing to trust her judgment? Brado's indomitable power, coupled with Linda's acumen, established them as the team to beat.

Linda took a few circling strides at a canter and then unleashed the might of Brado's raw power towards the first fence. They assaulted the course as Brado's robust hindquarters propelled them over the biggest and widest jumps with athletic ease and grace. Linda ignored the low-valued jumps altogether and twice repeated several of the higher-valued jumps. Brado soared over every huge obstacle, incurring no faults. Finally Linda ended the spectacular clean round by turning Brado's pricked ears towards a wide water feature and, as if overcoming gravity, they leaped across its wide spread with nary a splash. Then they raced to the finish line. Cheers erupted as their winning score was announced. Linda and Brado had won the Gamblers Choice Class and swept the Championship as well. It was a great day and a laudable showcase for a very courageous horse named Magyar Brado.

Marking one of their finest accomplishments, the following year Linda and Brado won this very event for a second time having just placed 9th together at the Tevis Cup Ride.

Spring PCERF Endurance Rides

Linda presents Dr. Richard Barsaleau with the trophy for winning the 1967 Sontag Evans Getaway 50-mile ride as Went and student look on.

"We're cookin' on the front burner now!" bellowed Went's voice.

In early spring plans were underway for PCERF's annual endurance rides that featured local trails around Badger and nearby Kings Canyon National Park. The Tellingtons' 50-mile ride was called the Sontag Evans Getaway, named for two marauding bandits of the 1800s who routinely robbed stagecoaches that traveled up and down Dry Creek Drive that ran through PCERF.

The other Tellington event, a 100-mile two-day ride, snagged its name from the 1892 Vienna to Berlin Endurance Race that paid homage to the Hungarian horses. The historic race covered a distance of 361 miles in 72 hours. According to documents, among its 217 entries only 145 horses and riders finished; many horses perished from exhaustion. Of the top 24 horses, two-thirds were bred in Hungary. Thereafter the popularity of the Hungarian horses spread throughout Europe, the Middle East and into America, and boosted the popularity of Hungarian horses in military breeding programs. Countess Bessenyey graciously donated the Athos Trophy for the winning horse and rider for the Tellingtons' ride in honor of her Hungarian horses.

Avid endurance rider Dr. Richard Barsaleau had his practice in nearby Visalia and was the veterinarian for the Research Farm. He's seen here riding his mare Good Trip.

The weekend list of guests included a who's who of endurance riding at the time: Dr. Richard Barsaleau on Good Trip, Pat Fitzgerald on Lanny, Phil Gardner on Cricket, Cliff Lewis on Black Jack, Marion Robie on Hailla, Julie Suhr on her Peruvian Paso mare Marinera, Susan Reilly and her Mustang mare, Bonnie. Former Hazard Canyon student Rho Bailey was a crew member. I was well-trained and ready for my first 50-mile ride on a tough buckskin horse named Ringo.

Veterinarian Dr. Murray Fowler examines Pat Fitzgerald's horse Lanny while Paige Harper and Lynn Blades assist. Pat is wearing his "party favor," a yellow cotton Cavalry scarf that was given to all participants in the Tellingtons' 1968 Ride.

The Tellingtons were also fortunate enough to have legendary photographer Charlie Barieau document their rides. He hiked his camera into remote locations along the trail, accompanied by his faithful companion, a little black poodle named "Shoes."

"There were so few rides back then that we would go to every one we could," said Phil Gardner — once a winner of the Sontag Evans Getaway 50 mile ride. "We would leave our jobs early on Friday afternoon, load our horses in the trailer and drive all night to get to the ride." Marion Robie proved her grit as a seasoned endurance rider by wearing a pair of skimpy canvas Keds sneakers and riding in English stirrups irons sans the rubber cushion. Her grandfather, Wendell Robie, had trained her well to be tough — especially if she wanted to ride with him.

In typical Tellington style, each competitor was given a "party favor" of sorts, a yellow scarf similar to those worn by the Cavalry. Its function varied. Soaked in water and tied around either the rider's or the horse's neck, it made an excellent cooling aid. Or in an emergency it could be ripped into bandages or used to mark a trail.

Before being rescued by two men, Pat Fitzgerald nearly drowned while riding (Rushcreek) Ken in 1967. Ken realized it was every man/horse for himself and made it to safety on his own.

Dripping wet, once Pat was back in the saddle, he said, "I can't swim, but I sure can ride!" PCERF student Peggy Potter looks on.

Went also mimicked the Cavalry by adding a number of obstacles to the course designed to earn time points. Dr. Barsaleau remembers, "We had the option of riding down banks, slides and over jumps. I chose to take a four-foot jump that included a drop, cutting two and a half miles off the trail." Riding his wonderful bay mare, Good Trip, he won the ride that year. "We also swam a pond and gained more time," he recalled. "That was the only endurance ride with those types of obstacles." But it was a tense moment when non-swimmer Pat Fitzgerald nearly drowned in that same pond. His horse Ken, unused to swimming, did his best as his completely-submerged rider held his breath and walked across the bottom of the pond while Ken swam above him. When Pat finally reached the near side of the pond, with the help of two men he came out sputtering and gasping for air as he climbed up the bank. Poor Ken scrambled to dry land with a dizzying look about him, a bit confused and soaking wet. Those were the days!

Dr. Barsaleau on Good Trip and author Shannon Yewell Weil on Ringo, wearing hunt boots and riding a McClellan saddle, strike a long trot through the Kings Canyon National Park.

Shannon rides Ringo down a steep slide to earn time points.

Martha Merriam waits to have her Arabian gelding, Green Acres Gaius checked by the veterinarian. Wentworth and Ernie Sanchez observe from the bank above.

I rode much of the day with Dr. Barsaleau and photographer Charlie Barieau captured us while we struck a long trot through the woods. *My* dear Great Danes (notice my feeling of ownership!) Tiger and Hara logged as many training miles as I did and ran with me during the ride. Tiger, however, surrendered at the 35-mile vet check and pulled himself with a "Canine Option" but the tenacious and beautiful Hara ran the entire 50 miles with me. Naturally Went prepared his famous Rattlesnake Stew for the barbecue during the awards presentation.

Later that evening after the awards were presented, I slipped away to check on Ringo, who was bedded in the lower barn. I opened the door to his stall and sat with him as he was munching his hay; I wanted to quietly thank him for the wonderful ride. The tough old caballo acted nonchalant, as if it was all in a day's work. I thought I was alone during my private visit and was startled when Wentworth entered the barn. In his Spartan way, he congratulated me for finishing the ride by giving me a nod and an approving grin. He said to me, "I didn't think you could do it." But as a young girl, I did successfully complete my first 50-mile ride. It felt great and I was one step closer to fulfilling another requirement to earning the coveted PCERF Silver Medal.

The following year Shannon returned to PCERF to ride a Thoroughbred gelding named Big Red. Seen here moments before the start of the 1969 Sontag Evans Getaway 50-miles Ride with Cliff Lewis on Black Jack, Phil Gardner on Cricket and Pat Fitzgerald on Lanny.

In the late 1960s, Val Pruitt (center of the three riders) continued to develop Sierra Spy (and changed his name to Spartan) and rode him on the Sontag Evans Getaway 50-mile ride.

CHAPTER 14

FROM THE STUDENTS' POINT OF VIEW

After a great year Shannon earned her PCERF Silver Medal and celebrated by riding the young Hungarian Tarter.

By June of 1968 I was facing my final test at PCERF for my Silver Medal examination. I studied my notes carefully and handily passed the lengthy and comprehensive written exam. Now with the required 50-mile ride under my belt, it was time to meet Wentworth for the mounted examination. I had prepared two horses, Red Fox and Hungarian Pallo, and readied myself for the appointed time at the Upper Field. Knowing Went's demanding and high standards, two of my buddies, Linda Day and Silver Brandon, accompanied me for moral support. The examination took three exhausting hours of riding over fences, banks, slides, and various obstacles and ended by performing dressage exercises. Finally it was over and I was elated when Went announced that I passed the rigorous requirements. I was awarded the coveted Silver Medal.

A few days later I packed my belongings and said a final farewell to the beloved dogs Hara and Tiger who I had cared for over the past nine months. I hugged my friends and then said goodbye to my mentors, Linda and Wentworth. It was a bittersweet day; I was torn about leaving the Research Farm but knew it was time to stretch my wings. I had grown immensely and in retrospect have always referred to that year as *the springboard of my life*.

Shannon (left) with fellow wrangler Tommy Tulles at the Peaceful Valley Guest Ranch.

Linda had arranged a position for me at the Peaceful Valley Guest Ranch in Colorado, the same place we had visited in the previous fall for the endurance ride. My blissful job there was to give riding lessons and train endurance horses. That summer we took two horses to the Bitter Root Competitive Trail Ride and at last, I received my sterling silver Tiffany & Co. pin.

After I graduated from PCERF, many wonderful young students followed in my footsteps coming to drench themselves in the well of knowledge that I treasured about the Tellingtons' school. When I began to write this book I contacted several alumni to learn their stories. Each fascinating conversation produced a common thread that tied us together. Everyone told about how PCERF changed their lives, just like it did mine.

Went assembled former Chadwick School students for a reunion at PCERF. Among those who attended was Roland Kleger, (seated, center) who later became Linda's third husband 32-years later.

Paula Stockebrand

Paula hadn't seen the Tellingtons since they left Hazard Canyon in 1965, when as a college freshman at the University of California at Santa Barbara (UCSB) she was driving to Northern California to visit her brother Steve over Easter break. "I decided to take a little side trip to see the new PCERF location in Badger. I never made it to see my brother. Linda invited me to join them and compete at the Easter Three Day Event at Ram Tap," an eventing center established in 1957 near the town of Fresno. "I was game and said yes. I rode the little half-Welsh horse Rebel and that began my dedication to the PCERF program."

Paula's parents, Archie and Bunny Stockebrand, who had helped Went and Linda build the Hazard Canyon facility, were now living in Paso Robles. "The Tellingtons pulled them out of retirement and gave my parents the job of renovating and managing the newly acquired (by Margit Bessenyey) M Bar J Guest Ranch just up the road, which was the equivalent of giving two fun-loving people a great big playing field," Paula said laughingly. "Plus my Dad could work on Went's new airplane, which was an antique Stearman biplane."

Thankfully dog-lover Paula Stockebrand returned to PCERF and assumed care of the Great Danes.

As a working student Paula became an integral part of the PCERF team and alternated semesters at UCSB and PCERF over the next two years. "I was a hard worker and the Tellingtons appreciated good work ethics," said Paula. "I helped with the food service for the students and staff. I also looked after Wentworth's hallowed comfrey garden."

Pulling weeds and nurturing the comfrey plants in the blazing sun left a lasting memory. In what Went described as his "esoteric" philosophy towards healing, the organically grown herb was a key ingredient in specialty products like VYM, a dark, pungent, vitamin-rich supplement that contained molasses and ground sea kelp. Comfrey contains healing properties used in poultices, a tip the Tellingtons learned from Will Caywood. Taken internally it serves as an anti-inflammatory and digestive aid, among other benefits. Another popular supplemental product called Horse Candy was constituted from powdered non-fat milk, finely ground comfrey and sea kelp. The powdery soft substance smelled of milk and made an odd, almost squeaky, sound when clenched in your fist. It possessed a healthy feel and the horses loved it.

Lynn Blades

Lynn brought the sport of foxhunting to PCERF and organized a mock hunt. At the end of the day, Hara, Jim Weir (left), Lynn Blades (center), Tim Durant (right) and Brado celebrate with champagne.

For a long time upstate New York native Lynn Blades had been looking for a riding school to attend. "I was a devoted reader of the *Western Horseman* 'Let's Go' articles that Went and Linda wrote and finally decided to go to their Pacific Coast School of Horsemanship," she said. "I was already well versed in their philosophy," she said. "So I signed up and thought I would be there for three months, then I would come home and become a school teacher and go on with my life." But it didn't turn out that way.

Like cream rising to the top, it didn't take long for Went and Linda to notice the exceptional talent that Lynn possessed. "I was in my twenties at the time and I remember wanting to make the most out of every single day. Being around so many exciting people was thrilling. I knew that I would ultimately come home to work in the family construction business, but those four years that I was out there were just amazing to me."

Lynn grew up as an avid foxhunter and steeplechase rider alongside her father. "While I was in high school, I would hunt six days a week. We had our own hounds at our farm and we loved it," Lynn said. "My Dad and I went to Ireland and I gained a lot of experience hunting there too." Lynn organized a mock Fox Hunt at the Research Farm. "We even had the renowned steeplechase rider, Will Durant, join us." Durant was called the "Galloping Grandfather" and rode in the Grand National Steeplechase when he was 67 years old. He was also an active member of the Los Altos Hunt Club and finished the Tevis Cup Ride in 1965.

By now Lynn had mastered the Tellingtons' program. When Eleanor Woltjes returned to Tucson, Arizona in the fall, she was confident that Linda had several students capable of filling her position. Linda offered the Assistant Instructor job to Lynn, who was honored to accept the position.

"Because I grew up in a family construction business I had a knack for scheduling and organizing classes and events so it all came very naturally for me. I loved it," Lynn said. Her skills lifted a lot of weight off Went's and Linda's shoulders, freeing them up for other projects.

The Tellington Team lined up at a horse show.

Lynn remembers several spontaneous whims. "It was so fun. We would throw a few horses in the trailer and go to the local horse shows in Porterville, Exeter or Visalia. Linda told us, 'We'll just get on their backs and jump around courses.' So on the spur of the moment we would decide what horse would go in which class. 'Let's ride Brado in this class, Taszilo in that one or Strider in this one,' Linda would say. Then we would enter the ring, jump around the course, make a few mistakes and come out and hop on another horse and do it all over again just to give the horses the experience."

It wasn't hard to spot the Tellington Team — they were the ones with all the ribbons and trophies.

Lynn recalled a moment that smacks of Linda's special gift. "Someone was having a problem with a horse and Linda was trying to sort it out from the ground. She was dressed in her typical attire of a front-pocketed jean skirt and a pair of clogs," explained Lynn. "After a few minutes of instructing from the ground the rider still wasn't getting the desired results from the horse, so Linda asked the rider to dismount. In her short skirt and clogs she hopped on the horse's back and straightened him out, just like that. It was her magic, her style — no one else could have gotten away with it but she did. She jumped off, the horse was fine, and we proceeded with the exercise."

Birch Jones

Birch Jones showed great promise as an equestrian while exhibiting his ability to entertain visitors.

When new students arrived at the school Linda would have her customary one-on-one conversation with them. It was a Friday evening when she set aside time to visit with a tall, lanky, young man of 19 years by the name of Birchall Jones, Jr. They met after dinner at around 8 p.m. and sat down on the bench at the library table near the office. The conversation started off about his riding experience and what his intentions were. He spoke of his interest in the Modern Pentathlon, which includes Pistol Shooting, Épée Fencing, 200m Freestyle Swimming, Show Jumping and a 3K Cross-Country Run. An athletic type, Birch wanted to do it all.

While Birch was talking, Linda suddenly felt a peculiar shift occurring. She couldn't put her finger on it but there was something uncharacteristically different about their meeting, as if she was receiving a glimpse into her future. It surprised her that she didn't even notice that two hours had passed when they finally said goodnight. She didn't talk about her odd experience but it stayed with her for quite awhile.

Birch was extremely athletic as he demonstrates jumping with arms open wide while bareback.

Birch performing a dressage test at Ram Tap.

Wentworth enjoyed having Birch at the school as he could tout his military training to an appreciative audience and help nurture the young man's preparation for the Pentathlon.

Shannon Yewell Weil

Michele Pouliot

A natural rider, Michele (right) is on Taszilo, Linda (center) is aboard Brado and Val Pruitt Sivertson (left) is riding Witch (Hungarian Tundra). The trio just finished a jumping demonstration at Prescott College in Prescott in Arizona.

Michele's introduction to PCERF was a little different. Growing up as an Air Force brat, her family moved to different bases wherever her father was stationed. She got her first horse while living in the Philippines and then, during her high school years, the Pouliot family moved to Louisiana. There she spent most of her time with a new horse that her father had bought for her. "It was really important to my Dad that I attended a good college," Michele said. "But after I watched the Disney movie, 'The Horsemasters,' I knew college wasn't for me. I dreamed of going to a fancy ivy-covered horse academy in England to become a riding instructor. I told him about my ambition but he kept hoping I would grow out of it." Michele argued that spending the money saved for college on something she really wanted to do was the better idea. "It took him awhile but he finally agreed to my plans," she gratefully admitted.

Just like in the movie, she fantasized about a magnificent British setting while learning the finer points of horsemanship. In those days England was the preferred destination for such schools and few were found in the United States. Her father disliked the distance that England would bring between them and sought closer options in the U.S. He found two possibilities: One was in Virginia and the other was the Pacific Coast Equestrian Research Farm in California. The PCERF tri-fold brochure adequately described the program Michele preferred. Her father's impending transfer to California meant he'd be closer to her, so she applied to the Pacific Coast School of Horsemanship.

"Dad asked me if we should go see the place but I said, 'No, I don't want to spend the money just to have a look.'" She was convinced that it would be as grand and beautiful as the school in the movie. Michele was booked for the 1969 Spring Session. "Dad drove me to Badger but when we arrived, we were shocked. We were not prepared for what we saw," said Michele, who was aghast at the sight of the rustic structures. "Where was the beautiful British school I had envisioned? I'll never forget the look on my Dad's face when we rounded the corner and pulled in. 'Is THIS IT?' I remember my stomach turning and I thought, 'Oh my God, did I make the wrong decision?'" There weren't a lot of pictures in the little brochure so her imagination had taken over. "All the other schools had nice buildings, beautiful barns, cobblestone walkways and fancy ironwork. When we pulled up to that rustic little office I thought, man, I can't look back now — we already paid my tuition.

"At first I was really disappointed, especially about all the money my Dad spent, which for us was a lot in those days," Michele said. "After he left it took me about five hours to come to my senses." It was the kindness of two residents, Birch Jones and Lynn Blades, that made Michele feel welcome, especially when she realized how much they loved being there. Then she settled in and shortly thereafter Michele hit the ground running and became a star student.

"I was a very good rider and spent many hours riding the Hungarian horses. They were incredibly high quality and I was able to show them a lot. Witch, Brado, Niscak — they were level-headed, honest, brave and had a lot of pizzazz. It's nice to recognize what Went and Linda did with those horses," Michele confirmed. "She deserves so much credit for how she campaigned the Hungarians."

After Michele received her PCERF Silver Medal, Went and Linda asked her to stay on as an instructor. "Throughout the next summer we did a lot of competing," Michele remembers. "The PCERF experience changed you internally and elevated your confidence level. I have to credit Wentworth for being a strong person, one whom I even feared a little bit, but the fact that he bolstered my ego was really good." What he said to Michele after she finished her Silver Medal test has stayed with her to this day. "He said that I had a gift that not many people had and that I should be proud about my talent. He really made me feel special, particularly since I was a pretty insecure girl when I arrived at the school." Both Linda and Went had that effect on many people who came through the PCERF doors, making the experience so extraordinary.

"Before I started working for Linda and Went they talked to me about staying amateur and taking a Hungarian on to the Olympics. But I was ready to start making money at that time," Michele stated.

Val Pruitt Sivertson

With arms open wide, Val confidently rides Brado over a jump while Roland Kleger looks on.

Val took control of her own destiny while at the Pacific Coast Equestrian Research Farm by attaching herself to her favorite horse, Sierra Spy. The young, gangly chestnut gelding that I cared for in 1967 was filling out and developing into a very handsome horse. His only fault was a rather rough gait, which deterred many riders from choosing him. Val, on the other hand, loved him.

Val talked about endurance riding with Spy. "Well, he had short pasterns and hit the ground like bricks," Val said flatly. "I picked him because no one else liked to ride him because he was so rough-gaited. That was my secret to success at PCERF; I always picked horses that no one else wanted to ride. Since I was the only one who wanted to ride him, I rode him every day while everyone else was taking turns riding other horses. That's why he came along much faster." She rode him in Three Day Eventing and endurance riding, including the Tevis Cup Ride.

Val went on to say, "Spy was eventually sold to someone in the Midwest and went on to become a Three-Day Event champion all the way up to Preliminary or Intermediate levels. I heard that he had won that region for a couple of years." It was an ideal ending for a wonderful horse.

Val tells a humbling story that left a lasting impression. "One day a group of three students joined Linda on an outing to look at a potential school horse. His owner had just had a baby, which was why she was selling him. For two years she won the California Appaloosa Jumping Championship on this horse; he certainly possessed talent," Val said. "I was really curious to see what this horse looked like." When they arrived at the ranch the owner saddled and rode the horse in the arena. As the three Tellington Girls sat back and watched the horse make huge sweeping arches over the jumps, they started to giggle at how bad the rider looked on him. They carried on about what a poor rider she was when suddenly Linda turned and said, "Val, get on that horse!" Feeling rather smug, Val got on the horse and rode him over the first jump. Even though she was an excellent rider, this horse nearly unloaded Val and by the second and third jump she was riding exactly like his owner was. Just like that, Linda politely made a swift attitude adjustment in her students. "From that day forward," Val said, "I never criticized people for what they look like riding a horse until I've ridden that horse myself." Lesson learned.

Alexis Flippen von Zimmer

Alexis Flippen (von Zimmer) and her Thoroughbred Ciri proudly receive a blue ribbon from Linda at a PCERF horse show.

An excellent rider in her own right, Lyn McKillip introduced Alexis to the Pacific Coast School of Horsemanship. Lyn shown here is exquisitely riding her horse over Cougar Rock on the 1966 Tevis Cup Ride.

When her horse trainer and mentor, Lyn McKillip, strongly recommended that she attend PCERF, Alexis asked, "What's a PCERF?" Lyn was a lovely rider and a natural athlete who rode jumpers, endurance horses, and dressage horses. Alexis explained, "Lyn knew of the Tellingtons through Combined Training Events and the Tevis Cup Ride, where in 1966 she campaigned her Arabian gelding, Sharif, and I was crewing for her. I had competed in and won various NATRC rides, often winning the horsemanship award, so that was an area of interest to me." She added, "I had also campaigned an Appaloosa horse named Ruff Spots Banner that was sold to Walt Tibbitts of Moraga, California. In 1969 the horse proved himself when he won the coveted Haggin Cup for best-conditioned horse at the Tevis Cup Ride."

Alexis was the youngest of three children in a family living in Danville, California — a small, upper-middle-class community just east of San Francisco. The area was still rural enough that she could ride her horse "downtown" at the time. Her parents implemented a brilliant method to teach their daughter how to achieve success. Every year the task was different, but for the summer between her junior and senior high school years, it was about horses. "I was required to submit a proposal to my parents describing why I wanted to attend PCERF. In this proposal I was expected to write of what I wanted to do, what the objectives were, why it was important to do what I was proposing, how much it would cost, and how much I was contributing to that cost.

"It was important to my mother. She saw English riding as something elegant, and that image has stayed with me for life — though the stall mucking part is just good, hard, honest and fulfilling work and maybe not the most elegant part. My mother read the PCERF brochure and agreed that this would be a suitable program for her daughter." Alexis had previously attended "charm school" which included a series of courses on proper etiquette and decorum; attending a proper Horsemastership school fit well with becoming a well-rounded young woman.

"Afterward, I was expected to write a report about what I learned from the experience and how it significantly added to my learning about life." Alexis admitted, "It was the first adult decision that I ever made." It also turned out to be early training for what she's done with the rest of her life — writing and being awarded many high profile research proposals in the aerospace industry.

"Selecting PCERF as my summer goal was an easy sell to my mother, who had ridden in her youth on her family farm." Alexis remembered her mother's brown Dehner boots around the house. "One of the reasons my mother, who was always well dressed, agreed to this school was reflected by what she said: 'Honey, you can do this but I never want you to look like a frump or to see dirty fingernails at the table.' So I promised her that." Since then Alexis has always been considerate of her appearance. "I dress well for riding and I dress well for work; it's just something that I've always enjoyed."

Both Lyn and Alexis are charter members of the California Dressage Society (Linda Tellington was a founding member). "We were fortunate to have participated in dressage clinics with Col. Alois Podhajsky, former head of the Spanish Riding School," Alexis said about her seriousness with horses. Podhajsky was in the United States coaching Kyra Downton for the 1967 Pan American Games in Winnipeg. She went on, "While I was not a very athletic rider, the theoretical foundation served me well when I was at PCERF and to the present. I was an avid reader and hungry for a disciplined approach to horse husbandry, so I was instantly captivated about the possibility of attending a full immersion horsemanship school away from home.

"After being accepted to the PCERF program, off we headed to Badger, California. I had a beautiful steel-grey Thoroughbred gelding named Cirrus, or Ciri for short. He was a green horse and what better place to learn than at PCERF! My mother and I followed behind the horse trailer in Mother's Ferrari. Of course, being a rebellious teenager, I was *sooooo* embarrassed by my blonde mother in a Ferrari, but somehow I survived this indignity!

"I will never forget the orientation meeting when Went Tellington made his opening statements to set the tone. He said, 'Riding is called the sport of kings for a reason.' He asked that we never forget that 'riding a horse is a privilege.' How right he was, and how wise to inculcate us with that message," Alexis reflects.

The Tellingtons were very thoughtful about what food they served. Alexis pointed out, "We were steered away from refined sugar and used honey instead. The dining room was properly set and the candles were lit welcoming all students who were required to dress well for dinner. Dresses or skirts for the girls and clean shirts for the men and created an inviting ambience. Because many of us were being weaned off of the high sugar foods in favor of more nutritious food, some of us did have 'withdrawal' symptoms — at least that's what we told ourselves when we sneaked into the kitchen after hours for a midnight snack."

Alexis was just one of many who had to learn the lesson of cooperation based on dormitory living. "During that summer, I met Liane Randall from Apalachin, New York, whom I instantly disliked as my upper bunkmate," reports Alexis. "She had ridden saddle seat and Tennessee Walkers and came with what I thought was an East Coast attitude. Then being a West Coast 'hick' by comparison, I thought she was from Appalachia! Not quite. By the end of the summer, we'd become best friends and maintained contact for many years. My hope is that Liane too has fond memories of that summer, as we were 'double trouble' but good kids at heart, despite the occasional kitchen break-ins late at night.

"Since I was a hard worker and disciplined, I was confident that I could easily pass the academic elements at PCERF, but that turned out to be no cake walk, and neither were the riding tests!

"There was the usual fun amid the hard work from dawn 'til dusk. The Tellingtons were far ahead of their time in terms of research, including taking temperature, pulse and respiration (TPR) for horses riding backwards in trailers to determine which trailering position (backward or forward) was less stressful on horses. Some modern trailers permit riding in forward or backward position and they have the Tellingtons to thank for that idea.

"Other areas where the Tellingtons were innovators included human and equine nutrition. We learned about the theory and benefits of feeding kelp (the most mineral rich food), wheat germ oil, and undistilled apple cider vinegar for improved digestion and as a fly repellant. They worked on kelp studies, nutrition and wound healing as well."

Near each barn and the Compound was a manure pile crawling with hundreds of Little Red Wonders. Alexis recounted, "These manure-eating worms were grown and sold as an ecosystem for manure removal. As students, we were active participants in how effective this was." These worms were sold by the Research Farm, packaged and sent across the country to many PCERF members. "I received the Little Red Wonder worm packages in the mail after leaving PCERF for use in my own barn at home," Alexis recalls. The Little Red Wonders had a unique quality of rapidly breaking down hot horse manure and were specially bred by Went.

Nothing was beyond the scope of learning at PCERF. "A horse had died on the property, and there was a necropsy performed that the students were invited to witness," Alexis said. "The cause of death was strongyle vulgaris infestation and intestinal strangulation. Seeing those live parasites — up close and personal — was far more vivid than textbook photos. It made me a believer in a good deworming program.

"All of this was consistent with the over-arching message from Linda about puzzling out a horse. What are they trying to tell us, the nuances of how much pressure do they prefer when you groom them, and how can we work with them and not against them. With regard to galloping a horse, we were taught the difference between a 12, 14 and 16 mph gallop and how to calibrate pace, which would serve us well when performing roads and tracks. This was the foundation for my competing on hunters where it's judged on style and even hunting pace.

"In preparation for horse shows, we had various practice shows at home with Linda or Went judging and sometimes outside guest judges. We'd all work hard to clean our tack and polish our boots, and clip and braid our horses. I treasure the photo of Linda pinning Ciri with a first place ribbon for a hunter round over fences. Of course in those days we did not have the luxury of three-way stretch breeches that we do today and we had only good quality wool jackets — and we wouldn't think of not wearing a coat — even in the scorching Badger sun!

"A milestone for me was earning a PCERF Silver Medal. That goal was at serious risk toward the end of the summer when time was running short. I'd met all of the academic and riding requirements, but one test stood in the way of earning the medal — mounting bareback. It seemed impossible. No matter how I tried, I'd end up hanging on the horse's side but never quite making it to the back. It seemed reasonable to at least use a smaller horse (mine was 16.3hh), and the instructors agreed. I was all but defeated until Linda said it's all about technique and timing — she seemed to effortlessly swing herself up, over and on. I did my best to emulate Linda — clumsily, but was never able to get the feel of it. So I set out to practice before the final test. I don't know how, but somehow I managed to pass the test and earn my medal. I was the only student that summer to do so, and I still have pride in that accomplishment. But I admit that I do use a mounting block at home if I want to ride bareback.

"It was a fascinating summer for me," continues Alexis. Like so many other students, Alexis was deeply enriched by the summer of 1968. She said, "PCERF was far ahead of its time in many respects, and their program was a sort of 'shock treatment' and represented unwavering standards of horse husbandry and excellence. To this day, people ask, 'Where did you learn all of this about horses?' Easy, I say – from Linda and Went Tellington at PCERF. The basics and classics are enduring."

While Alexis was a PCERF student, she and her horse Cirrus won the Grand Championship at the Oakland National Horse Show.

During a horse show class entrants are asked to demonstrate their ability to mount bareback. Although a difficult technique for nearly everyone, it was a requirement to achieve the coveted PCERF Silver Medal.

CHAPTER 15

THE TEVIS CUP RIDE IN *ERNEST!*

A Sign of the Times – 1968

Although Linda was constantly surrounded by dozens of people and swirling activity, amongst all that whirlwind she took just a moment in June to read a small advertisement in the *San Francisco Chronicle* newspaper that caught her eye and ultimately influenced her life. It said that for five dollars she could receive one of the first computer-generated astrological charts assembled by famed local astrologer, Fritzie Armstrong.

"I was celebrating my 30th birthday and I thought why not, it would be a fun gift to myself," Linda said. So she mailed the envelope containing the required background information. When Linda received the chart it held some surprising insights about her life. "It said I would always be taken under the wing of royalty," she smiled while reflecting on the good fortune that Countess Bessenyey, obviously of royalty, had bestowed upon her. "It became clear to me that everything in my life was all in the stars since the beginning," Linda went on to say. "There was another gem embedded in the chart that definitely caught my attention. It indicated that a life-changing shift lay in my future.

"Fritzie's chart predicted that I would develop a form of communication that would spread around the world," Linda continued. "But in order to develop such a method I would have to learn to trust my intuition." The chart encouraged Linda to spend time with like-minded people who were dedicated to making a difference in the world. Linda pondered the revealing information and kept those profound insights close to her heart. This astrological prophecy turned out to become the guiding blueprint throughout her extraordinary career. "I continued to follow this thread during my whole life," Linda said.

Meanwhile, sitting on the desk in the PCERF office was a four-page brochure. The front cover read, "The 14th Annual Invitation to Riders of All Nations, FOR THE WESTERN STATES OF AMERICA TEVIS CUP 100 MILES ONE DAY RIDE, Saturday August 10th, 1968." The dates were logged into the

Research Farm's dizzying schedule. In addition to the on-going school sessions, there were many more events planned.

California native, rancher and former Governor of the Western States Trail Foundation, Paula Fatjo simply said, "The great thing about the Tevis Cup Ride is that it goes somewhere." The attraction of the Tevis is somewhat like an E-ticket adventure through time and space. Simply speaking, riders attempt to cover 100 miles of trail starting near Lake Tahoe and crossing the Sierra finishing in Auburn, California. Sounds easy enough, but in a nutshell the Tevis Cup Ride is the culmination of over-zealous riders, their horses, their crews, veterinarians, volunteers and a few spectators that are formed into a massive, passionate ball of energy. As if under high-pressure force, it's all squeezed through a 24-hour keyhole and then this mass pops out on the other side by 5:00 a.m. Sunday morning. *Whew!* The journey produces a fair amount of friction, dozens of amazing stories and memories to last a lifetime. It's the greatest dusty and dirty day imaginable.

In 1960 the winning Tevis Cup was presented to Ernie Sanchez (center). Behind him (L to R) are two very serious men (names unknown), Will Tevis (behind Ernie), Wendell Robie and Nick Mansfield.

Ernie Sanchez (black cowboy hat) holding court at PCERF during the 1968 Sontag Evans Getaway, tells his story of winning the Tevis Cup. Shannon is center, facing Ernie.

Because the school was booming, Went felt more help was needed. The Tellingtons invited their old friend, stellar horseman and 1960 Tevis Cup winner Ernie Sanchez to join their staff. Ernie was a man small in stature, standing about 5'4" in height. He was a member of the Navajo nation, experienced as a former jockey and movie stunt rider, and his knowledge added to the Research Farm's vision. A proven champion, Ernie rode Marko B, his 13-year-old Spanish Mustang to his Tevis win and placed second the following year. His wife Laurie, who adored and towered over him, and along with their daughter Marcie, joined him at Badger.

PCERF student Alexis Flippen von Zimmer simply described Ernie Sanchez by saying, "I called him the magician. Ernie had a gift with a horse, the likes of which I'd never seen. Today, he would be among the true horse whisperers. One day, sitting on a stump, I asked Ernie if my horse Ciri was happy with the way I was riding him. Ernie immediately asked me about his Thoroughbred bloodlines. I said he was from the Khaled and Hyperion line. Ernie declared, 'I knew it!' He explained about the Thoroughbred foundation sires and the joy of the gallop. He asked if he could ride Ciri and I was thrilled at this request. Ernie took up a racing cross with the reins, and off they went — at a full gallop. It was joyful to watch! I had never really let the horse gallop like that. When they returned from the lap around the field, I recall Ernie — who was sporting an ear-to-ear grin — saying that 'it's in his blood … he's a blood horse … and you need to give him a free rein sometimes.' That changed how I approached the horse. Instead of trying to fight him when he was fresh, we went for a gallop! Then he could concentrate and learn."

Ernie introduced the Cherokee Bridle, a thin string that ran through the horse's mouth, giving Linda and her students more freedom and trust with the horses.

A unique element that Ernie introduced to Linda and her students was called the 'Cherokee Bridle.' It consisted of a simple thin rope or string that encircled the horse's lower jaw and tongue, then ran back up to the rider's hands. Linda and her students adapted quickly to giving demonstrations for thrilled crowds while riding the Hungarians with a Cherokee bridle. The drills included jumping two, three or four abreast with the riders' arms stretched out horizontally.

In the meantime Ernie ramped up the endurance training on horses that included Brado and Taszilo and a tall and lanky 16-hands-high chestnut Anglo-Arab named Strider. Assisting Ernie was Pam Parker who had returned for her second summer with her sister, Nancy Corbett, in tow. Pam described the numerous hours she spent riding with this special man by saying, "Ernie was a phenomenal horseman. He was excellent at communicating with the horses in a very special way — as if he could read their minds. Ernie taught me so much about bringing the most out of a horse," she fondly remembers of her mentor. "He taught me how to track another horse and rider and said, 'Look carefully to see which way a twig or branch was broken. See the way a hoof print hits the ground, and how much dirt was pushed up, would indicate a trot or a deeper foot plant would mean a horse was at a gallop.'" All of these details were shared with Pam during miles of training and the hours passed by quickly. "We would stop and drink crystal-clear spring water flowing into stock tanks; we never carried water with us," she remembered back to those days of pristine conditions.

If horses did not measure up to Ernie's rigorous training schedule, they were immediately dropped from his program. That year Linda took her training seriously and spent many hours training with the team.

As summer rolled into August, the Tellingtons loaded the grey five-horse van and headed to Auburn to finalize their Tevis training. Then they drove to Tahoe City and parked in the 'Cabbage Patch' campsite among other buckle seekers. The air was filled with excitement as they went through the registration process. They picked their group numbers and weighed in with all their tack. All of the Tellington horses passed the pre-ride veterinary inspections. Brado was fit and ready to go. Linda, Ernie and Pam were ready to tackle the dusty trail traveled by the pioneers of yesteryear.

Passing the pre-ride veterinary examination is the 'needle's eye' of the Tevis Cup Ride. Ernie is applying Linda's ride number 84 on Brado's hip.

Also toeing the starting line were the biggest names in endurance riding, including Pat and Donna Fitzgerald, Wendell Robie, Marion Robie, Dru Barner,

Shannon Yewell Weil

Bud Dardi, Phil Gardner, Walt Tibbitts, Paige Harper, Dick Barsaleau DVM, James Steere DVM, Dave Nicholson DVM, Julie Suhr and her daughter Barbara Suhr (White), to name a few. Barbara had failed to finish the previous year but was about to begin her reign as the all-time highest finisher with 32 buckles (as of 2012) and still counting.

The 125 riders mustered in front of Tahoe City's Post Office and at 5:00 a.m. they set off into the crisp darkness as they rode the nine-mile riverside stretch towards Squaw Valley. It was a 40-degree morning heading for a 90-degree day.

The peach and blue rays of dawn fanned across Lake Tahoe and its surrounding mountainous horizon. In an attempt to reduce trail congestion, the riders started in groups in Squaw Valley and were released in two-minute intervals. The Tevis Cup Ride was underway as excited riders followed the historic trail across the Sierra Nevada mountains to Auburn. It was an awesome day of glory!

Although I was in Colorado training horses that year, it didn't take me long to piece together the Tellington Team's experience. Here's what I gathered.

Linda was riding Brado in an original McClellan saddle and a simple hackamore. She was dressed in jeans, black Dehner hunt boots, a long-sleeved white shirt and a cowboy hat that kept the sun at bay. Pam and Ernie were similarly dressed but Ernie rode in a western saddle and mechanical hackamore. His attire was simple and his Navajo concho belt reflected his distinctive heritage. All three riders wore the Cavalry yellow scarves.

Linda recalled, "It was a beautiful morning when we reached Emigrant Pass. We looked south and saw the volcanic outcropping called 'Fort Sumter,' which was named for the American Civil War's flashpoint in Charleston, South Carolina. We were awed by the 360° view that included Lake Tahoe behind us, surrounded by spectacular panoramic mountainous views in all directions." To the north jutted Lyon Peak with Needle Peak standing guard over the Little American Valley that tumbles below the foot of Mt. Mildred to the south. Wedged next to Mt. Mildred is a sheer granite cliff called Picayune Bluff. Lyon Ridge sprawls along the distance and the panorama just keeps going for miles.

At 9:23 a.m. the anxious crowd at Robinson Flat greeted Nick Mansfield, a Nevada rancher riding a stout Standardbred/Thoroughbred cross named Lucky as he led the first riders into the one-hour veterinary check. Mansfield was one of the original four men who accompanied Wendell Robie on the first 100-mile ride in 1955. His fast pace would catch up to him later as none of the riders traveling in Mansfield's company would finish the ride. Only four of the horses that finished in the top ten arrived at Robinson Flat before 10:00 a.m.; the other six arrived almost 50 minutes later.

Leaving Robinson Flat, Linda and Brado are refreshed and ready to hit the trail again, with 36 miles down, 64 miles to go.

Right behind Linda, Ernie and Strider looked fresh and ready to challenge the rough terrain.

Robinson Flat offered up its grassy meadow oasis among towering forest pines under a cloudless blue sky. Linda on Brado and Ernie on Strider clocked in at 10:31 a.m. Went, Laurie and crew scurried to assist with the riders' needs, and both horses eased through the vet check. Linda and Ernie were having a great day.

About 44 minutes behind them, Pam Parker and Taszilo arrived at Robinson Flat. After Pam took some time to refresh her horse with water and hay, she was ready for the vet examination. The horse passed all criteria with excellent recoveries: 53-pulse rate and a respiration of 14 breaths per minute. Then she was instructed to trot out Taszilo for the soundness check. To Pam's alarm Taszilo took a couple of off-steps, which puzzled her because he hadn't had any issues on the trail. Without the courtesy of consulting another vet's opinion, the examining veterinarian pulled Taszilo for lameness. It was final. But it turned out Taszilo was fine; he had flinched as he stepped on a rock at the most inopportune moment. The veterinarian jumped to conclusions, took her rider card and essentially said, "You're pulled!"

Heartbroken, Pam was told by a ride official to saddle up and ride her *lame* horse several miles down the road towards Foresthill where she could catch a trailer ride back to the fairgrounds in Auburn. A different veterinarian was driving down the road and came upon a very sound horse and rider trotting briskly ahead of him — it was Pam and Taszilo. He eased his pickup truck alongside the pair and said, "What are you doing on this road? There is nothing wrong with your horse, he's perfectly sound!" To which she explained the unfortunate circumstances, revealing her extreme disappointment.

Robinson Flat, known for flushing out the speed demons, didn't slow down Bud Dardi and Pancho, a 12-year-old half-Arab, who held the lead for the remainder of the day. Bud felt pressure coming into Michigan Bluff from close competitor Frank Moan riding an Arabian named Sun Shalejma, but that pair fell back at Michigan Bluff, a small Gold Rush community where remains of the old mining town are scattered amongst a few dwellings. Dardi and Pancho were on a scorching, record-setting pace and no one would catch them that day.

Upon completing their one-hour rest, the Tellington duo headed west down the hot and rocky Cavanaugh Ridge that emptied into Deep Canyon. Gladly leaving the rocky ridge behind, Linda and Ernie made a left turn onto a logging road and their pace quickened for the next ten miles. They came upon vine-covered and rusted mining equipment that lay scattered in the heavily-forested area exactly where it was abandoned 100 years earlier. They had arrived at Last Chance. The riders grabbed a quick drink of cold water and fruit offered by descendents of the town's founders.

Then they were back on the trail, which immediately dropped into the first huge chasm of a canyon. They rode the long switchbacks to the bottom and walked across the Swinging Bridge, followed by a long, hot crawl up innumerable switchbacks. The unfaltering Brado led others up the canyon trail to Devil's Thumb – named for a lava tower that juts up near the brim of the canyon, which is the steepest climb on the entire Ride. A veterinary checkpoint awaited them at Deadwood a few miles from Devil's Thumb. Just past the historic Deadwood Cemetery (dating to the 1850s) the trail drops into El Dorado Canyon. It's late afternoon now, about 4:40 p.m. Linda and Ernie slowly pulled out of the oven-like canyon into the vet check at Michigan Bluff as the sun-drenched old mining town surrendered to the heat of the day.

For Linda, Brado was indeed giving her a heavenly ride. After refueling the horses with hay and water, the crews waited on the riders as the horses rested. The horses' vital signs were excellent as they passed the veterinary examination and were released by the timers. Soaking their yellow scarves one more time, Linda and Ernie tied them around their necks to cool themselves. Leaving Michigan Bluff the trail then swings around the old Byrd's Valley Ranch and climbs up to the ridge above Volcano Canyon. The six-mile stretch comes out at a small town called Foresthill. The next vet check would be at Echo Hills Ranch.

Almost four-and-a-half hours after Bud Dardi and Pancho blazed through Echo Hills, Linda and Ernie reached the third hour-long checkpoint at 8:16 p.m. Nearly an hour before, Nick Mansfield's luck ran out — his lame horse was now named 'Un-Lucky' and was pulled from the Ride.

In the final minutes of twilight, the vanishing light gives way to darkness. A memorable day has just been logged into these people's lives. Soon afterwards the brilliant full moon rose in the evening sky, emulating a great big light bulb hanging from a star. It was a special hour indeed.

Linda and Ernie left the Echo Hills vet check at 9:16 p.m., fully prepared for night riding. Behind them to the east, the lunar glow silhouetted the Sierra Nevada mountain range, the very range they had crossed earlier in the day. They had already been up for 17 hours when they forded the Middle Fork of the American River. The moon shed enough light for the horses to pick their way across the smooth rounded rocks that made up the riverbed. The horses were refreshed by the brisk flowing water that nearly reached their bellies. The watery dip cleaned and soothed their dusty legs as they climbed the far bank and the pair struck a long trot on the road that followed the bends of the river.

After crossing Highway 49, the trail went up a small climb through Pointed Rocks Ranch. As if being pulled along by an invisible force, Linda and Ernie flew down the mountain narrow trail with the moon casting shadows from the trees. At the bottom of the trail they crossed the historic Mountain Quarries Railroad Bridge, nicknamed 'No Hands Bridge,' that spans the Middle Fork of the American River. They made a hard left turn, picked up the pace again and headed for Auburn. That great big light bulb in the night sky reflected like shimmering diamonds on the flowing river below. "I felt like we were on winged horses flying across No Hands Bridge," Linda remembers fondly.

Linda riding Magyar Brado and Ernie on Anglo-Arab Strider crossing the finish line in 9ᵗʰ and 10ᵗʰ places at the 1968 Tevis Cup Ride.

With only a half mile left to Robie Point, they could almost smell the finish line. "I don't remember any fatigue at this point. The adrenalin was pumping and Brado and Strider spurred each other on," Linda accounted. "It was really exhilarating!" They had successfully ridden 100 miles from Tahoe City to Auburn, California in one day. The riders safely made their way to Auburn's Gold Country Fairgrounds Stadium, the finish line of the Tevis Cup Ride. At 12:43 a.m. a smiling Linda, Brado, Ernie and Strider crossed the finish line in 9th and 10th places. "We were so happy to have finished in the coveted Top Ten," Linda beamed.

Winners Bud Dardi and Pancho crossed the finish line at 8:44 p.m., a mere ten minutes after dark. Second place was captured by Marion Robie on Hailla, followed by Paige Harper on Raskela, a 7-year-old Arab stallion who was awarded the Haggin Cup; Lona Sweet on Safarr; Ed Bailey; John McCullough on O' Blue; Dick Barsaleau DVM on Good Trip; Karen Iversen on Jamait and tying for ninth and tenth were Linda on Magyar Brado, an 8-year-old Hungarian stallion, and Ernie Sanchez on Strider, a 7-year-old Anglo-Arab. Three stallions finished in the Top Ten.

The tired but cheerful crowd reveled in the celebration dinner the following day, honoring the glorious Sierra Nevada crossing. After all 68 buckles were awarded, Ernie approached Pam and handed her a small silvery pink box. Inside was the beautiful sterling silver Tevis buckle that he had just received. He said, "Here, you deserve this. You've earned it and you shouldn't have been disqualified," and gave her a sincere hug. Pam was deeply touched by his altruistic gesture. She gratefully accepted the buckle that exemplified Ernie Sanchez's generous heart. "He was such a dear friend, almost like a father to me," Pam reflected. "I still have his canvas pinney with number '85' printed on it, hanging on my dresser," she said sentimentally. The Tellingtons had chosen wisely when they invited Ernie to join their team. Ernie Sanchez died several years later but his legend lives on.

1970 Tevis Cup Ride – Countess Bessenyey's Buckle

"I remember being so exhausted when I finished the Tevis Cup Ride and going to bed thinking 'I'll never do that again!' and then waking up and saying, 'When's the next ride?'"
— Linda Tellington

The year 1970 marked the 16th Tevis Cup Ride with 75-year-old founder Wendell Robie still playing a very vital role. With his one-of-a-kind gold-plated 1,000-Mile Ten-Day Tevis buckle always proudly displayed on his belt, Wendell shared his infectious enthusiasm with riders everywhere. He created a sense of place for those searching beyond typical trail riding. Wendell provided a challenge with his slogan, "Ride, Really Ride!" Always shod in cowboy boots, this charming man served up a handshake that made some wince.

Margit Bessenyey, who at age 59 was eager to toe the Tevis starting line, would give Taszilo another chance. The training at PCERF was again under Wentworth's command. The horses that made the trip that year were Hungarian Graflo, Taszilo, dear ol' Sierra Spy (the blossoming chestnut Thoroughbred gelding who was renamed Spartan by his constant rider Val Pruitt), a grey gelding named Hungarian Csengo, and the Anglo-Arab named Strider that Ernie Sanchez had ridden to a 10th place Tevis finish two years before.

When I telephoned Val Pruitt at her Washington home, she took pleasure in recalling her Tevis Cup experiences. But I could hear her voice stiffen when she recounted Wentworth's training regime. "We trained brutally hard for the Tevis. Went pushed us so much and he was ruthless," she remembered of his demands. "Margit, who was back and forth from Montana, bought us all hiking boots," recalls Val. "So Went decided we should all start running to get in better condition. We would run down to the Compound and then run with our horse back up to the top of the highest hill overlooking PCERF. Then we'd mount our horses and gallop the ten miles over to the M Bar J Ranch and back again. After we got back to PCERF, he made us get off our horses and run up that dang hill again. That's how well Went conditioned us," Val gasped. "I had some massive blisters to work through from those hiking boots too." Went had them trotting for long periods of time during the heat of the day and even at night, which was a particularly excellent task in preparation for the actual day of the Ride. They were ready.

Years ago, it was commonplace for people to come to Auburn a couple of weeks before the Tevis and to familiarize themselves and their horses with the trail. That's just what the Tellingtons did. The Tevis, part serious, part social and a whole lot of fun, is *the* place to be for endurance devotees. "It is," as Went would say, "the whole ball of wax!"

Many still believe the hardest part about the Tevis Cup Ride is getting to the starting line, which in 1970 had been changed to Squaw Valley. Linda and her quartet of riders including Margit Bessenyey, PCERF student Val Pruitt Sivertson and Roy Smith, Director of the famed Colorado Outward Bound School, at Arizona's Prescott College, had their own last minute problems. Margit was going to ride Hungarian Graflo but a girth sore forced him out so she switched to Hungarian Taszilo. Count Ernest Szechenyi, Margit's distant Hungarian relative who lived in Hamilton, Montana, was bumped off the roster completely when Linda took over his mount, Hungarian Csengo. Since he was the least fit horse and Linda was the fittest of the riders, she could dismount and walk up the steep canyon climbs, optimizing the horse's chance of finishing. Val stuck with her buddy Spartan and Roy Smith stayed with Strider. The four good-sized horses averaged 1,050 pounds each. Everything was set.

The afternoon of the pre-ride vet exam drew to a close. Everyone tucked in for a restless night. The next day promised an early start when the sounds of voices, feed buckets and nickering horses broke the slumbering camp around 3:30 a.m.

By 5:00 a.m. 164 horses started up the stunning five-mile climb to Emigrant Pass. No view matches the dramatic easterly backdrop of Lake Tahoe at dawn.

In the distance and to the west sits Auburn — farther than the eye can see. FINALLY it's Tevis Day again.

Along Red Star Ridge riders encountered the famed Cougar Rock where the most spectacular photographs are taken of horses and riders climbing the steep volcanic escarpment. White arrows are painted on the barren steep rock to guide the best way to the top. It's a short but daunting climb and makes for a magnificent photograph that heralds the fact that you have ridden the Tevis Cup Ride.

"I *love* the challenge of Cougar Rock," Linda declared, "because every horse I ever rode, when we came to the bottom of the rock I always had the feeling that they knew that together we could just head up that treacherous steep climb and not have a stumble or misstep. As I think about the Tevis in retrospect, that to me is one of the most exhilarating moments on the trail while traversing the formidable passage over that outcropping. It has really driven fear into the hearts of many riders." Linda went on to say, "I always felt grateful when riders who were with me made it safely over Cougar Rock too."

Because Hungarian Csengo was not well conditioned, Linda covered many miles on foot to assist his progress in the canyons, which includes the most arduous sections of the trail.

The group takes a refreshing break at the river where the Countess holds the horses while Linda takes her turn to dunk in the cool water.

By the time they reached the Last Chance vet check about mid-day, it was darn hot, dry and dusty. Linda was concerned about Margit and made an unusual decision to rest for an extra hour. They were the last horses to leave Last Chance, and slowly descended down into the North Fork of the Middle Fork of the American River Canyon. To help Csengo, Linda was on foot much of the way but now the group faced the cut-off times — even a few minutes overtime at a vet check meant certain disqualification. After refreshing themselves in the cool flowing river, they mounted their horses and crossed the familiar Swinging Bridge. Linda led her horse and team up to Devil's Thumb — the most demanding and steepest climb on the trail with dozens of switchbacks. Just after reaching Devil's Thumb, Strider, Roy Smith's horse, was pulled for fatigue at Deadwood.

It's not often that one finds a Hungarian Countess leading her horse, Hungarian Taszilo, through El Dorado Canyon but that was the case on the day of the 1970 Tevis Cup Ride.

VALERIE SEVERTSON AND LTJ
ON THE TEVIS CUP TRAIL

Spartan (Sierra Spy) leads the way up the long steep rugged trail through El Dorado Canyon. Linda is 'tailing him' from behind. Both horses and riders are draped in wet towels to shield themselves from the oppressive heat.

Spartan (Sierra Spy), a Thoroughbred, in front as the riders head for the top of the endless switchbacks in El Dorado Canyon. They will find Went and their crew at Michigan Bluff.

The remaining three riders passed the Deadwood vet check and dropped into El Dorado Canyon where they made the grueling three-mile switchback climb to Michigan Bluff. The oppressive heat kept their pace slow but consistent. Right about now, Val was thanking Went for all the arduous training.

Countess Bessenyey's expression reflects the long hot day while riding up El Dorado Canyon. Yet in the end she conquers the 100 miles on her Hungarian Taszilo.

Through Foresthill and on to the Echo Hills veterinary inspection, they were riding in the cool evening air. The horses perked up and were getting their second wind soon after sunset. "Because we went to Auburn a week ahead and trained the horses on the last 15 miles of the trail three or four times, they knew it very well," remembers Linda. "The night of the Ride we left the last vet check and passed 33 riders on the way into Auburn. They were all dragging along in the dark but our horses knew the way and felt great. As we rode over No Hands Bridge, we moved out at a good pace for that last five miles. It was a sensational feeling."

By the time they reached the finish line, and having moved up in the pack, Linda, Margit and Val came in 59th, 60th and 61st places. Out of 160 horses that started, 93 of them successfully completed. Margit received her first buckle and Val and her three-name horse, Sierra Spy aka Speed the Wonder Horse aka Spartan, had finished the Tevis Cup Ride.

"For us the highlight of the 1970 Tevis Cup Ride was bringing Margit Bessenyey through. She was a wonderful rider and she rode a lot for pleasure but she was not conditioned for that distance. She showed her endurance and perseverance by finishing the Tevis," Linda proudly said of Margit.

"There is something magical about finishing the Tevis Cup Ride," Linda went on to say, "Nothing comes close to finishing it, you and your horse have built a great partnership after the long hours you've spent training together. The exhilarating sense of accomplishment is like no other competition. There's just nothing like that feeling," Linda declared passionately.

Linda, Birch Jones and Margit Bessenyey campaigned the Hungarian horses in endurance rides on the east coast in the early 1970s.

Margit aboard Hungarian Csengo and Birch aboard Hungarian Pallo at the Virginia 100 Mile in Three Days Ride.

In 1972 Linda rode the Tevis Cup Ride for her final time and was accompanied by Birch Jones and Countess Bessenyey. Linda ultimately notched a total of five finishes out of six attempts over the years of 1961, 1963, 1964, 1968, 1970 and 1972.

CHAPTER 16

HERALDING THE HUNGARIAN HORSES
ACROSS AMERICA

Linda's school at Badger was at its apex by 1970. Gifted students filled the sessions and more Hungarian horses were sent down from Montana. Countess Margit Bessenyey and Linda had grown extremely close and Linda proved she was the ideal person to promote these horses. The versatile Hungarians blended perfectly into PCERF's rigorous all-around program. Margit could have had anyone on the planet train and ride her beloved Hungarian horses, but she chose Linda Tellington.

After miles and miles of endurance riding on the Hungarian horses, Linda and her students also competed with this breed in other disciplines. Pleased with Linda's results with Brado, Judith Gyurky sent two mares named Magyar Godiva and Magyar Duna to PCERF. "Godiva," Linda began, "was the only horse in our string that I never allowed anyone else to ride. In retrospect there was something very special about that mare and I really enjoyed riding her. I won many trophies and ribbons on her and she made me feel like a Centaur — the same way I felt with Bint Gulida," Linda commented. "So that's the reason that I turned Brado over to Lynn Blades who was a brilliant rider and horsewoman. She deserved to ride him."

About 100 miles south of San Francisco where California's voluptuous hills roll down to the jagged Pacific Ocean coastline, sits the Monterey Peninsula. Towering Monterey pine trees guard the shoreline lined with granite rock outcroppings that resemble smooth patterns laid by the hands of a skillful mason. The fresh ocean air stimulates the Del Monte Forest surrounding the famous Pebble Beach Golf Course and Equestrian Center. From Badger, the Tellington Team made the six-hour drive to Pebble Beach to attend some of the best hunter horse trials in California. When the big gray PCERF five-horse trailer pulled into the center, everyone on board felt the pride associated with arriving with Linda Tellington.

When Linda received more Hungarian horses she turned Brado over to Lynn Blades, who, for good reason, felt like the luckiest girl in the world.

Adding to the fairytale experience at Pebble Beach, the Tellington Team stayed in a beautiful cottage that resembled a birdhouse in the nearby quaint town of Carmel. "Looking back," Lynn Blades said fondly, "I've done a lot of traveling and campaigning with the horses over the past 20 years and nothing compares to those experiences at Pebble Beach while riding the Hungarian horses. There is simply nothing like it anywhere. The fact that the course wove through the golf course with the ocean in the background — spectacular!" Linda smiled and added, "What great times we had!"

Lynn, who also felt very connected to Brado said, 'I was grateful that Linda assigned me to ride Brado because I had complete confidence in him. I cringed at the upcoming competition but Brado made me feel safe. I'd never seen the ocean before and the next day I was galloping along the beach stepping on seaweed that had washed up onto the sand," she said of her rare opportunity.

Lynn went on to say, "The next year when we went to Pebble Beach Linda rode the mare Duna, crazy Duna!" As Linda settled into the memory she said, "Yes, I competed on two different Hungarian horses the second year and for some reason I don't remember, I'm sure I walked the four-mile course twice. This was my first steeplechase riding Duna on this 24-obstacle course. Lynn referred to her as crazy but actually I should have been called the crazy one to ride her on this course because she had no brakes.

"When Countess Gyurky shipped Duna from Virginia to PCERF, I was, of course, expected to campaign her," said Linda. "However, Duna had just been started under saddle in Virginia, and had almost no understanding of rein aids and was very hard to slow down or stop. In retrospect, I wonder if she was exhibiting the Hungarian characteristic that gave the warhorses the reputation of being 'the secret weapon' of the Hungarian Cavalry. They were taught that when their rider was separated from them, they would not let anyone else mount them, rendering them useless to another soldier.

"This may have been true because all the other Hungarian horses I had in training were ridden not just by me, but also by my best students. But then there was Godiva, another mare Judith sent out to us. Maybe it was intuition that prevented me from sharing her with other riders. Maybe I tried it and she would not tolerate another rider. I don't remember. But I loved riding Godiva and I rode her almost daily for the years I had her in training.

"Later when we closed down Westwind I sent both Godiva and Duna home to Judith in Virginia. Both mares turned out to be unridable by others and Judith was unhappy at first. Perhaps the one rider only was responsible but, of course, I had the winning trophies and ribbons to prove that they had been campaigned!

"I had especially won so much on Godiva but she was a typical, classic Hungarian and by being her only rider, that may have activated that genetic warhorse trait of 'one rider only.'" Linda ends with saying, "I never made that mistake again with any other horse."

"But Duna was another story. I didn't dare have anyone else ride her because she was unstoppable. I so wish I could turn the clock back and start her over with Tellington TTouch and develop a trusting relationship with Duna, and be able to work her from the ground through 'The Playground for Higher Learning' that is a big part of the 21st Century Tellington Method.

"Back then I didn't have those tools, so my only choice for successfully showing Duna was in 50-mile endurance rides and steeplechases. In a steeplechase all I had to do was climb aboard, line up for the start, and let her take over. She had the courage of a lioness and perfect control and judgment over jumps. Flying over those sixteen-foot-wide brush jumps on that spectacular Pebble Beach course, blasting around the turns to avoid trampling the famous Pebble Beach golf course, and feeling the ocean spray coming off the waves that were breaking alongside the track, remain some of the most treasured memories of my riding career.

Los Altos Hunt Race Meet at Pebble Beach, 1969 – Linda is racing on Duna in the four-mile Steeplechase. Just after she abandoned her helmet, Linda lost her right stirrup, yet she still rode in perfect form on her way to victory.

Duna is about to overtake her competition in the last few strides before the finish line of the Pebble Beach Steeplechase.

"Looking at the photos of me flying over that fence without a helmet and without my right stirrup, I can feel the thrill as though it was yesterday. Note that in those days we were not required to wear helmets with safety straps, and after the second jump my riding cap was bugging me so I threw it off to the side of the course," laughs Linda. "After the jump that I took without my stirrup, I reached down and shortened both stirrups between the obstacles at a flat-out gallop. That was not a problem thanks to Went's strict Cavalry discipline. All students learned to shorten their stirrups at the trot and the canter so it was no problem for me."

Linda Tellington and Duna were the victorious winners of the Pebble Beach Steeplechase Race that day. "The look of triumph and exhilaration on my face as I finished that race really says it all."

Also riding at Pebble Beach was PCERF student Michele Pouliot who said, "I rode Hungarian Tundra, whose nickname was Witch, on the Steeplechase at Pebble Beach, which, by the way, was the scariest thing I'd ever done. When I started the race I felt very confident," she said, but things changed in a hurry as she went on to describe how her race unfolded.

"At the start I took off like a shot and gained a huge lead over the rest of the field. Witch and I approached the first turn that was a pretty sharp corner. Then I heard Duna behind me and Linda was yelling, 'SLOW DOWN!'" The two riders had widened their lead but at the next fence, Michele grimaced when she stated, "Witch hit the coop really hard and we went down on the far side of the jump." Startled by the crash, Michele, who was still mounted, said, "Witch was on the ground sitting like a dog with her front legs stretched out in front of her." Michele described the astonishing sight by saying, "She looked as if she were a sphinx. So I jumped off her and she swiftly sprang to her feet again. Then Witch promptly shook off the entire mishap and was fine so I climbed back on her and we took off at a gallop. All of this took place in less than 90 seconds and because of the lead we created, Witch and I still had enough time to escape being mowed down by the field of horses barreling down on us." Michele and the mare continued on and finished the race.

"Pebble Beach holds special memories for us all," Lynn Blades remembers. "We always came home sunburned, very happy and with a lot of ribbons and trophies."

The following year, 1971, the Tellingtons returned to Pebble Beach for the season's final steeplechase for the Los Altos Hunt. This time Linda was riding Witch and her sister Robyn Hood was riding a big Quarter Horse named Top Hand. During the race Linda and Robyn were in the lead and on the second lap they approached a big coop festooned on each side with two colossal black-and-white whales. Another horse and rider had knocked down one of the rails on a coop on the first lap. "I sailed over the last jump," Linda remembers. "Witch landed on the rail on the other side of the jump and flipped over. I landed really hard and broke my collarbone. I was lying there in a heap on the ground when I looked up and Robyn was coming fast right behind me. We were ahead of the field and she PULLED UP! And I remember lying on the ground waving with my good arm and yelling 'GO ON, GO ON! Don't stop! I'm okay.' Robyn was in tears but she finished the race, but I think she had lost her lead. Oh, those were fun times," Linda reminisced.

Linda was attended to for her collarbone and said, "The next day I was hoping I could ride in the final hunt of the season. I had to be helped onto the horse with my arm in a sling," recalls Linda. "I thought I could ride in spite of my broken collar bone because I had danced at the Hunt Club Ball the night before, but Duna took about ten steps at the walk and I had to be helped off! I wasn't as tough as I thought."

Since Linda had logged so many miles on both Hungarian and Arabian horses the question arose about the difference between riding the two breeds. "There's a huge difference between riding a Hungarian and an Arabian," states Linda. "Every Hungarian I ever rode felt like I had a solid leg at each corner, giving it a solid and dependable balance. The horses always felt like they knew where they were putting their feet. Whereas with Arabians, it's more like riding a bicycle. They are so flexible and with the exception of a few, they don't provide that same feeling of a sturdy leg at each corner. I love Arabs but that is definitely one of the differences I've felt.

"The Hungarians give a clear sense of balance from the substance they draw from their solid chests and hindquarters. The spring of the ribs is another important quality — Bint Gulida had that but she was one of the few Arabians I've ever ridden that gave that feeling of having a really solid horse under you."

East Coast Tour

The Tellingtons took their show on the road to promote the Hungarian horse. Shown here: Linda on Niscak, Lynn Blades on Brado, Paula Stockebrand on Taszilo and Birch Jones on Pallo.

Countess Bessenyey wanted to promote the Hungarian horses by showcasing them in various cities in the Midwestern and Eastern states, so Linda and Went created a schedule of state fairs and horse show appearances across the country. They loaded up the van with Brado, Taszilo, Niscak and Pallo and off they went for another adventure that included Went, Linda, Birch Jones, Paula Stockebrand, and Lynn Blades who had gone east to visit her family. "When Linda and everyone arrived in Syracuse for the New York State Fair, I reunited with them," Lynn said. "We rode the horses in demonstrations with just a thin rope that ran through the horses' mouths called a 'Cherokee Bridle.' While jumping four across in unison we had our arms held out at shoulder height."

Lynn carried on, "Can you imagine! It was a magical story and as a young girl I felt so special while driving my little red VW bug around the country, riding Brado in the exhibitions and loving every minute of it.

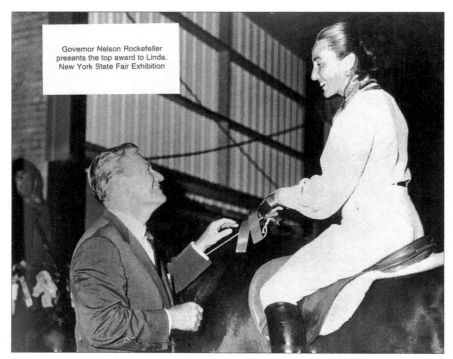

Governor Nelson Rockefeller presents the top award to Linda. New York State Fair Exhibition

*It was in New York that Linda was presented
the winning trophy by Governor Nelson Rockefeller.*

"We went to Chicago where we met horse enthusiast Arthur Godfrey at an exhibition. We would drive all night between cities. However, the highlight of the trip was an exhibition in Kansas City," Lynn said. "To our complete surprise, Countess Bessenyey was there to meet us. She took us all out to dinner at a Hungarian restaurant where we could share in her traditional culture. She was happily speaking in Hungarian with the owners and catching up on their beloved homeland. After dinner she arranged for the waiters to come to our table and play their violins while she continued to reminisce about her extraordinary life in Hungary. Linda, Went and everyone had a wonderful time and we were all swept away by this treasured occasion with Margit Bessenyey. Conversations between Linda, Went and Margit became storybook tales to us. I must confess, I was spellbound by Countess Bessenyey; she was so mystical, so enchanting. To me that night was the highpoint of the entire trip."

Linda riding Niscak and Lynn Blades on Brado show the two elegant Hungarian stallions to an enthusiastic crowd.

Linda recalled the fun they had while jumping the horses in Kansas City. "We had the two stallions Brado and Niscak and two geldings, Pallo and Taszilo. We were there to promote the horses and Went had bought beautiful scarves for us to wear."

"I may still have my scarf!" Lynn beamed. "Are you serious?" Linda asked. "And remember we had those flowing beautiful blouses with puffy sleeves?" Lynn went on to say, "I felt elegant for the first time in my life."

Shannon Yewell Weil

Linda spoke of one of the many times Margit called her to come to Hamilton, Montana. "It was so typical of Margit Bessenyey — every few months she would ask me to leave the horses and come up to the Bitter Root Stock Farm or go to her beautiful farm on the Potomac River in Indian Head, Maryland. Oh my God, that was so spectacular. I would usually go for a week," Linda remembered.

"One time when I arrived at Bitter Root Margit had a little black dog with her. Frequently she would load up the car and horse trailer and take a horse to ride up in the mountains. She had recently returned from camping above her ranch where she had been for several days. Over the course of her stay a shy black-mop dog showed up around her campfire. She fed it and talked to it but it wouldn't let her touch it. Finally on the day she was ready to go home, she said to this dog, 'If you want to come home with me I will take care of you.' So when Margit opened the car door, the dog jumped in and went home with her and became a constant companion." That was part of Margit's mystique; she had a really special way with animals.

Linda was moved by Lynn's stories that brought to life many happy memories of Margit. Lynn recognized a trait shared by the two women, "And you, Linda, you and Margit shared the same qualities and love for animals and that is why she loved you so much." Lynn went on, "That is why you have been such a great teacher; you pass your knowledge on to others. You taught me more than I can ever remember," she emotionally revealed to Linda. "That is what I felt about those remarkable years at PCERF."

Val Pruitt Sivertson remembers Margit in the same way, confirming Lynn's remarks. "I got to know Margit quite well after experiencing the Tevis Cup Ride with her," Val began. "She was a self-assured person, very smart and dedicated to her Hungarian breeding program. She did not let anyone tell her how to breed; she was very independent and didn't like to be told what to do."

Val later went to the Stock Farm in Montana and purchased some of Margit's Hungarian mares to form her own foundation herd. Val continues to breed Hungarians today. Val recounted Margit's admiration for Countess Judith Gyurky, who was Margit's senior by about 15 years, by saying, "When she was young growing up in Hungary everybody looked up to Judith Gyurky — she was the wild woman who showed horses and competed against men and beat them. All the girls thought she was really remarkable and they all looked up to Judith."

CHAPTER 17

THE PEAR THAT BROKE THE CAMEL'S BACK: THE PARTING OF LINDA AND WENTWORTH

In an attempt to grow the potential of the Pacific Coast Equestrian Research Farm and with financial backing from Margit Bessenyey, Wentworth spent months working on a deal to create an equestrian housing development in Badger. He was optimistic about its success; he would market it in the Los Angeles area as a getaway from the busy urban life. Each parcel would be designed to include horse facilities so that the horses were kept near to the homes. The centerpiece of the community, of course, would be the extensive riding program directed by Linda.

Badger resident Helen Reilly, whose daughter Susan was a frequent rider with PCERF students, was now holding down the PCERF office. Wentworth was enlisting people to become involved with his lofty plan and even summoned former Chadwick student Roland Kleger. "We stayed in touch over the years and in 1969 Roland brought his family to PCERF to assist Went with the big equestrian project," Linda said.

Roland was enthusiastic about becoming involved because he says in retrospect, "PCERF was a true learning institution at a level that is disappearing from our world today. Horsemanship was a big part of it but developing your own skills was another important part." That philosophy was the synergistic core of Went's and Linda's teachings.

During the early 1970s, PCERF hosted a group of students who were involved in the Outward Bound program at Arizona's Prescott College. Their leader was the program Director, Roy Smith and the participants were required to confront their fears through physical tasks. In Badger, they would learn to ride horses. In exchange, Linda had taken a group of riders to Prescott where they gave a demonstration with the Hungarian horses. The PCERF students then challenged their fears by rappelling down the side of a steep cliff.

Roland Kleger, the ever-present friend in Linda's life, appreciated the Pacific Coast Equestrian Research Farm as much as anyone. He even considered moving his family to Badger to assist with the community development project.

By this point in time, in addition to the regular mail order business of PCERF products and the School of Horsemanship, there was a broad spectrum of endeavors swirling around the Research Farm. The scope of the program broadened with Birch's passion for Olympic Pentathlon training, a full training program for endurance riding, and the equestrian community development. According to Lynn Blades, who was helping Went with the logistics of the development project, it's possible that Went was feeling the effects of a self-induced mental pressure cooker. The atmosphere was becoming a bit unwieldy and there was tension growing between Went and Linda.

At last all the arrangements were made for a big party that would serve as a press conference and celebration of the new equestrian community. Margit Bessenyey (who provided cases of champagne for the event) and her attorney Henry Hyde arrived, as well as others partaking in the festivities. The champagne flowed, entertainment was provided by a dancing bear (of all things!), and the dozens of guests celebrated the new project.

During a conversation with Tim Durant and an unidentified woman, the gaze in Linda's eyes reveals the pressure she was under.

However, during the weekend a sour note was struck between Went and Mr. Hyde. Suddenly the entire development plan sank into jeopardy. In addition to growing signs of Wentworth's impulsive behavior, something was definitely amiss — perhaps related to his whiskey consumption.

Later that evening, cook Dottie served pears for dessert at dinner. Went looked at the pears and said, "Pears? I told her to serve peaches!" This minute detail struck Wentworth as absolutely incomprehensible after he had carefully planned peaches, his fruit of choice, for the dinner menu. Sitting at a table of eight guests, he became incensed, shoved his chair back, abruptly stood up and walked into the kitchen. A hush fell over the dining room, yet people tried to behave nonchalantly and returned to their conversations. Went came back to the table and said, "Well... she may quit." No one heard what he said to Dottie but Linda, who heretofore had never questioned Went's actions, responded calmly with four words: "I wouldn't blame her."

Went clenched his jaw and said, "What did you say?" and Linda repeated her remark to which Went ordered, "Step outside." They went outside and closed the heavy wooden door, in an attempt to muffle their conversation from the guests.

"This was *the* turning point in our relationship," revealed Linda. "Outside, Went said to me 'Say that again,' and I repeated my comment, 'I wouldn't blame her.'"

Within a matter of minutes their dialogue escalated to what would become the most intense moment of their marriage. Went's fuse was lit and he unleashed his pent-up frustration.

"Went struck me with a right hook to the chin. I hit the ground but jumped up like one of those dodo birds perched on the rim of a cocktail glass! Actually, I felt nothing," remarked Linda. "No pain. No emotion. I just stood up without comment and looked at him. He repeated the question with escalated anger, *What did you say?'* and I responded once again with 'I wouldn't blame her.' And he punched me and knocked me down again. It's so strange that I felt no emotion and I just stood up looking at him again without comment."

"I think we better go for a walk and talk about this," Went said through clenched teeth. "I replied with, 'Yes, I think we better,'" said Linda. Apparently her disapproval was enough to jolt Went into acknowledging what was at stake. Finally Linda spoke up for herself. "For the next 30 minutes I told Went in very clear terms all the mistakes I felt he had made in the dealings with attorney Henry Hyde plus everything that I'd been holding back for all those years. It proved to be the pivotal moment in our marriage. At the end of the conversation Went decided to go to our apartment in San Francisco and think about the situation for a while."

Over a decade of hard work had gone into building the Research Farm and in an instant Went was finished. San Francisco provided the cooling retreat he needed to reflect on his life. Went wanted to attract fascinating people and projects to Badger, but instead the energetic cost was too great and he departed like a rock propelled from a slingshot. Linda remembered, "When Went drove out the front gate I experienced a huge feeling of relief." That moment would become the genesis of a major change in Linda's life.

Linda said in retrospect, "In all of the sixteen years that I was married to Went, it never crossed my mind to leave him. In spite of a lot of difficulties with him, the Research Farm and the School meant so much to me that it never once crossed my mind that I could run the school alone."

The tone of the Farm changed dramatically without Wentworth's presence, but he left a great deal of knowledge that was deeply woven into the program. Now Linda was left with the daunting task of running the School of Horsemanship on her own. Lynn Blades remembered, "The Research Farm started drifting but I stayed because Linda and I were working on a proposal for a school of horsemanship program at Prescott College that I wanted to see materialize."

Lynn was hit hardest by Went's departure. They had worked closely on the development project that lay in a heap of rolled-up plans. She admitted she felt dazed and confused; things had changed drastically.

It wasn't long until Lynn departed too. Now Linda was without an Assistant Instructor. She began relying on the assistance of Went's son, Jay Tellington, and Roland Kleger to keep the operation running. Although Linda continued to remain strong after Went left, the Research Farm was a lot of responsibility on her shoulders. Went, who was now coping better in San Francisco, stayed in touch by telephone. Linda recalls, "I am so grateful that I lived in gratitude for everything we had at that time."

Linda continued her every-morning, hour-long telephone conversations with Margit, the focus of which usually centered on the progress of her horses and plans for upcoming competitions. "Then one day we were discussing the situation with Went and Margit said to me, 'Why don't you divorce him?' The thought had never even crossed my mind," said Linda. However, now she thought 'why not?' and began considering the option.

Shortly thereafter during a telephone conversation with Went, Linda suggested the idea of divorce and he agreed that it was the practical course of action. Their separation was completely amicable, without any blame, and they proceeded to divvy up their possessions. Linda bought him out of all of the Research Farm assets and he took the product line, which he later marketed under the name of Whitehurst Products.

It was apparent to everyone that Wentworth had become too isolated at Badger. While coaching the bright aspiring equestrian instructors was gratifying, it was clear that he missed the brilliant engineering minds with whom he had once interacted. He was a very complex person, full of wit and intelligence, who just ran out of steam in the tiny town that boasted a population of 13. It finally took its toll on him. It's likely that whiskey on the rocks veiled his tedium and the residual pain left by old athletic injuries. Who's to say?

Went was a geologist, an accomplished classical pianist, and an engineer; he had so many interests that were simply not being nourished enough in Badger. Years before they parted, Went told Linda that one day she would go out on her own; now the time had come.

It was clear that Went always had love and respect for Linda and she for him. Wentworth taught Linda by expanding her thinking process, instilling confidence, fine-tuning her capabilities and giving her the tools to reach lofty goals. After they parted ways, they stayed in touch, even to the degree where he twice asked her to come back to him. But it was too late; Linda was already moving down her own path.

As for the School of Horsemanship that followed after Went left Badger? Judging from my own phenomenal experience with Went and knowing his contribution to PCERF, I believe that after he left the School, the students certainly learned a great deal about equitation and horsemanship, but they truly missed out on knowing the magnificent genius of Wentworth J. Tellington.

Because Went left a positive impression on me, I stayed in touch with him and visited him when I could. In the early 1970s Went married Kathy Cashion and became a professor at Prescott College in Prescott, Arizona. He eventually moved back to California's Sierra Nevada foothill town of Auburn. There Wendell Robie asked him to join the Board of Governors of the Western States Trail Foundation, sponsor of the Tevis Cup 100-Mile One Day Trail Ride that Went so revered.

Endurance riding had brought him a long way since publishing his first manual on long distance riding. In 1979, along with Linda, they wrote a revised and updated book, "Endurance and Competitive Trail Riding."

Went then later moved to North San Juan in California's Nevada County where he had a gold mining claim. He later returned to Tucson and Prescott, Arizona where he commenced working on and eventually patented an invention that had simmered in his mind for years. His engineering feat consisted of a floating platform that was capable of enlarging landing strips for airports located near bodies of water.

Years later Linda and I had a retrospective and cathartic conversation about the magnitude of influence that Went had on both of us. She revealed many details about their complex relationship and said, "After staying quiet for so long I finally told Went what I was really thinking. Remember I was twenty years younger, and he was a brilliant raconteur — always story-telling, entertaining and intriguing people. Went had an explosive side to him that most of you students never saw, thank Heavens. I had never once in sixteen years had a real conversation with him. It always went one way. Him lecturing. Me listening. There were some really hard times when I think the whiskey got to him and he completely lost control.

"I've been asked a few times by friends what I thought when Went punched me and knocked me down. The answer is I didn't think anything. I had disciplined myself to have no feeling because it was necessary in order to survive my life with Went.

"The fact is to be punched in the jaw with a right hook by Went Tellington was no small deal," reports Linda. "He had been on the Golden Gloves boxing team while at Harvard and he knew how to throw a mean right hook. One would wonder how it was that I felt unfazed and bounced back on my feet without comment each time he punched me. I have wondered about that myself occasionally over the years.

"Remember the 'she's as tough as a boiled owl' comment about me by Arabian horse breeder, Mrs. Jackson, twelve years earlier when our Thoroughbred racing stallion Fault Free stood straight up on his hind legs in the most extreme rear I had ever experienced? I was pretty sturdy. I remember when my jaw was broken in 1969 from the kick of a horse while I was waiting to enter the ring at a Pebble Beach dressage show. There was a doctor friend of mine sitting on the horse behind me who witnessed the incident. She told me later that had he horse hit my face 1" higher, the lethal blow would have killed me instantly. To this day, that is why I approach life with a positive point of view. It was the first instance that made me see the 'glass half full, rather than half empty.' I was not even knocked down, and due to the shock, mercifully, I felt no fear or pain."

And yet there was something more. "Practicing self-control was a key to survival over the years with Went," Linda continued. "Because of his habit of daily whiskey consumption, I had to be very careful not to react because of his short fuse. In fact, that practice of 'acting rather than reacting' has become a cornerstone of the Tellington Method in the 21st century.

"After much thought," Linda explains, "I tell this story now to shed a positive light on these events in my life. Not to seek sympathy, but if there is even one woman who can learn from my experiences and stand up for herself, it is worth revealing what happened to me.

"But in spite of some hard experiences, I would not trade a moment of my time with Went Tellington. He was my teacher in so many ways. He encouraged me to read the classics, to go to night school and summer school at UCLA, and study trigonometry and history as a foundation for learning, which I would never have done. I enrolled in the creative writing classes he taught at Chadwick School, which prepped me for the joy I feel while writing today. I am so grateful to say that we remained friends and in contact until the day he died. He was a brilliant organizer and a strict taskmaster. In later years he developed a horrific case of emphysema. He took a practical approach to life and promised that if he were ever sick he would shoot himself rather than end up sitting in a wheelchair in a senior home. And that is exactly what he did. In 2000, he wrote a very poignant letter to me the week before he died saying he had sold his household goods and his car. When I read it I had the strong premonition that he was announcing his departure. Sure enough, he took cash in hand, paid to be cremated, and walked out behind the crematorium and shot himself. It was a dramatic but fitting end for a Cavalryman dedicated to action."

Shannon Yewell Weil

A Tribute to Wentworth Tellington

"I want to be sure to give Went credit for his remarkable contributions to PCERF. I was in charge of the horses and the training and teaching," remembers Linda, "but Went's organization skills, his genius, his amazing creativity and his ability to write the syndicated columns, articles and advertising were the backbone of the operation.

"I would not be where I am today without Went Tellington. Being married to Went was not always easy but I am deeply grateful and clear about the advantages that certainly shaped and developed my character. Plus my passion for reading books was directly influenced by Went.

"I like to memorize inspiring quotes, and three books have influenced my philosophical approach to life. The first is the book, "The Prophet," by Kahlil Gibran. The chapter on Sorrow and Joy lifted me up when I felt like melting in a puddle of tears. The quote, *'The selfsame well from which your sorrow flows, shall also flow your joy'* took me from a state of hopelessness to one of trust for myself. Whenever I felt down I remembered those words and thought, 'Come on tears. Someday this well will be overflowing with joy.' And that is precisely what has happened.

"When Went was critical of me, I would be uplifted by the words of the Russian philosopher Peter D. Ouspensky in his book, "In Search of the Miraculous": *'It's necessary to go through the crystallization of fire in order to hone the soul.'* I experienced maybe more than my share of 'honing' but I would not trade a day of it. I've thought a lot over the years of Went's sometimes-violent side. Fortunately for both of us there were only a handful of times over sixteen years when he lost control. But I have developed a deeper understanding of violence from the teaching from "The Course In Miracles," a one-year self-study course that had a huge influence on me. The concept that *"Aggression comes from a place of fear, and is a cry for help"* has allowed me to understand Went's behavior and forgive him. This teaching has become a basis for understanding and working with aggressive horses and dogs with The Tellington Method. I hold the intention that Went, who 'changed addresses' over a decade ago, is aware of my deep gratitude for all the gifts he contributed to my life."

CHAPTER 18

THE END OF THE DREAM

Simply put, Margit Bessenyey was Linda's safety net, a fabulous client and a friend. By 1971 her voice of prudent wisdom said to Linda about Badger, "Why don't you look for a smaller place? I'll buy it for you and send down more Hungarian horses for you to train." The enormous responsibility of the Research Farm was weighing heavily on Linda and she was ready for a change. The pursuit to downsize and relocate the School of Horsemanship began.

It wasn't long before Linda found Westwind Barn, a wonderful historic horse facility in Los Altos Hills, California, just south of San Francisco. Originally built in the 1940s by Frank Ellithorpe, it began as a six-stall barn where he raised Morgan and Arabian horses. Ellithorpe sold the land in 1965 to Robert D. Clement who added 17 more stalls, a tack room and an arena. Margit, who was now taking a more active role in Linda's life, leased the adjacent property that already had a spacious home. The acquisition totaled 13 acres, and Margit also leased another parcel next to it that we used for pasture. A new sign at the entrance read "Westwind Hungarian Horse Farm."

As much as Linda loved PCERF, she was always very good about moving on in life and this transition was essential. Leaving the rural setting in the Sierra Nevada foothills for the last time, Linda and her entourage were figuratively airlifted by Margit from Badger, drawing closure to the Pacific Coast Equestrian Research Farm. Lock, stock and barrel, everything was transported over the four-and-a-half hour trip to the swank community of Los Altos Hills. Linda's country life was compressed into an entirely new dimension. Everything was different now.

Wentworth's son, Jay Tellington, and Roland Kleger were there to help Linda close down the operation and prepare for the move to Los Altos Hills. Hard worker Val Pruitt also remained at Badger to see that everything was finalized.

Roland remembered, "I was saddened to oversee the closing of PCERF. However, in hindsight, it was an essential step in the evolution of Linda's work internationally – through her books describing the Tellington Method, her development of TTouch and the establishment of Tellington Training which teaches these methods to many more people each year than she could have reached at PCERF."

As Linda was closing down the Badger location, aside from the Hungarians, she listed all the school horses for sale. Several of the bombproof horses like Earthaquake and Chuckwagon Son made an easy transition to the Stockebrand's corrals at the nearby M Bar J Guest Ranch. The all-time-favorite Dakota was sold to a student who adored her. Several other horses were privately sold. Sierra Spy went to the Midwest and became a regional champion eventing horse. Val Pruitt bought an Arabian gelding named Fahr for a bargain price of 50 dollars, based on the fact that she took exceptionally good care of him throughout his recovery from a bad injury.

Michele Pouliot had already left the Research Farm when Linda received a call from Cynthia Evert in Fargo, North Dakota. Cynthia was hiring riding instructors for a public riding center called Winfield Manor School of Horsemanship. Linda put her in touch with Michele. "I was the first one hired to help start Winfield Manor in about 1971," remembers Michele, "and I recommended to Cynthia to buy ten or twelve of the best school horses that were for sale when PCERF closed down.

"A huge truck left Fargo and returned with a group of PCERF horses that included Red Fox, Caper, Rebel and UFO, Bay Rum, and Dauntless. I was able to tell her which horses we could use for public lessons immediately," continues Michele. All the horses knew each other. When the truck arrived, Michele was there to greet and welcome the herd that she knew so well. That was a perfect transition for the horses who had taught so many students at Badger.

"Several other PCERF graduates also worked at Winfield Manor including Val Pruitt, Barbara Van Etten, Sally Schwartz and Judy Hale, which made it a great program with all those talented instructors," said Michele. "I left after one year at Winfield and in the summer of 1972 drove back to California."

Linda's extraordinary endurance mare Bint Gulida, who was now 15 years old, had been sent to Montana the previous spring to live under Margit's care. By then she had produced five foals; stallion Cougar Rock by world-famous Arabian Bezatal (who won the Tevis in 1965 and 1967 with Ed Johnson in the saddle) would become her most significant get. When Bint Gulida's heartthrob Brado (who was the same age) arrived they produced a filly together.

Linda reflected on the dozens of students who came to her school representing nine countries and 36 states. She realized that there was one final detail to which she had to attend as she was packing up the PCERF office. She held up a Bronze Medal in her hand and thought, "This needs to go to Merrilee Pruitt," who had been unable to take her final riding due to a serious spill she had taken off of the Thoroughbred, Resolute several weeks before. In the mailing envelope she slipped a note that read, "I know you would have passed your test; here's your long overdue medal. With love, Linda."

As the remaining days in Badger were drawing to a close, with boxes packed, the enchanting photographs removed from the walls, items tossed away or wrestled into trucks, the details of silencing the once bustling and robust Research Farm were falling into place — as if bringing a fast-moving freight train to a halt. Linda had already left Badger; she was carrying her life forward in Los Altos Hills.

Tiger was the last Great Dane at Badger.

235

No more would the melodious clang of the bell outside the PCERF kitchen call everyone for meals, no more Great Danes roaming freely, no more black hunt boots scuffling along the concrete sidewalks. No more students lucky enough to find their courage, confidence or better yet, their life's purpose. No more horse breeders, veterinarians or endurance riders with their finely-tuned horses coming to meet at this training epicenter for long distance riding. No more excited students training for the Tevis or setting off for their first horse shows; the dormitories were vacated and scrubbed cleaned. The barns and pastures were now empty of all the beautiful horses; every one of them had moved on. Soon the only sounds that could be heard were that of the doves and quails.

The only remaining person heard the final thunk of the screen door at the Pacific Coast Equestrian Research Farm. It was Val Pruitt Sivertson. She turned around and locked the door, then walked to her car and drove away for the final time.

The great PCERF dream had ended.

CHAPTER 19

WESTWIND HUNGARIAN HORSE FARM
LEADS TO A TIME FOR CHANGE

Countess Margit Bessenyey was uncomfortable with the fact that Linda, who was now the director of the Westwind Hungarian Horse Farm and living in the posh area of Los Altos Hills, California, was a single woman. She felt it more socially acceptable if Linda had a husband, and it didn't take long to resolve the situation. Despite the fact that Birch Jones was some 11 years younger than Linda, who was now 36, Margit felt he was a proper consort for Linda.

Birch created a dashing vision when dressed in his formal riding attire.

"He was tall and handsome and dressed very well. Birch had more pairs of expensive riding boots than anyone I knew," Linda said describing her young husband. "He played polo, belonged to the Los Altos Hunt and was training to compete in the pentathlon event, with Olympic dreams." Linda even joined Birch while taking fencing lessons in San Francisco.

Plans moved swiftly as improvements were made to Westwind. The large, three-bedroom, rambling ranch house is where Linda and Birch lived and was adapted to accommodate guests. A fourth bedroom was added later. The remodel job transformed the property to suit the needs of Linda's new school. In addition, there was a one-bedroom guesthouse for the Assistant Instructor as well as the leased house with a swimming pool next door for the eight students.

"For the main house we didn't want pavement so we had the driveway coated with a special sand colored gravel. We also had brick floors installed that had a classic European feel," Linda remembered. "I enjoyed transforming this house. My neighbor was an antiques dealer and she helped me fill the house with beautiful pieces of antique furniture, as well as decorating the guest house." Linda was thrilled with furnishing her new home and planning for her upcoming nuptials. "My favorite part of the wedding was the preparation."

I was again living in Altadena, California when the mailman delivered an invitation to Linda's wedding. "Well, look at this," I thought, "she's going to marry Birch." And yes, of course, I would be in attendance. On the wedding day, my sister Susan accompanied me as we drove to Los Altos Hills from her home in San Jose. Westwind was a stark contrast to the dusty ranch in Badger that I loved so well, but certainly an idyllic setting for the new chapter in Linda's life.

"It was a small yet fun wedding," Linda recalled. "That morning several of the students made trays of food while I sped up to San Francisco to pick up a huge pot of Spanish Paella that I had ordered from a fabulous restaurant."

Many friends and family, including Linda's parents, were there to celebrate. It was the first time I met the omnipresent person throughout Linda's life, Roland Kleger, who was also there to witness his dear friend's wedding. Little did any of us know that Roland and Linda would celebrate their own wedding 28 years later.

In a beautiful, small church a few miles from Westwind, Linda walked down the aisle with her father, Hoodie. We witnessed the simple ceremony uniting Linda Tellington and Earl Birchell Jones, Jr. The reception followed at the Westwind house as guests celebrated while overlooking the impressive facilities.

We toured the immaculate Westwind Barn filled with magnificent Hungarian Furioso horses. What a grand life — not only for the horses, but also for the very fortunate students who had enrolled in the first session at Westwind. Birch was a lucky guy and had plenty of activities to occupy his time.

After the wedding he entertained the guests with an impressive fencing demonstration. *En garde!*

Linda joined Birch in fencing lessons while they were still living at Badger.

Westwind frequently provided Hungarian horses for the Los Altos Hunt Master of the Hunt, Tony Vascek.

Tony Vascek is looking fabulous riding Hungarian Lazlo.

Aptly named, the Westwind Hungarian Horse Farm became center stage for the Hungarian Furiosos and provided far more exposure for them than the Central California location did. Linda became a recognized member of the Los Altos Hunt and accompanied by her students, frequented the combined training and steeplechase events held at the familiar Pebble Beach Equestrian Center in Monterey where she continued to sweep the prizes.

From a sepia-toned brochure touting the Hungarian horses and Westwind…

> *Westwind was established in 1971 as the California base for the training, showing and selling of Hungarian horses. In addition to the program for Hungarian horses, Westwind is also offering a six-month program for riding instructors, limited to eight students selected for their potential as instructors and trainers. The instructor program was developed by the Pacific Coast Equestrian Research Farm and became nationally recognized as the Pacific Coast School of Horsemanship.*

The Hungarian mare, M. Godiva, became Linda's favorite riding horse. Seen here Linda is teaching a class with the Westwind Barn in the background.

At Westwind Linda continued the drills while teaching her students. In the background is the leased 5-bedroom house with a swimming pool for the students.

Agility exercises keep the riders supple.

The rewards of all their hard work and training paid off by winning the 1970 Oakland Preliminary Combined Training Event.

Eleanor Woltjes joined Linda again at Westwind as her Assistant Instructor.

Eleanor Woltjes, a graduate of PCERF, met Linda's high standards for riding, and joined the Westwind staff as the Head Instructor. A strict and proper dress code for attire while riding or instructing was precisely executed by everyone at Westwind: tall black riding boots, breeches, a belt and a ratcatcher shirt. One day Linda looked out of the kitchen window and saw Eleanor standing in the arena giving a lesson, wearing blue jeans and sneakers. Linda was aghast. After the lesson she asked Eleanor what was going on. Why had she ignored the strict dress code, a clear *faux pas*? Eleanor's pointed response was unexpected and out of character when she said, "Well, if you don't like it, you can fire me."

Eleanor's response took Linda by surprise. She commented to me, "We had worked closely together for years, but I already had a clear sense of trust that there must some reason for this dramatic turn of events, so I let her go. What happened next had a major influence on my life. It was the first glimpse I had of seeing a half empty glass as half full — it made me aware that we all have guardian angels. Over the years I've had a few times when I had to let people go, but I always remember what happened to Eleanor.

"In order to understand that statement you need to know something about Eleanor. She was a very pretty woman, about thirty-five at the time with lovely, long blond hair. She was very smart and well read but had one huge empty area in her life. She had never had a boyfriend. She was simply too shy with men. Well, her guardian angels were preparing to answer her prayers.

"As it turned out, while Eleanor was visiting her parents in Hayfork, a handsome young man was also visiting his parents there. Coincidently, while strolling down Main Street, they met. As if out of a fairytale, Eleanor and her Prince Charming fell in love. After waiting years for her true love, Eleanor had at last found what she had been longing for. She was ready to move on in life with her new love.

"And so, after many years of working together with mutual respect and admiration, we parted ways," remembers Linda. "Within a couple of months, Eleanor married the man of her dreams and they lived happily in the Santa Cruz Mountains. Sadly, Eleanor succumbed to cancer and passed away several years later."

In her search for another instructor, Linda was fortunate enough to hire the well-known and accomplished riding instructor, Jim Forderer, who was a student at the Pacific Coast Equestrian Research Farm in 1966. He was now teaching horsemanship at nearby Stanford University in Palo Alto and was willing to make the move to Westwind. His standards of excellence mirrored Linda's. Jim continued as the Head Instructor until 1974 when Westwind closed.

Robyn Hood brought her awesome talents from Canada and spent six-month stints at Westwind. Her primary focus was to start the young Hungarians sent from Montana. She also assisted Jim with teaching classes and enjoyed many happy hours competing.

Countess Bessenyey bought the Mount Aventine Manor House in 1954 to have an east coast base for her Hungarian horses. Today it is widely known as Chapman State Park and is in the National Registry of Historic Places.

Margit set Linda up in sublime fashion at Westwind. At the time Linda was one of the highest paid horse trainers in the country. She had anything and everything she wanted right at her fingertips. She was even given six months of medical leave should she become injured or ill. And to top it off, Margit insisted that Linda join her at her spectacular Indian Head farm in Southern Maryland called Mount Aventine Manor House, on the banks of the Potomac River every few months for rest and relaxation.

Countess Judith Gyurky lived about 160 miles from Margit at her 90-acre farm called Port-A-Ferry Farm in Piedmont, Virginia, just outside of Charlottesville. The pair of Countesses were like two doting aunties who relished in the activity of pampering Linda, the equivalent of their shared niece. They were delighted that Linda was showcasing their Hungarian Furioso horses.

When visiting Countess Bessenyey in Maryland, she insisted that Linda "Sleep in until at least 10:00 a.m.," Linda reports. "Then Margit would personally bring me a huge breakfast in bed, served with gorgeous china and linens, and we would look over fashion magazines and discuss anything but horses." This was unusual for Linda since she was an early riser, but she loved the intimate connections and education she received from Margit. "Countess Gyurky would often come for dinner and then we would talk horses into the wee hours of the morning.

"I remember sitting at the kitchen table at Margit's place in Maryland. She would let her staff go while I was there and she would do all the cooking herself — we had wonderful meals. One of her favorite desserts was whipped cream with fresh apricot jam folded into it," Linda swooned.

During these visits, Margit would reminisce about her mother who possessed the admirable traits of the Hungarian Magyar, whose characteristics reflected intense vitality and enthusiasm. They would fling themselves into every cause that excited their interest and sympathy, regardless of the consequences. Margit remembered her mother's work with charities and her tireless efforts in relieving misery. Linda recalled a story Margit told while preparing a delicious meal in the kitchen. "It must have been at an elegant dinner in New York when Margit's mother, a renown hostess, observed a guest picking up an hors d'oeuvre and eating the paper doily along with it. In true grand fashion, this elegant lady did the very same thing so as not to embarrass the guest."

Like so many young American heiresses of the early 1900s, Margit's mother, Harriot Daly, married into European royalty and became the wife of Count Anton Sigray von Febre of Hungary.

Even though Linda relished her time with the Countesses, it was not her intention to remain idle. The early 1970s were awash in social and behavioral change throughout the country, and Linda soon discovered that she wanted more out of life. She returned from each respite with the Countesses fortified again, but she still had a thirst to find her true calling. Linda had lived a fairly regimented life. She had taught riding classes at Briarcrest from the time she was 14, taught 8th grade Social Studies at Chadwick School, taught riding students and had run PCERF, and had been married to a taskmaster for 16 years. She was ready for a hefty dose of *joie de vivre*; she wanted to venture out and grow. She had been the teacher for all those years and now she longed to be the student again.

Manifesting Destiny

A short drive south of Los Altos Hills is the Monterey Peninsula, which is embraced by the Pacific Ocean. Nestled a little farther south is the Big Sur coast and the international personal development center called the Esalen Institute. It offers tantalizing visions of adventure, of unexplored frontiers, and human possibilities yet to be realized.

In 1974 Linda signed up for a workshop with Robert Monroe, the founder of the groundbreaking Monroe Institute. "My interest in the use of logic and intuition was awakened," remembers Linda, "and there I participated in a study conducted that weekend by Russell Targ, co-founder of the Stanford Research Institute with participants of the Monroe Institute. The results showed that I had an equal use of left and right hemispheres of the brain, representing equal use of logic and intuition. Most people are weighted on one side — either more logical or more intuitive." Tantalized by this new world of exploration and knowledge, Linda was hooked!

Linda and Birch were drifting apart and she began attending more and more weekend seminars at the Esalen Institute. She loved the intellectual caliber of the seminar leaders, as well as engaging in fascinating conversations with other attendees. She enjoyed indulging herself in massages in the out-of-doors overlooking the rugged coastline of Big Sur, while enjoying the fresh smell of sea air and listening to seagulls cawing and waves crashing on the rocks. Linda invested time at Esalen to discover who she really was.

It was at Esalen where Linda was led to the blueprint that was affirmed in Fritzie's Astrological Chart from many years earlier. Internally Linda's life was transforming as her mindset changed and her persona shifted. No longer was she bound to the strict conservative clothes and drab color palette that Wentworth required her to wear. No longer was she confined to the status quo of what she thought and taught. Linda's world was opening and she was going to grab as much as she could to expand her thinking. Esalen opened many doors for Linda, including introductions to people who were expanding their minds and furthering their potential. She was becoming a liberated woman.

The rigid mindset was crumbling; tweeds were replaced by fun, colorful clothing. No longer tethered to the daily routine of teaching, Linda was learning how the mind, body and spirit worked together. She was free to spin her curious thoughts and questions into brewing ideas.

Enter Roger Russell

While attending a workshop at the Esalen Institute, Linda was drawn to an unusual-looking young man named Roger Russell who ultimately played a major role in her life and career. Linda recalls, "On the first day of a Gestalt workshop taught by Ilana Rubenfeld, a pioneer in the integration of body-mind-spirit, I met Roger. We were asked to choose a partner for an exercise, and although I usually waited until someone chose me, we looked at each other across the room and it was clear we would partner together. When I first noticed Roger I was immediately attracted to him but he was certainly not a guy who would pass in my social circle of the Los Altos Hills Hunt Club. Although I never met one, he fit my vision of a Moroccan hash dealer — he was one of those males with brooding brown eyes, and totally wild, uncombed curly black hair that stood out in all directions. And he looked like his jeans would stand up alone if he took them off and put them in a corner. But his looks were completely deceiving. After that first day we began hanging out together after every class and having deep conversations. It was the first time I had a chance to discuss spirituality in depth, and in our first conversation we discussed our relationship to a loving God."

Linda was finally getting the chance to speak her own mind. "All those years with Wentworth were spent listening, never having a chance to engage in a philosophic conversation because Went, being a genius and a raconteur, never gave anyone else a chance to get a word in edge-wise. Besides he was twenty years older than I, so what did I really have to contribute to a conversation? However, thanks to Wentworth's guidance I had read many classics, practiced speed-reading with Homer's 'The Iliad' and 'The Odyssey,' and was a great fan of 'The Great Books of the Western World' and historical novels."

Recounting the dynamics of her second husband, Linda revealed some insight to her growth. "Birch was eleven years younger than I was and he was totally different. With Birch, however, I finally found *my* power and *my* voice, but he was totally the opposite of Wentworth on the intellectual scale and I found myself bored stiff in any conversation with him. I had been attracted to Birch in the beginning because he told me he remembered 'seeing' his parents entering the San Francisco Opera House *before he was born!* Intriguing thought! In retrospect, I must have thought he would have an interest in opera and culture because of his parents' cultural background, but as it turned out, I was way off base. His choice of reading material was limited to cartoons and comic books. Yikes! On a scale of one to ten, his intellectual curiosity was zero," Linda proclaimed.

But Roger was something else. He was highly intelligent, had won a national science award as a student, worked for a bank in Denver, Colorado and had accumulated a respectable nest-egg from playing the stock market. Like herself, Roger was at Esalen to reinvent himself in a new phase of life. After the workshop he returned to his home in Colorado but he stayed in contact sporadically with Linda.

Meanwhile at the Westwind Hungarian Horse Farm, a position became available and Linda had an idea. "I telephoned Roger and asked him if he wanted to come back to California and take on the job of temporary gardener," explaining to him that one of the Mexican staff had to leave the country to take care of his ailing mother. Roger was intrigued and accepted the invitation. He quickly settled in to one of the guest rooms in the spacious house. Linda added, "At the same time I had a intern student from Germany who was also living in the house. Some years later she told me how curious she thought it was that the gardener often got up late and sat in the kitchen drinking coffee and reading poetry!"

Roger stayed to himself while caring for the landscaping, about which he knew nothing, but he made a modest stab at satisfying his new job description. Linda integrated him into the equestrian atmosphere and he soon began to learn the basics of riding. Linda now had someone at Westwind with whom she shared the Esalen experience. Roger was settling into the household quite comfortably and he and Linda were spending more and more time together.

By now, Birch had reconnected with a former girlfriend closer to his age and had moved out of the house several months earlier. He then declared her as the love of his life. Much to Linda's relief, he was off the property and starting a new chapter of his own. However, after several months he rethought his decision, apparently realizing what he had forsaken by leaving Linda and the splendid opportunities afforded him at Westwind. Now he wanted to return. But it was too late — Linda told him that she and Roger had already struck up a relationship.

"I was slightly flabbergasted when Birch announced to me that he wanted to challenge Roger to a fencing duel – and whoever won had the right to be with me!" Linda said shaking her head, hardly believing that really happened. "You'd have to know Birch to appreciate the nature of his idea," she began. "His dream of making the U.S. pentathlon team was a big part of his life. I think he really saw himself as a reincarnation of a knight from the Middle Ages." Linda fueled his dream, however, and confessed with a smile, "I probably didn't help matters when I gave him a full suit of armor for his 22nd birthday gift." The shiny figure of metal had occupied a place of honor at the front entrance to their home.

"My first response to Birch's dueling challenge was to remind him that Roger was not adept at combat sports with bladed weapons and this was completely out of the question and certainly not sporting." So Birch replied, "Then I will challenge him to a polo match!" My reply was, "But Roger has only ridden a few months and has never played a game of polo! How fair is that?

"Looking for a way that Birch could save face by 'losing me' and knowing full well that Roger was an accomplished chess player, I then suggested, 'How about challenging Roger to a game of chess?' Birch agreed. Roger won." And Roger stayed with Linda for nine years. They remain close friends to this day.

The 1970s were all about liberation and proved to be a major turning point in Linda's life. She felt there was more to her life's purpose then showing and riding horses. She was certainly ready to explore the next phase of her life in full Technicolor.

"I had Margit's horses for thirteen years, from 1961 to 1974," Linda reflected. "I had competed with horses ever since I was thirteen years old. I was riding to school, riding after school and competing for so many years. After twenty-seven years I was ready for something new. I wanted to learn, not just teach."

Finally the day came when Linda's daily morning telephone conversations with Margit turned towards Linda's future. Margit had created a perfect world for Linda. After all, Linda was showcasing her marvelous Hungarian horses that she worked so hard to bring to light in America. Linda told Margit that, after their long connection training and competing with the Hungarian horses, it was time for a change.

Over several weeks, their discussions were salted with emotion. The outcome was inevitable for Linda to find her life's purpose. "Deciding to part ways was really hard because of the depth of our friendship," Linda said. "She was one of the most important mentors in my life." Finally Margit and Linda felt it was time to close the doors of the Westwind Hungarian Horse Farm. It was a sad decision but necessary for Linda to pursue her future goals, whatever they might be. Countess Margit Bessenyey, who was the ever-present champion of Linda Tellington-Jones, understood her choice and agreed to dissolve Westwind. They also agreed that all the horses at Westwind would be offered for auction and those unsold would return to the Bitter Root Stock Farm.

All of the horses were sold at a Fasig-Tipton auction held in a big tent erected near the Westwind barn.

Dispersal Sale

Linda called the west coast office of Fasig-Tipton Sales Company that was then connected to the California Thoroughbred Breeders Association (CTBA) in Arcadia. She scheduled a date for the auction company to come to Westwind.

By this time, I had already spent five years working in the Thoroughbred racing industry including time at the CTBA. My friend Ralph Kraft, liaison for Fasig-Tipton and the CTBA, told me that he spoke with Linda regarding the sale. Naturally I made arrangements to travel to Westwind for the event. After all, it was yet another milestone in Linda's life and I had to be there. Hundreds of people attended the sale as the beautiful equines were offered one-by-one to their perspective new owners.

Many of Linda's excellent riders had already lost their hearts to their favorite horses and anxiously signaled bids in hopes that theirs would be the top dollar when the auctioneer's gavel fell. Years of excellent breeding, patience, and high-level skilled training had been poured into these steeds. To watch these eqine partners load up into horse trailers and depart for their new homes was a melancholy moment, marking the end to a magnificent era in Linda's life. It was like the final curtain call in a long-running Broadway play. It was also the closure that Linda needed to hang up her tack and bring her years as a beautiful, magnificent competitive rider to an end.

After the property was vacated, the generous and altruistic Margit Bessenyey donated the Westwind Barn to the town of Los Altos Hills. The community graciously embraced it as the gem that it is. In 2010, this historic facility was given a complete overhaul. It now boasts a new roof and foundation, and is energy efficient and seismically safe. The Westwind Barn hosts a Pony Club and a 4-H Riding for the Handicapped program among other activities.

From Los Altos Hills, Linda moved with Roger to Big Sur to be closer to Esalen. They spent months attending seminars and expanding their minds as well as nurturing their new relationship. Roger, who was intellectually stimulating, brought a broad dynamic to Linda's life.

Now in total green-growth mode, Linda was exploring, learning, searching, but all the while not knowing exactly what she wanted. For the first time she didn't have the responsibility of a school, students, or dozens of horses.

Reflecting back on that period of time in her life, she said, "I was discouraged that there was so little respect for horses in the equestrian world. I felt it was hopeless in terms of changing the way people related to horses. I wanted to do something different with my life. I'd been teaching horsemanship classes for the

University of California at Santa Cruz. One day I made an appointment with the Dean at the University to discuss changing my career. I was considering the pursuit of a Masters degree or a PhD in animal behavior. His prophetic advice set a new direction for my life. 'Listen, Linda, university is for people who don't know what they want to do. You know what you have to do in the world, just go out and find it.' I decided to take two years and travel around the world to figure out what I was *supposed* to do.

"It was 1974 and I had an invitation to join a former student from Chadwick School, Lee Lyon, in Zaire where she was filming gorillas. I thought this was perfect and made arrangements to spend several months with her," remembers Linda. Roger and Linda flew to Europe and on their way to Zaire they stopped to visit her friend Ursula Bruns in Germany. "This visit was a major sidetrack in my life and it was seventeen years later that I finally made it to Zaire!

"But I must digress for a moment," Linda paused, "and go back a few years to introduce Ursula Bruns who represents a major milestone in my life."

Settling in her chair, Linda's mind slipped back to her years at PCERF. "I first met Ursula in 1970 when she visited my school in Badger and was very impressed with our style of riding and teaching — particularly by our bridleless riding and jumping.

"Ursula was the publisher of a German horse magazine, *Freitzet im Sattel* (Free Time in the Saddle), dedicated to pleasure riders and the first of its kind in Germany. She had written a horse book for children that had sold more than half a million copies. She was an innovator and a mover and a shaker in the German horse scene. With this connection to Ursula Bruns, my guardian angels were setting the scene for my future.

"After Ursula's first visit to PCERF she returned to Germany and established the Reken Freitzet im Sattle Test Center and developed an innovative Eleven-Day Course for Beginning Adult Riders, called the Bruns/Behr Method. The course content was very much influenced by the Balanced Seat style of riding and classroom theory Ursula had observed at my school, and she incorporated the idea of riding without a bridle as she had seen us do with the Hungarian horses."

Expressing a great sense of accomplishment, Linda reflects back, "Our school for riding instructors stemmed from a single phone call in 1962 from a woman rider in Pasadena wishing to take lessons over the Christmas holidays. Her only choice for lessons was in a class with children at the famous Flintridge Stable, and the kids seemed to learn so much faster than she did. That phone call was ultimately the inspiration for the opening of our Pacific Coast Equestrian Research Farm and School of Horsemanship at Badger in 1964. Ursula's program was the most effective and safe method for adults learning to ride and it is still in operation today directed by Jochen Schumacher, who as a teenager, was a member of my four horse quadrille when I introduced bridleless riding at Equitana in the mid-1970s.

"The following year she invited me to Germany and I spent a month with her, visiting stables and breeders around the country." It was then that Linda saw the evidence of the Tellington and PCERF influence.

As they grew closer, Ursula visited Linda a second time at Westwind, this time accompanied by Dr. Ewald Isenbugel, a recent graduate from the University of Zurich Veterinary School, along with his fiancée, Menge. Linda continued, "Ewald later became the head veterinarian for the Zurich Zoo and has been a staunch friend to this day. It's fascinating to contemplate how my friendship with Ewald and Menge Isenbugel has impacted my work in zoos around the world, but that's another story.

"On Ursula's second visit to California I took her to horse shows in the San Francisco area and in Woodside, introducing her to the American way of keeping horses at home, which includes in stables, with separate paddocks for each horse. This was so very different from the German way of keeping horses in stalls with no turnout possibilities," Linda explained.

As a consequence of this second trip, Ursula went home and used the influence of her magazine to start a whole new movement of horse-keeping in Germany. She teamed up with Professor Potoff who worked for the German Department of Agriculture. Together they urged horse owners to build open-sided turnout barns for their Icelandic Horses as well as other breeds.

"Ursula's Reken Test Center became a model for a new way of keeping horses that has influenced tens of thousands of horse owners in Germany, Switzerland and Austria. It's interesting to note the parallel with our Pacific Coast Equestrian Research Farm, which had a significant influence on the emerging new class of back yard horse owners. It all started with our magazine articles and syndicated columns a decade earlier in the 1960s," Linda said.

"Ursula asked me to give a presentation at Equitana, the world's largest equine expo, located in Essen, Germany. I was to demonstrate the American style of riding based on the demonstrations she had seen with the Hungarian horses. I had the next four months to train four horses and three other riders for a bareback and bridleless jumping quadrille exhibition. It was a great success and generated articles in many of the European horse magazines. As a result, I was invited to teach all over Germany and Austria.

Shannon Yewell Weil

"After Equitana I put an advertisement in the *Freitzet im Sattel* magazine for the first clinic I ever gave in Germany. It was for anyone who had horses but were fearful, or adult riders who had fears due to injuries or accidents. The advertisement attracted a full clinic with twenty horses and twenty riders," she said, pleased with the turnout. Linda was informed that there was no need of a translator because every German speaks English. "But when I got there not one person spoke one word of English — that was the perfect challenge for me." Right away the opportunity to learn a new language was stimulating for her.

"To prepare for the clinic I wrote down the ten most important German words I needed to teach the class. It worked. Everyone had a wonderful weekend and people and horses made giant leaps forward," Linda happily reported.

"After that first workshop I just began using German words. It was only possible because I had four years of Latin and French in school and could conjugate words. Today I speak German as easily as I do English," Linda concluded.

Linda pondered for a moment and asked, "Have you ever looked back at your life and tracked the people and events that have laid the trail upon which you are tied? For me, Roger Russell was responsible for the next propitious turn of events," Linda declared. "After seeing the success at Equitana, Ursula asked me to be a part of a huge new government-sponsored center for German riding instructors where she was a consultant. I was invited to teach the American style of Balanced Seat riding. I agreed to teach a pilot program for one year and then turn it over to someone else." The center was expected to take form in about a year and that would give Linda some slack time to explore new directions.

"In the meantime Roger was looking for something he could contribute to the program and hit upon the idea of teaching the Feldenkrais Method to riders. We had both been impressed with a Feldenkrais Awareness Through Movement exercise we had experienced with Ilana Rubenfeld at the Esalen Institute two years earlier. Roger wrote to the Feldenkrais Institute in Tel Aviv and learned that Moshe Feldenkrais would be teaching a four-year Professional Training at the Humanistic Psychology Institute in San Francisco, beginning that summer.

"When we received the brochure describing the course, I read it through one time and had one of those rare epiphanies," Linda confirmed. "I knew instantly that I was meant to take the Feldenkrais training.

"I've been asked how I chose the paths I've followed. At that time I had several other offers for teaching and I had an unusual way of making decisions that brings a smile of recognition to my face as I say this," she said letting us in on her little secret. "I used to imagine I had invisible antenna (don't ask me where that comes from!) and if I had to make a choice, for instance, between offers to teach trainings or other issues, I would imagine I could feel those antennas reaching out in the direction of imaginary doors. The doors would be labeled with the offers I had. I would imagine pointing my antenna to the doors and see which door opened. That would determine my choice. It worked like a charm and my life has been as magical as that system of decision making." Linda, who is always ready to investigate new possibilities, went on to say, "But today I often use a simpler decision-making process with a form of Body Kinesiology that I teach in my classes. It also has scientific validation," Linda acknowledged, "but the 'fairy antenna' worked well in past years."

Feldenkrais Training

During the summer of 1975, Linda began a four-year program at the Humanistic Psychology Institute in San Francisco, California that became the turning point for her work. "On the second day of the training, sixty-three eager students were lying on the floor being guided through an 'Awareness Through Movement' exercise," Linda recalled. "During that exercise Dr. Feldenkrais made a statement that made my ears prick up and set me on a path that would change my work with horses and ultimately all animals. To paraphrase, he said, 'It's possible for a human to learn in one experience, without constant repetition, by moving the body in gentle non-habitual ways that activate unused neural pathways to the brain, thereby activating new brain cells increasing human potential for learning.

"I remember thinking, 'If non-habitual movements can enhance the learning capacity of a human, it must be true for a horse.' My immediate thought was, 'How could I move a horse in ways that would activate unused neural pathways to the brain, enhancing a horse's ability to 'learn how to learn' and actually getting the horse to enjoy the process of learning?' Over the ensuing weeks that summer, I worked with horses exploring gentle movements a horse could not do itself, searching for ways to enhance the animal's ability to learn without the widely-accepted use of force, dominance or repetitive exercises."

Over the next six years Linda and Roger traveled back and forth from California to Germany on a regular basis, continuing the development of her new work. This led to the incorporation of the Feldenkrais work with horses, coupled with Linda's vast equine knowledge and Roger's interest in how the brain functions. The results were outstanding.

An example is the development of the Tellington Labyrinth for horses in 1975 during the first summer of Linda's four-year Feldenkrais training. The labyrinth is formed by laying six poles, each 10 to 12 feet long, on the ground in a pattern unique to the Tellington TTouch® Method.

Roger and Linda laid out the first labyrinth to see how the horse's brain and attitude would respond while working the horse through the design. The results were encouraging; a new body of emerged called The Tellington-Jones Equine Awareness Method (TTEAM). In 1978, together with Ursula Bruns, Linda wrote her first book on the subject.

Roger Russell and Linda Tellington-Jones were constant companions and traveled around the world together in 1979. They are seen here on Japan's Bullet Train.

CHAPTER 20

GREAT AMERICAN HORSE RACE
AND PONY EXPRESS RIDE

After several years of being out of touch with Linda, we were about to be reunited again for another grand adventure. This time we would meet in New York for the start of the Great American Horse Race, an epic event from New York to California.

For the past seven years, I had been working with Thoroughbred horses and I was now eager to return to endurance riding. I joined the newly formed American Endurance Ride Conference (AERC) and the membership included a subscription to *Saddle Action* magazine. The January 1976 issue ran a classified advertisement that changed my life.

"WANTED: Crew Member for Bicentennial Horse Race rider. Will pay expenses and 10% of winnings." I responded immediately, describing that I was a PCERF graduate and adding my experience with endurance horses and years in the Thoroughbred industry — hoping to be selected for the job. Soon I received a reply from my old endurance riding friend Phil Gardner. I got the job.

At last the beautiful spring day in May 1976 arrived when all preparations were complete for the New York to California challenge, and we hoisted the camper on the old 1968 Chevy pickup truck. When all the supplies were secured, the two Lanigan Arabian chestnut geldings, Natomas and Haseful, hopped into the trailer for the week-long drive to New York.

Meanwhile Linda and Roger Russell were in Germany where they had been developing the groundwork for what would ultimately become the Tellington Training Equine Awareness Method (TTEAM). While they were visiting friends, Icelandic Horse breeders Claus and Ullu Becker of Saarbrucken, Germany, Linda received a telephone call from the United States telling her about an organized race on horseback across the country.

The Great American Horse Race was billed as "the longest race in history." The route would cross 13 states in 99 days and the entry fee was $500 per rider, with the carrot of a $50,000 purse to the winner.

Shannon Yewell Weil

Because of Linda's extensive background and success with long distance riding, she was tapped as the International Rider Coordinator. She agreed to join the team.

"I told my German friends about the Great American Horse Race and Claus and Ullu were intrigued about riding 3,500 miles across the United States," Linda remembered. "As it turned out not only were the Beckers interested, but four other Europeans wanted to go too. So late in November we outlined what would be necessary for the group of six to ride in the race: four months of free time, a few extra bucks and some damned good horses."

"Oh, no problem with the horses," the Beckers said, "we'll take our Icelandic Horses." Roger added, "We knew they had good horses, but where would they find a fat bank roll?" A budget of $50,000 for six riders and 15 horses was estimated for the adventure.

"The Beckers were among the first people in Europe to import the breed from Iceland," Linda added. "They knew that the Icelandic farmers' co-op, Samband, which had a monopoly on the exportation of horses from Iceland, had been looking for an opportunity to publicize the Icelandic Horses in America. The Beckers thought that the race would be a great opportunity." Linda went on to say, "When we approached Samband, they thought so too and agreed to sponsor the team, with a $50,000 pledge, that included four Germans, one Swiss and one Austrian."

Details of their plans were falling into place like a large puzzle. "These tough little horses have been bred in Iceland for the past thousand years to carry Icelandic men across some of the most rugged and God-forsaken terrain on the face of the planet. Icelandics have a very comfortable four-beat gait called a tolt. Claus and Ullu Becker were certain their horses would take the trip in their stride," said Roger.

The riders met at the Beckers' farm and at 2:00 a.m. they made the mutual decision to commit to the race although they had only a verbal agreement for financial support from the Icelandic government.

"At 6:00 a.m. the following morning the phone rang," Linda comments. "After only four hours of shut-eye I answered sleepily. It was the Beckers' neighbor and good friend, Kurt Hilsensaur, who was also an Icelandic horse breeder. He was calling to ask me if I was planning to attend the International Press Conference for the Great American Horse Race that was scheduled for 2:00 p.m. that very same day in New York City. I thought that if we could get good press coverage the Icelandic government would be more likely to honor their $50,000 commitment.

"Kurt's early morning wake-up call cinched the decision. New York was beckoning. I dressed quickly, threw a few show clothes into a suitcase and just managed to make the 8:30 a.m. plane out of Luxembourg to New York. Thanks to the six-hour time difference I landed in New York early enough to get my hair done, and slipped into the press conference in time to take the microphone and tell the story of the 'Viking Horses,' as they were referred to.

"This race had attracted the attention of some of the big-gun newspapers and the only story they carried about the Great American Horse Race was about the Icelandic Horses. Splashed across a third of the front page of the Living Section of the *New York Times* was a map of the United States with a photo of me riding an Icelandic Horse and leading another horse in traditional Icelandic style." The Times also ran a comprehensive article praising Linda's in pulling this complicated plan together about bringing the Icelandic horses and this historic trip across America for the country's bicentennial celebration.

But the really tricky complications were yet to come. While in New York, Linda was instructed to contact a Canadian cattle dealer who had assured Claus Becker that they could ship the horses to North America at half the normal rate because he was sending a load of cattle to Germany.

Linda continues, "It was February when I called the shipper he said there was confusion about the dates and he had no plans to ship before next year! The horses were all gathered at Ullu and Claus's farm waiting to fly to California to start their long-distance riding. I called Pan American Airlines to inquire about the standard cost of shipping and it was double the amount we had budgeted. Airline rules required that each horse ship in its own crate, and the crates weighed almost as much as the horses. I argued that this is a special breed of herd animal and that they would be more comfortable on a palate built to hold four horses. I was told that only the head veterinarian for the Department of Agriculture could make that call. It just so happened that I had met the head veterinarian at a conference some years before. The horse angels were on our side because I managed to get him on the phone. He listened to my reason for shipping them four to a pallet, said he trusted my judgment, and gave his permission. A miracle!

"I called Claus with great excitement to announce the success of the shipping dilemma and then he dropped the bomb!" After Iceland's Samband agreed to the deal, at the last minute the government sponsorship was denied. The entire country of Iceland was engulfed in a general strike and everything was at a standstill. It was very tense at this point and it was uncertain whether or not this large-scale plan to ride across the United States for the $50,000 prize would succeed or fail.

Linda flipped! "When this happened I called the director of Samband in Iceland, whom I knew, and declared that because the *New York Times* had run a feature on the horses they had to come up with the money or Iceland would be disgraced," Linda stated vehemently. "I told him I was flying through Reykjavik in three days on my way to pick up the horses, and he had to meet me with the check at the airport."

It worked. Linda picked up a check for $50,000 in Iceland, flew to Germany, loaded up the horses and she and Roger headed west. But there were more bumpy spots on the road ahead. When their plane landed in New York they were told the health certificates were not acceptable in German. Linda was told the horses would have to stay in quarantine on the plane under Roger's supervision while she caught the next plane back to Germany, picked up the correct papers, and return to clear the horses through customs. After much persuasion, however, Linda was allowed to translate the papers and the horses were cleared.

Linda carried on, "Based on the barriers we had to overcome getting the horses to California to start their distance training, we might have suspected that trouble was brewing regarding the race officials, the route across the U.S. and the mysterious disappearance of the $50,000 prize money."

The horses finally arrived in San Francisco. They were then delivered to the California training center that belonged to a friend of Linda's in a small Gold Rush-era town called Murphys in the central Sierra Nevada foothills. Thankfully, Linda's sister Robyn Hood and her husband Phil Pretty were there to meet the horses and assist with the training, aided by Robyn and Linda's mother Marion Hood who also helped with the conditioning.

"It was wild," Robyn remembers. "These Icelandic horses were brought in from Germany with long winter coats and we were expected to train them in ninety degree heat." But in typical Hood family fashion, they made the impossible possible.

Within a month the horses were going 20 miles a day, four days a week with an easy ride on the fifth day and then two days off. "We started slowly, often climbing hills to condition the muscles and tendons and gradually working up to longer, faster rides, making certain that the horses never tired," said Linda, drawing on her extensive endurance riding background. "We used a special endurance saddle that we brought from Germany, called the Hestar. The horses never had sore backs," Linda added.

Off to New York!

It was the end of May, 1976. Linda had already enlisted the services of friend Woody Riggs to haul the horses from California to New York in his huge green horse trailer that easily held all 12 Icelandic horses. He would then serve as a crew member for the Europeans for the summer. The riders, all of whom were riding Icelandic horses, were Germans Claus Becker, Ullu Becker, Lothar Weiland and Walter Feldman; Max Indermaur of Switzerland; and Count Johannes Hoyos of Austria.

The Great American Horse Race camp with Linda's gray van in the background.

Woody Riggs' huge green stock trailer with canvas sides served as a second transport for the Icelandic horses.

An operating budget of $300,000 was approved by the Great American Horse Race to pay for salaries of staff and veterinarians. Head Veterinarian Hank Cook from California was accompanied by veterinarians Homer Webb, DVM from California; Bruce Branscomb, DVM of Nevada; and Dave Nicholson, DVM from Wyoming. Kate Riordan had come in from California to serve as the Head Veterinarian Secretary and a group of veterinary students including Rick Stewart from the University of California at Davis, came along for the adventure. Kate's vet secretaries included Lori Stewart, Lona Webb and Patti Jameson, and there were eight trail markers, timekeepers and logistic personnel.

Each contestant had two horses or mules: one to be ridden and the other one ponied (led) throughout the daily races. The format of each day was set up like an endurance ride with vet checks and certain criteria for the safety of the horse.

By now Linda had developed a stylish look of her own.

At 4:00 a.m. on May 25, 1976 Phil and I pulled into the Herkimer County Fairgrounds in Herkimer, New York. As I surveyed the group that first morning, across the campground I spied Linda, who was coordinating the international riders for the race. She had blossomed since I had last seen her and had abandoned the conservative tweeds she once wore while married to Wentworth. Now she was wearing bell-bottomed blue jeans and wide-brimmed straw hats. We laughed about being together at this remarkably weird and zany 3,500-mile horse race.

Sitting on top of our horse trailer, I could see the entire camp.

Natomas and Haseful, Phil Gardner's two Lanigan Arabian chestnut geldings.

Shannon Yewell Weil

Ride Secretary Lori Stewart (L) records vital statistics gathered by her vet student husband, Rick, in the striped shirt.

The 101 race competitors had stories to tell that were endless, priceless and ridiculous. The riders ranged from a Florida alligator wrangler, a recently-released convicted murderer, a pediatric cardiologist, a sheriff, an Austrian Count, to colorful endurance character Smokey Killen. The horses ranged from Arabians, a Russian Orloff, Icelandics, Appaloosas (one rescued from a slaughter pen), Connemara ponies, Mules, Morgans, Pintos, Mustangs, Quarter Horses, Thoroughbreds, Standardbreds and Paso Finos.

The stories were almost unbelievable. Who would ever think that it was a good idea to have your husband drop you off at the starting line of a 3,500-mile race along with your stallion (and only horse), a cooler, tack trunk, rain slicker, sleeping bag and a Muscovy duckling named Mary Lou? Note: No truck or trailer. With all good intentions of being swept into the fold of the traveling community and the kindness of strangers, one lady did just that.

At the end of the first week, when all the vetting and paperwork was finally completed, every contestant was introduced at a "launching" event staged at the local rodeo arena. A sizable crowd consisted of local curiosity seekers, families (including my sister Susan), and friends who were gathered to see what all the hoopla was about. Dressed in whatever passed as their finest attire, the contestants rode one horse and ponied the other as they were presented; various forms of bucking, bolting, balking and rearing entertained the crowd.

Claus Becker carried the Icelandic flag.

The Icelandic Horses presented the most impressive show with their riders turned out handsomely in tall black boots and blue blazers. Their well-executed drills demonstrated the abilities of these horses, including jumping over picnic tables with people seated at them. The crowd went nuts, leaped up in their seats and cheered until they were hoarse. It was indeed a moment in time — it was the opening ceremony of the 1976 Great American Horse Race.

The unfolding of this event became more and more bizarre each day, with clashing personalities, broken promises, and the unveiling of the truth — that there was no purse money and that the race was broke before it even began. Snippets from Linda's diary explain how the race progressed from that first day forward...

May 31, Monday – New York To California or Bust! The beginning of the Great American Horse Race! Nice cool weather, 5,000 people there to see us off – CBS TV and newspaper included! Rode 31 miles – mostly on pavement.

June 1, Tuesday – Influenza epidemic broke out among the horses.

June 3, Thursday – IT WAS ALL OVER – We were told the GAHR was BANKRUPT; we were to go home. HOME! A few riders had sold their possessions; quit their jobs – anything to join in "the chance of a lifetime." Crisis meeting called – it was decided we'd continue across the U.S. – come what may. (Ride manager and founder) Randy Scheiding left the race.

June 7, Monday – On the go again – for how long is anybody's guess. Trailered 165 miles, rode only 7 miles.

June 11, 12, & 13 – Trailering, trailering and more trailering. Not enough trailers, plastic and rubber shoes on some horses were slipping – problems, problems – and more problems.

July 1 & 2 – Illinois. Expected grand reception in Springfield a flop (not enough advance publicity – darn!)

July 9, Friday – TIME TO TAKE A STAND – riders' meeting: THE RIDE IS OFF – it's now called the "Great American Trailer Race" (we had trailered our horses 990 miles and ridden 600). YET, only a few have dropped out.

Virl Norton riding his two handsome mules Lord Fauntleroy and Lady Eloise was the ultimate winner of the GAHR.

July 10, Saturday – Kansas City, Missouri. Remaining riders trying to reorganize. Virl Norton and his magical mules are in first place!

July 14, Wednesday – 15 riders traveled to St. Joseph, Missouri to join the Pony Express Race.

Mary Lou Arrives in Camp

Mary Lou, a juvenile Muscovy duck moved into our camp.

While we were with the Great American Horse Race in June, we camped in a huge but crowded orchard. I arrived late as usual after serving as the horse taxi for the group and the only place left to park meant I had to take the quintessential test for backing a horse trailer. It required backing up a long, narrow, muddy and slippery lane between two rows of apple trees. After successfully maneuvering the rig, I found a suitable spot next to the folks who were kindly lugging gear that belonged to the duck lady.

As I was setting up camp, I noticed the juvenile black-and-white feathered duck, Miss Mary Lou, making her way through the thick grass and heading at a substantial waddle straight towards me. I swear I heard her say, "Hey! Can I move in with you?" and on second glance she had a suitcase under each of her little wings. She became my constant companion and would make little chirping and whirring sounds as she chattered away. Mary Lou was an absolute nut and soon everyone adored her. Including Phil.

Linda kept close to the management pulse as she had a lot at stake for the success of the European riders and the Icelandic Horses. Overall, the GAHR was a magnificent dream that was lacking a solid infrastructure, not to mention money.

With the amount of commitment, preparation and expense each person heaved into being there, no one wanted the GAHR to fall apart. But the frustration was building as day after day the horses were trailered instead of ridden just to stay on schedule; the outcome was not looking very optimistic. The S.O.S. flag was flying high.

This is how Hal Hall hauled his two Hyannis Arabians, El Karbaj and Koszar. They both willingly jumped up into the back of his pickup truck and saw America from their crow's nest.

The Pony Express Trail Comes to Life

As the GAHR struggled down the road it landed in Kansas City, Missouri where it lingered for several days. Dissatisfaction and frustration ruled as we faced yet another managerial meltdown, which once again stalled progress. Despite Linda's efforts to keep the international riders happy, there was no hope left in the GAHR. She needed a solution for the disenchanted Germans who had come for a riding adventure, not a soap opera.

By this point Linda was fed up. She decided to take matters into her own hands, which led to a discussion with veterinarian Dave Nicholson. "Can't we find an alternate way to get to California and end this aggravation?" Linda insisted. So Linda and Nicholson hatched an enchanting plan to find and ride the original Pony Express Trail to California.

Dave had long been enchanted with the history of the Pony Express Trail, which started in St. Joseph, Missouri. In its day St. Joseph was the far western edge of civilization and was known as the jumping off point for not only the Pony Express Trail but also the Oregon Trail. And as fate would have it, the Pony Express Trail terminated in Sacramento, California. As fate would also have it, St. Joseph was just an hour's drive north of Kansas City.

Linda and Dave invited several people from the GAHR to spin off and join the German riders on a new adventure. Kate Riordan, who had also seen enough of human weirdness and damaged horses, abandoned her post as the GAHR's Head Vet Secretary and joined them. Linda kept pressuring me to join them, and I wanted to go, but Phil, who never quit anything he started, was very reluctant.

Count Johannes Hoyos of Austria and Walter Feldman from Germany were the only members of Linda's international group to stay with the GAHR, so Linda split up the support crew to accommodate both factions. Woody Riggs and his huge green stock trailer stayed with Walter and Johannes. Robyn and her husband Phil, who went with the Pony Express group, picked up an old post office truck with right-hand steering (and no door) that they turned into a mini motor home and puttered it all the way across the country.

At first it was a tough sell for Phil Gardner to leave the GAHR and join the Pony Express group. After some deliberation, I said, "Let's just drive up to St. Joseph and check it out." When we arrived it was a breath of fresh air and we liked what we saw. I persuaded Phil to make the switch and Linda was delighted about this decision. So I left Phil behind at the Holiday Inn to stay with Dave and Kate while Mary Lou and I hurried back to Kansas City. I quickly broke down our camp, at which I had become very adept. Mary Lou and I made a hasty circuit of the camp to bid farewell to several people. I loaded Natomas and Haseful in the trailer and we barreled straight north to officially join the 1976 Pony Express Ride.

The newly emerging Pony Express Ride was formed from 22 people who included Linda Tellington-Jones; David P. Nicholson, who served as our leader and veterinarian; Kate Riordan, who adroitly administrated the record-keeping system and helped with the horses; several pre-vet students from Cornell University; Hal Hall; Rick and Lori Stewart (who had served as vet student and as vet secretary on the GAHR); Patti Jameson, who now transitioned from vet secretary to rider; Bill Kean and his crew, Etta Marie Beecher and her two children; Camille Druge and her crew Joy Hutchison; Dave Frank and his crew Rod; Max Indermaur; Lothar Weiland; Claus and Ullu Becker; Linda's sister Robyn Hood and her husband Phil Pretty; Louise Geffert and her young son

Shannon Yewell Weil

Billy crewed for Lothar; trail chief Chris Closs; and Phil Gardner and me. Plus Dave Frank's Queensland Blue Heeler dog named Henry, who fell in love with Kate that summer.

Lori Stewart had developed a hankering to ride. So Dave gave his Nebraska friends Gloria and Gene Fells a call to see if they had any available horses. They did indeed. Rick and Lori borrowed a rig, disappeared instantly and returned within a few days. A grey Arabian named Retro Rocket and a tall chestnut Thoroughbred named Red stepped out of the trailer. Pulled right out of the pasture, they were both fat as could be. Phil Gardner put some shoes on her new horses and just like that, Lori was all set.

Patti Jameson also wanted to jettison her job as vet secretary so she could ride. Somehow she managed to put together two Rushcreek mares (Rushcreek Audrey and Rushcreek Belle) and saddles and tack. She disappeared one day before the ride started and came back to camp with a truck and trailer (and a cowboy; we never asked). Patti always got the job done.

The undoing of the 1860 Pony Express, which was an epic business endeavor for its time, came only 18 months after it began. While the riders were galloping across the country they actually watched the installation of the telegraph poles (some of which were still standing in 1976) and telegraph lines that ultimately eliminated the need for the Pony Express altogether.

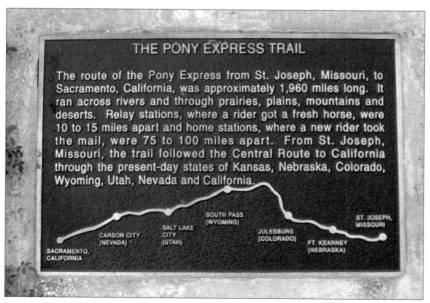

The Pony Express Trail marker

270

From Veterinarian Dave Nicholson's Website

In 1976, during the bicentennial year of the United States, a small group of endurance riders from the United States and Europe set out from St. Joseph, Missouri in an attempt to ride to Sacramento, California on the original Pony Express Trail. At that time there were no maps of the original route. The only contemporary description of the trail was the itinerary of Sir Richard Burton's 1861 book, "On the Road to the City of the Saints." Burton had kept a fairly accurate record of the trail and the stations along the way. With a copy of the book and less than a weeks planning, 14 riders and their support crews, with two horses apiece, were able to follow the trail descriptions written 116 years earlier. Within a few days the riders, crews and management were caught up in an experience that none of them have ever gotten over. The farther west they came, the easier it was to follow the itinerary and by the time that they reached Wyoming it was virtually impossible to get off the trail, as it became more and more distinct. The western half of the trail remains today, for the most part, just as it was when the last travelers used it over 100 years ago.

In the drizzling morning Patti Jamison holds Mary Lou while her horse can't decide if the sidewalk or the street is more comfortable. Phil Gardner is jawing with a spectator while holding his newly Easy Booted horse, Natomas.

Dr. David P. Nicholson is riding an Icelandic with a mochila thrown over his saddle, ready to lead the group of 1976 XP riders.

The riders received a cheering farewell by local well-wishers.

Excerpts from My Journal

Monday, July 17, 1976 began as a cold and drizzling morning fit for a black-and-white duck. At 10:00 a.m. we assembled in front of the historic Pony Express Patee House. The City Mayor conducted the starting ceremonies for our new adventure. Other city dignitaries and Pony Express buffs stood by to view the spectacle. The riders were swallowed up in their wet-weather gear and the horses were already soaked. As we stood under umbrellas and breathed the smell of wet pavement, Mary Lou, who was flush with her adult feathers by now, played in the puddles in the street as only a duck could enjoy.

Dave Nicholson rode an Icelandic horse for the start of the 1976 Pony Express Ride, with a calliope playing in the background.

Our humble group was braced with only maps, books, photographs and the lure of the legendary Pony Express Trail beckoning us forward. So under the leadership of Dr. David P. Nicholson, we charged full steam ahead into the wild blue yonder.

The 1,960 miles of trail started at St. Joseph, Missouri and crossed parts of Kansas, the length of Nebraska, kissed the corner of Colorado, went up into Wyoming turning south at the Green River, across Utah and Nevada, then halfway across California to Sacramento.

Shannon (right) is reminiscing about the wonderful days at PCERF while gazing at the well-traveled X-2 Trail-Van. It was now serving as a workhorse in its own right on the Pony Express Trail.

Never without a stethoscope, Kate Riordan was always on the ready to check horses.

A new routine quickly found its own rhythm and we formed a collective personality that became the 1976 Pony Express Race. All horses thrived in the camp life. The daily exercise and constant attention proved to be a perfect blend for horses and humans alike.

Everyone had a job —horses, riders, crews, veterinarian, and vet students. We forged remarkable friendships that have lasted for decades and the group became a finely oiled machine.

The Germans were having a marvelous time. They loved the new regime and every evening their camp was full of music and singing. The Icelandic Horses were doing very well; to see those thick forelocks, manes and tails tolting across the desert was quite a sight.

By now Linda Tellington-Jones was well into her split week routine of returning to San Francisco to participate in her second summer of a four-year program studying with Dr. Moshe Feldenkrais.

Linda's schedule was commendable that summer. On Thursday afternoons she would leave San Francisco and fly to the airport nearest to our location on the trail, rent a car and find us wherever we were camped. She'd spend a long weekend and then on Sunday afternoon return to San Francisco where she would be fully present in her Feldenkrais class on Monday morning. She would repeat the routine again on the next Thursday.

"Do you remember the time I showed up in camp in that red convertible?" Linda laughed. "That was so much fun!" "Yes, I do," I said, "I remember the surreal sight of you driving into camp with the top down as the dust boiled up from the back of that crimson car." She looked like a movie star driving into camp.

Ullu Becker is enjoying watermelon on the long, dusty Pony Express Trail.

"I remember bringing watermelon out to the riders," Linda laughed, "and back then of course the trail was in the middle of nowhere and fresh food was almost impossible to find. One day I remember going with Nicholson in his green pickup truck to scout the trail. We were following a riverbed, not knowing if we could get out the other end or not." Linda started getting wound up at the memory and continued, "We didn't know where we were so we left the riverbed and stopped at a ranch to ask if we could get through at the end. They invited us in and made us sandwiches with tomatoes out of their garden. It was the best I've ever tasted. Beefsteak tomatoes; I can still taste them."

Lessons in Utah

By now we were in Utah, and a delighted Linda loved being with us on the trail and in camp. She squeezed in as much as possible on each visit. Her summer course in San Francisco with Moshe Feldenkrais was going very well; she was having two grand experiences over one summer.

After our trail master Chris Closs left to return to school in Vermont, trail marking became an arduous job, and everyone chipped in to fill his duties. Even Linda.

"Oh my God! What an experience," Linda got excited gearing up to tell this story. "It was before Salt Lake City. Roger had joined me for a couple of days, so Nicholson sent me off with Roger on two Icelandic horses to mark the trail," Linda recounted. "We were following posts in lake country, and our horses were almost up to their knees in water for more than a mile," Linda explained. "It was a full moon night and the plan was for us to ride across the lake, find the XP trail in the moonlight, and head to the top of the mountain. When we got to the top of the mountain we were to set off flares signaling to Nicholson that we had found the trail. Then he would set off his flares and we would supposedly ride down the mountain and connect the trail," Linda accounted. A perfect plan, so they thought.

"But the problem was the cloud cover. The cloak of night descended just as we reached the shore of the lake and we could not find the trail that was to take us to the top of the mountain so we could connect by flares with Nicholson. I'm sitting there thinking, what are we going to do in this complete darkness?" At this point Linda and Roger were quite concerned about executing their mission. There they were, riding in unknown territory in near total darkness, not knowing where to go. "We had to figure something out because Nicholson was waiting on the other side," Linda continued. "Plus the trail had to be flagged for the next day's ride." Linda was beginning to get worried. "Just as I'm pondering our problem, an owl flies overhead. There was just enough light that we could see the silhouette of his wings and body. It flew past us and flew back and forth, barely ten feet above our heads, displaying a most unusual behavior.

"Suddenly I got this really strong communication to 'just follow the owl.' And that's exactly what we did. The bird kept flying back and forth, leading us up the mountain in the darkness. We were so thankful. When we got to the top we lit our flares and a few minutes later Nicholson lit his flares; he was right below us just a few miles down from where we were. It was clear to me that the owl showed the way. This was indicative of what happened during that summer. I call such a miracle a PIC – Profound Interspecies Connection," said Linda.

Camp Life

While Hal Hall was napping in his bachelor's camp his horses were content to be tied to the stock rack.

Mary Lou waited all day for Phil to arrive in camp so that he would tickle her tummy.

Hase and Natomas were comfortable anywhere. It was a wonderful feeling living within feet of our horses for four months straight.

Similar to Bedouins living in the Middle East, our horses were a part of our families and social structure. Over four months time we lived right next to our horses every day and slept a mere eight feet away at night. It was blissful to trust the horses enough to let them loose and know that they wouldn't wander away. They preferred to hang their heads over our shoulders while we sat with friends under the shade of a tree.

Hollenberg Station. Every day brought a new adventure and we checked out many old Pony Express Stations that were still standing.

Each day started before daylight so we could beat the afternoon heat. We routinely fumbled in the dark to feed the horses, saddle up and rally some breakfast. At that subtle moment when the pristine sunlight separates the night from day known as "the crack of dawn," the horses and riders assembled near Dave's rig as Kate checked the horses in anticipation of another day's ride. The crews would then break down camp and depart in search of the next campsite. In the open range of Utah and Nevada the shield of darkness provided privacy for a short walk into the sagebrush when nature called.

The monotony of foraging for food left us all many pounds lighter; even the horses lost about 100 pounds each. Still no one had time to cook decent meals even if we had good food. Living in the dirt and thick dust meant numerous trips to the laundromat to wash our filthy clothes — an utter luxury. Most of the time we all smelled pretty bad but we were simply living our own truths. Almost three months had passed since we left California.

From being taken care of by royalty to roughing it on the Pony Express Trail,
Linda enjoyed it all.

Both Went Tellington and Roger Russell paid a visit to our camp at Stateline Stables at Lake Tahoe in California. Linda was in the company of two significant men in her life! "It was a propitious event to have Went and Roger there together," Linda grinned. "I remained friends with Wentworth throughout his life and it was fun for me to share this experience with him and have him meet Roger."

Phil Gardner rides Natomas through the unforgiving Nevada desert.

There were only three days left of our XP excursion after departing Strawberry, California on Highway 50 in the Sierra Nevada mountains. The inevitable end of this journey was on the horizon. Stress, strain, pull, tug, sigh!

Reentering civilization was awkward, as if we were coming out of a time warp and the home stretch was nearing. Through Placerville and down Green Valley Road towards Sacramento we traveled, knowing the end of our story was in sight. We didn't want to see the final chapter unfold.

Our weary, yet elated, collection of people arrived in Sacramento, signaling the final days of our magical summer adventure. We staged in Discovery Park before riding to Old Town Sacramento and the trail's terminus. The riders mounted their horses and for the last time, Lori, Lothar, Camille, Phil, Hal, Dave, Claus, Bill, Ullu, Max, and Patti rode together, along with a guest Hal Hall had invited to join them, Judge Sherrill Halbert, a 75-year-old U.S. District Judge who had a penchant for the Pony Express. We put him on a tame and short Icelandic Horse.

The final three miles into Old Town Sacramento happened on September 14th, 1976. The group stopped in front of the old Hastings Building, which was the western terminus of the 1860 Pony Express route and the finish line for our riders. The media swarmed with enthusiasm.

We had been traveling across America for four months. As the journey was ending the riders headed towards Old Town Sacramento from Discovery Park. Lori Stewart on Retro Rocket (white hat and horse) was the overall winner.

The Pony Express statue in Old Town Sacramento, California marked the end of the trail and finish line for the 1976 XP Ride.

We followed these plaques for 1,960 miles all the way from St. Joseph, Missouri to the last one in Sacramento.

In Old Town Sacramento there is a life-sized bronze statue created by Tom Holland of the Pony Express Rider that stands next to the signature plaque of Pony Express entrepreneurs Russell, Majors and Waddell — many of those plaques helped us "connect the dots" all the way from St. Joseph, Missouri. Under the towering statue I sat down on the curb and cried, releasing both joy and sadness that our trip was over. It was a memorable day for us all.

Lori Stewart was the ultimate winner of the 1976 Pony Express Ride in her first ever attempt at an endurance ride. She has since gone on to capture two wins of the Tevis Cup — on Don Van Witt in 1980 and again on Risque Rocket in 1986. As of 2012, she has 18 Tevis buckles. She remained good friends with Gene and Gloria Fells, who furnished her XP horses Retro Rocket and Red.

End of the trail . . .

Slowly everyone packed up their gear and we said our final farewells as people headed home. Linda remembered how they dispersed everything. "My sister took some of the Icelandic horses home to Canada where over the years her herd grew to over 100 horses." Robyn Hood went on to become the biggest breeder of Icelandic Horses in North America.

We put 9,979 miles on the truck over the summer.

Shannon Yewell Weil

Dave Nicholson and Kate Riordan put on another Pony Express Ride in 1979 that was sponsored by the British Post Office. Dave eventually made staging 50-mile endurance rides over the Pony Express Trail a full-time business.

It was just a week after we got home when Phil and I walked down to the barn to have a chat with the two Pony Express horses. Haseful and Natomas stood before us and Phil said, "Which one of you wants to go do the Virginia City 100-Mile Ride in Nevada?" There was a moment's pause and then Natomas stepped forward. He and Phil finished and Phil received his 10th buckle at Virginia City that year. Phil later went on to be the first rider to earn the 20-day 2,000-mile buckle at the Virginia City 100.

Both Phil Gardner and Hal Hall were inducted into the American Endurance Ride Conference (AERC) Hall of Fame in 1999.

Eight years later Linda shifted gears slightly and her work morphed into the Tellington TTouch® Training Method, with focus on cellular function, and influencing behavior that is used worldwide today.

EPILOGUE

After the Pony Express Ride Phil and I shared a brief marriage and I lived in Auburn for the next six years. Phil and I trained for and rode the Tevis Cup Ride; it was 1977 and there were 14 runners sharing the trail with the riders. As the day unfolded it gave me a bird's eye view of how this seedling of an event for runners had all the makings of a grand event of its own. Halfway to Auburn on the Tevis Cup Ride, I thought to myself, "This (the Run) is going to be a hit and I'm going to make sure it is." Phil, myself and two other friends, Mo Livermore and Curt Sproul, became the co-founding four that created the infrastructure for the Western States Endurance Run as an event. The genesis of what is now a world-renowned competition was based on Gordy Ainsleigh's solo inaugural running of the 100 miles on August 3rd, 1974 when he covered the course on foot amongst the Tevis horses.

I remained involved with the Run until 2010 when I retired from its Board of Trustees after 32 years. I am grateful to Linda and Went Tellington for introducing me to all things surrounding the Tevis Cup Ride, the Western States Trail, Wendell Robie and Phil Gardner for making my involvement with the Western States Endurance Run possible.

I didn't see Linda for many years as she began spending more time in Europe building her Tellington Method. In 1978 I met Jim Weil, a runner who came to challenge the Western States 100 miles on foot, and in 1981 we married and moved to the South Pacific.

While there I discovered a jungle-born female puppy that had been paralyzed in an accident — she faced certain death had I not intervened. Named 'Amber' for her color, her little body was useless and she cried in fear if left alone. I adopted her for two reasons. First, because of her young age, I knew her body was in full-tilt growth mode and secondly, based on what I had picked up from Linda about the Feldenkrais work and non-habitual movement, I thought I could give the puppy a chance at recovering. (This was two years before Linda developed TTouch.) I commenced this healing journey by constantly massaging and stimulating her limbs, organs and daily functions. Jim pitched in with her too, and after about a month we began to see improvement. The feeling returned to her hind end first and she gradually learned to push her lifeless front end around like a wheelbarrow. She was in my hands nearly all day every day and after months of work, little Amber was able to walk and even run, albeit clumsily, but she adapted to her own style of mobility. She ultimately learned to run, climb

285

stairs and play with other dogs but always had a distinct gait of her own. It worked, she recovered, and I credit her success directly to what I learned from Linda and Went Tellington.

After leaving the island life Jim and I returned to Marin County, California where I spent over a decade in the corporate world. That's when in the 1980s I saw Linda's television infomercials. She looked fabulous, dressed in beautiful Southwestern colors demonstrating TTouch on her dog Jesse. I realized how much I missed her as great memories flooded my mind. To find out what she was up to I purchased her book, "The Tellington TTouch: A Revolutionary Natural Method to Train and Care for Your Favorite Animal" that she wrote with Sybil Taylor. The next day I called in sick at my job and spent the day reading the book. It struck a chord in my heart and I couldn't wait to hear Linda's voice again, so I called her Santa Fe, New Mexico office. It was 1995.

In 1997 Linda held a meeting of the Veterinary Advisory Board for Animal Ambassadors in Santa Fe, New Mexico. (front row: l to r) Shannon Weil, Mrs. Rusty Fletcher, David "Doc" Fletcher, DVM, Jessica Bradley, Allen Schoen, DVM (middle row: l to r) Betsy Adamson, DVM, Kate Riordan, Kerry Ridgway, DVM, Christine Ridgway, Joyce Harmon, DVM, Linda Tellington-Jones, Christine Jurzykowski, Robyn Hood, –, Carol Lang, Susan Harding (back row: l to r) Tom Mitchell, Audrey Johnson, Tom Beckett, DVM

She invited me to join her Advanced Tellington Method Training in San Miguel de Allende, Mexico. Out of respect to her students and practitioners in the training, I brought myself up to speed by taking a crash course in Feldenkrais Awareness Through Movement classes. Then I headed south of the border for a wonderful reunion with Linda and the assembly of TTouch and TTEAM practitioners. The following spring I moved to Santa Fe and became her Executive Director. Linda deemed me the PCERF historian, which prompted this book.

How the Tellington TTouch was Born

Linda explained to me how the Tellington TTouch began by saying, "It was birthed on a warm July day in 1983 while I was teaching a workshop at the Delaware Equine Veterinary Center in Cochranville, Pennsylvania. I had been asked by one of the vets to check out his mare who was extremely resistant to grooming and saddling, often threatening to bite or kick. This was thirty-years ago before it was common to check backs and necks for inflammation. When I placed my hands lightly on the mare's shoulder, and began the gentle movements of Feldenkrais Functional Integration, the mare became very quiet and accepting of my contact. The owner of the horse was amazed at how this normally cantankerous horse seemed to enjoy the movements. Within minutes the mare's eyes softened, her head lowered, she took a deep breath and relaxed. Her owner asked me in a surprised voice, 'What are you doing to effect my mare in this way? What is your secret?'

"Without thinking I responded with the prophetic words, 'Don't worry what I'm doing. Just place your hand lightly on the shoulder and move the skin in a circle,'" Linda said.

"Moving the skin in a circle was not a part of the Feldenkrais Method, but I learned many years before to trust my intuition. Much to my surprise the mare became as quiet and accepting of the light circles as she had been for the Feldenkrais movements.

"That was an 'aha' moment that changed my life and shifted my direction. It takes years to learn the brilliant Feldenkrais Method but anyone could move the skin in a circle. I began experimenting with a variety of circular movements that morphed into the Tellington TTouch Training, the technique that has spread around the world. It is used for horses, companion and exotic animals, as well as for human healthcare. TTouch enhances behavior, performance, well-being and relationship between animals and their people," she concluded.

One day while sitting in Linda's living room I spied a letter on the table from the venerated Japan Racing Association. Because of my background in the Thoroughbred horse racing industry I was well aware of its importance. The letter was an invitation for Linda to go to Japan and teach TTouch. I said to her, "You *are* going to accept this invitation to Japan, *aren't you*?" Linda was non-committal at first and said her schedule was just too busy to fit in the trip. I replied, 'No! You must go now, Linda. This is too great an honor to miss the opportunity to teach your work in Japan — especially when invited by the JRA. It's immensely important that you go!" I said flatly, insisting that she agree with me and I ended with, "Just let me handle this!"

The next day I sent a proposal to the JRA in response to the letter. After some negotiations the JRA accepted our terms, which included having an assistant travel with Linda. We chose Kate Riordan to accompany her because of Kate's knowledge of Linda's work, and Kate's self-proclaimed role as the "world's largest Sherpa," a worthy title as she had wrangled Linda's luggage and boxes of equipment around the globe in their travels together. The Japanese people enthusiastically received the pair and their visit was a huge success.

In 1997, Linda and Kate Riordan were invited to Japan to teach the TTouch and the Tellington Method to members of the Japan Racing Association.

Sometime later Linda vacationed in Hawaii where she participated in a seminar with her friend Joan Ocean, who provides opportunities for people to swim with Spinner Dolphins and whales. About that time, coincidentally, Linda's brother, John Hood, had unearthed the whereabouts of her long-time friend and Chadwick student Roland Kleger. Lo and behold, Roland was living in Hawaii not far from where Linda would be, so she gave him a call while she was there.

Roland flashed his handsome smile and his eyes lit up as he reflected on the fortuitous occasion, "Forty years after Linda taught me to ride at Chadwick fate brought us together again. For the first time since we had known each other, neither of us was married and the smoldering but unacknowledged attraction we both had but never acknowledged over all the years, burst into flames." Shortly thereafter, Linda moved to Hawaii. "Two years later we married. What a treasure to now have fifty years of history to share," Roland beamed.

Longing to be closer to the Sierra Nevada foothills again, in 1999 Jim and I moved from Marin County to Placer County where we bought a ranch literally on the Western States Trail just outside of the tiny and remote Gold Rush town of Michigan Bluff. In 2000 Linda and Roland Kleger married in Santa Fe, New Mexico on the same day as the Tevis Cup Ride. Torn between attending her wedding (a three-day incredible celebration) or keeping my promise to work on the Tevis, I chose to stay in Michigan Buff. However, my sister Susan, then a Santa Fe resident, represented me and joined the 90 guests who came together from many corners of the earth to spend three days in celebration with Linda and Roland. Susan became one of a handful of people who can say they attended two of Linda's three weddings.

Together after 50 years — wedding guest and equine photographer, Gabriele Boiselle, captured this joyful moment with Linda and Roland the day after they were married in Santa Fe, New Mexico in July, 2000.

Constantly in motion, Linda continues to travel the earth teaching her work that was once only a prophecy in an astrological chart. Now she's teaching and honing TTouch and the Tellington Training Method around the globe, exploring and embracing newly-discovered scientific proof of why the effectiveness of TTouch bridges the worlds of magic and science.

Over the decades that I have known Linda, she has changed the lives of thousands of people, horses and other animals. She has demonstrated for princesses, lived with countesses, lectured at veterinary universities, worked on Olympic horses and hopped over fences to help the pony next door. She has met extraordinary people along her path — you may even be one of them.

Dating back to when the Tellingtons met the leggy three-year-old Arabian filly that prompted Went's quote, "Well, she was *some* horse!", I have to wonder what would have become of that filly had she not fallen into Linda's hands. Would Bint Gulida have been tested to her fullest capabilities under anyone else? Probably not. Today it's commonplace to compete in two or more 100-mile rides in one year on one horse but when Linda and Bint Gulida did so in 1961 it was uncharted territory. Would Linda have been able to achieve her success on another horse, attracting the attention of Countess Bessenyey? Perhaps it would have been a long shot, but I, for one, am pleased with that particular convergence in time. Because of Went and Linda, Bint Gulida became a foundation mare for endurance horses by breeding her to the great Bezatal. Although Linda only campaigned Bint Gulida for a few short years, her broodmare career began in 1963 when she produced a foal by Arabian stallion Lothar. Five years later in 1968 she produced her fourth foal, a chestnut colt named Cougar Rock by Bezatal. Ed Johnson rode Bezatal to Tevis wins in 1965 and 1967. Cougar Rock became Bint Gulida's best-known progeny and stood for many years at Rushcreek Arabians in Lisco, Nebraska with a descendant count of around 80 horses.

Bint Gulida produced a foal by Brado when Margit Bessenyey took ownership of her after Linda left Badger. California-based Arabian breeder Danica Cuckovich DuBois dreamed of having the mare and convinced Margit she was worthy after being properly vetted (Danica, not the horse!). Danica then delivered two more purebred foals from Bint Gulida, bringing the mare's foal count to eight.

Linda played a pivotal role in establishing the Hungarian Furioso in the United States, which is now referred to as the Hungarian Felver. Between Linda, the Countesses Margit Bessenyey and Judith Gyurky, Steve and Wanda Cooksley of Nebraska and rancher Jim Edwards, they saved this breed from disappearing altogether in this country. Today there are many breeders of Hungarian horses across America.

In 1976 Linda introduced the Icelandic horses to the United States where they've become a popular breed. Her sister, Robyn Hood, continues to raise these horses at The Icelandic Horse Farm in Vernon, British Columbia, Canada.

As an instructor and coach, Linda has had a great impact on riders. She remembered back to 1978 and said, "I traveled to Goodwood, England to assist Gwen Stockebrand when she competed in the world dressage championship and entered the Musical Kur on her Morgan/Tennessee Walker gelding, Bao. I sat with Gwen in the stall with the horse and we visualized the routine prior to the competition." Although commonplace today, Linda began practicing this technique decades ago and could be considered a pioneer of visualization in equestrian sports. Bao and Stockebrand won the bronze medal in the Kur, and were the highest-placed Americans at both Goodwood and Rotterdam. That same year they won the U.S. Grand Prix Championship.

Retracing the Footsteps of Grandfather Will Caywood in Russia

In 1985 when Linda made her second of ten trips to Moscow, Russia as a Citizen Diplomat to work with the Esalen Institute's Soviet/American Exchange project, she found reference to her grandfather at the Moscow Equine Museum. She writes, "On this trip to Moscow I visited the Equine Museum with my Russian friend and translator, Andre Orlov, wondering if there would be a reference to my Grandfather's award from Czar Nicholas II. You can perhaps imagine my astonishment when the elderly attendant at the museum recognized the name of William Caywood, and responded with enthusiasm. He asked us to wait while he went into the archives and came back with a copy of a 1905 Pravda newspaper containing the report that William Caywood was awarded a jeweled cane by Czar Nicolas II, in recognition of being the Leading Trainer at the Moscow Racetrack with 87 wins.

"When I returned from that trip, I told my Aunt Irma about the visit and she sent me copies of the Russian newspaper article, along with other fascinating documents that shed new light on my grandfather's time in Russia. The file contained a letter of agreement from Will's agent to an Austrian count who hired Will to ride his horses at the Moscow and St. Petersburg racetracks. The file she sent me also contained his Russian visa and a postcard, I think the date was 1905, from my grandmother describing a scene she observed from the hotel across from Red Square of Russian Cossacks shooting into the crowd of demonstrators. It is such a déjà vu experience to read this since I stayed at this very hotel seven or eight times on various visits to Moscow between 1984 and 1987. Those were the years when I was working with the Russian Olympic dressage team, the Academy of Science, and the Moscow Zoo, as well as teaching a group of veterinarians at the Bitza Olympic Center where we did a stress study on twenty horses and how TTouch affected their stress levels.

"One of my most poignant connections to my grandfather was sitting in the Hippodrome restaurant in the same room where he would have been drinking tea and observing the workouts of the horses."

Looking Back at a Long Career

"I've had many people express surprise that in demonstrations I ride horses that I have never ridden before," continues Linda. "It's because I had the opportunity to ride so many different horses as a junior rider and I learned to connect with their minds and their hearts.

"And speaking of hearts, today I understand why horses like me so much and connect with me in such a short time. Of course, I had no explanation for it at the time, but today it's understood that when a person is in a state of 'heart coherence' that animals naturally gravitate to them. Heart coherence, as researched extensively by the HeartMath Institute in Boulder Creek, California, is achieved by controlling one's breathing and quieting one's thoughts while coming from a place of gratitude. I was intuitively very good at all three, and today I understand the value of learning to monitor my emotions, giving thanks for small things, and *smiling*. And heart coherence is actually teachable to riders.

"In retrospect, I find it fascinating that I learned to smile while riding at the Edmonton Spring Horse Show. One of my treasured memories is of my Mother standing at ringside in this huge exhibition hall that I believe held at least 5,000 spectators. Each time I rode by she would softly call out in her encouraging, musical tone, 'Smile, Dear.'

"I so wish Mum were alive today so she could understand just how important those words are to me still. I won far more than my fair share riding horses that I had only been on for maybe 10 minutes before the class. I would send each horse a mental picture that we were going into the ring not only to win, but to have a really nice time and to do the best we could. And it paid off big time time with many blue ribbons!

"I believe the smile was a big part of the 'secret to success.' When we smile, there is a release of serotonin, the 'feel-good hormone.' Research has now shown that those feelings can be transmitted and that's a part of the reason horses felt that potent energy Shannon observed so many years later at PCERF.

"That habit of smiling is so ingrained that I've been known to laugh even when a student's horse I'm riding for the first time takes a few unexpected little bucks or jumps. It's just fun. And I sometimes jokingly warn spectators when

I am giving a one-hour demo at an expo to be prepared for me to go over my allotted time when I take the bridle off a horse I'm riding for the first time, which I often do in demos — much to the owner's surprise. Riding bridleless with a Liberty Ring around the horse's neck is so much fun. You may not be able to get me off because of the connection that I feel between the horse and me when the bridle is not getting in the way. It's an indescribably magical feeling.

"But I digress," Linda continues. "Back to the reason I am so comfortable riding horses I meet for the first time... From the time I was nine years old until I was fifteen, I rode at Briarcrest Stables after school almost 365 days a year, and each day I rode two to three horses. And at the huge nine-day Edmonton Spring Horse Show each year, I would normally 'catch-ride' two to four horses each day, in Hunter and Jumper classes and many Hack and Hunter Hack classes. These were horses belonging to riders who were not comfortable showing in the big classes in which there were often fifty or more horses.

"This background of riding so many horses laid the foundation for my lifetime of having a special trust that I feel when I put my hands on a horse for the first time. It is with a sense of honor and gratitude and respect for the heart and mind of that individual. I feel a cell-to-cell and heart-to-heart connection, without words. It's a gift from the Divine Spirit and the Horse Angels. How can you tap into it? Many years ago I learned to trust that inner feeling from a statement made in Richard Bach's Jonathan Livingston Seagull classic novel by that name. When asked how it was that birds could fly, the answer was, *They think they can.*

"Thanks to the new understanding of the power of intention and the merging of quantum science and spirituality, I now understand this precious connection I have with animals, and I know that anyone can develop this ability. Trust, and know that you can too." A succinct comment came to mind that I always reference after watching Linda work with a horse, or any animal, "Always Amazed — Never Surprised!"

When I asked her if she has any regrets, Linda said, "Very few but if I could turn back the clock, there are two invitations that I wish I had accepted. In 1972, Margit invited me to join her on a trip to Hungary to take a two-week course on learning how to drive a four-in-hand carriage and I didn't go." I thought what on Earth could equal that lost opportunity when she added, "A few years later I was invited to play elephant polo against the Nepalese Army Polo Team. It was a fundraiser for an elephant sanctuary near Kathmandu. Since I had trekked on the trail headed for Mount Everest Base Camp several years before, I didn't make the extra effort to go. Later I learned that the elephants really get into the game and will kick the ball themselves to help their team." What an experience that would have been!

In retrospect, I learned a valuable lesson from Linda. She taught me that if I could Strike A Long Trot while riding a horse and set a worthy pace, I could cover 100-miles in one day and reach the finish line. In my life, this became a metaphor for accomplishing any goal, including telling this story, which I am honored to share with you.

Over lunch one day I asked Linda, now age 75, what her future plans hold and if she was considering slowing down. She said, "My grandfather, Will Caywood, was still getting on difficult two-year-olds at the racetrack at age of 80. Retirement is not a word that's in my family genes." Having known this incredible woman for nearly half a century, I shook my head at the pace of her inspiring life and said, "It's hard to keep up with you, Linda."

HIGHLIGHTS OF AWARDS AND HONORS

LINDA TELLINGTON-JONES PhD (Hon)

1969 – Governor Ronald Reagan presented the Award for Creative Citizenship to Linda and Wentworth Tellington in recognition of their contributions to the State of California through the work done at the Pacific Coast Equestrian Research Farm

Master Instructor Award from the American Riding Instructors Certificate Program.

1978 – Graduated from the 4-year Feldenkrais Professional Certification Program at the Institute of Humanistic Psychology in San Francisco, CA

1987, 1997, 2001 Consultant for U.S. Endurance Team to World Championships veterinary team

1992 – ARICP Lifetime Achievement Award (American Riding Instructors Certificate Program). Recognized an individual whose lifetime experience and accomplishments exemplify the pursuit of excellence and uncommon devotion to the art and science of riding instruction.

1994 – North American Horsemen's Association (Horsewoman of the Year)

2002, 2003, 2004 – Taught TTouch at the University of Minnesota Center for Spirituality and Healing

2004 – RFD-TV Magazine Personality of the Month for January

2007 – Hall of Fame sponsored by the Western States Horse Expo.

2007 – Massage Therapy Hall of Fame Inductee

2008 – Linda Tellington-Jones received an Honorary Doctorate degree from the Wisdom University and was granted the position of Director of the Institute for Interspecies Connections.

2003 – In celebration of Trail Blazer Magazine's 25th Anniversary, Linda Tellington-Jones was awarded the "Publisher's Silver Star Award of Recognition."

The Equine Industry Vision Award, finalist, sponsored by Pfizer Animal Health. The award is intended to recognize innovation, leadership and service.

Linda's contributions to equine behavior, health and communication are recognized and acclaimed internationally; her TTouch and TTEAM methods have been successfully used by Olympic contestants and trail riders alike. As part of Linda's legacy, she has authored 20 books in 14 languages and has produced

Shannon Yewell Weil

21 videos of her work with animals. To help spread her work around the world, there are 1500 Tellington Training Method certified practitioners in 29 countries, as well as Tellington Training Method Centers in Canada, Germany, Austria, Slovenia, Switzerland, South Africa, the United Kingdom and the United States of America.

Books by Linda Tellington-Jones

Dressage with Body, Mind & Soul, A 21st-Century Approach to the Science and Spirituality of Riding and Horse-and-Rider Well-Being with Rebecca M. Didier, Trafalgar Square Publishing, 2013

The Ultimate Training and Behavior Book for the Twenty-First Century, Linda Tellington-Jones with Roberta Lieberman, Trafalgar Square Publishing, 2006

Improve Your Horse's Well-Being: A Step-by-Step Guide to TTouch and TTeam Training, Linda Tellington-Jones, Trafalgar Square Publishing, 1999

Getting in TTouch with Your Dog - An Easy, Gentle Way to Better Health and Behavior, Linda Tellington-Jones with Gudrun Braun. Trafalgar Square Publishing, 2001, 9,700 copies sold, revised and republished in 2011

Let's Ride With Linda Tellington-Jones: Fun and TTeamwork with your Horse or Pony, Linda Tellington-Jones with Andrea Pabel, Trafalgar Square Publishing, 1997

Getting in TTouch: Understand and Influence Your Horse's Personality, With Sybil Taylor, Trafalgar Square Press, 1995, 41,000 copies sold

The Tellington TTouch: A Revolutionary Natural Method to Train and Care for Your Favorite Animal, with Sybil Taylor, Penguin Books, 1993, 69,000 copies in paper back, Republished in 2011

An Introduction to the Tellington-Jones Equine Awareness Method with Ursula Bruns, Breakthrough Publications, 1985

Endurance and Competitive Trail Riding, Wentworth and Linda Tellington-Jones, Doubleday, 1972

PCERF ALUMNI PROFILES

While interviewing former students for this story, I enjoyed hearing about their lives over the past four decades and discovering how they had been influenced by their time with the Tellingtons at the Pacific Coast Equestrian Research Farm. They all felt extremely fortunate for their PCERF experiences.

MARTHA MERRIAM – Loomis, California

Martha was affiliated with the Tellingtons for nearly ten years during the 1960s and began riding with Linda in her early teens as a member of the Rolling Hills Pony Club. That led to week-long stays at the Hemet Thoroughbred Farm and later, summers at PCERF, both the Hazard Canyon and Badger schools. Martha remembers the fun of riding down sand dunes and going on trail rides with Linda, picking out downed trees to jump and steep slopes to tackle with the variety of horses available at the Research Farm. "Seeing which horse you were assigned to each today was a thrill. I remember when I saw 'Earthaquake' or 'Kilsythe' written next to my name, I was delighted. Both mares had successful show careers and they took care of us when we learned to jump fences."

After attending several Tevis Cup Rides as a crew member for the PCERF team, Martha rode in 1968 at age 16 years old but did not finish the Ride. Her horse lost a shoe, became lame and was pulled at Michigan Bluff. However, Martha was determined to finish another year. In a postcard to her, the late photographer, Charlie Barieau, wrote, "Greetings from Auburnville, the home of the 100-mile ride, that summer madness of the horsefly set." Charlie urged Martha to spend a summer in Auburn before starting college at the University of California, Davis. Martha and her roommate, Barbara Suhr White, lived on Robie Drive, only a few blocks from the finish line. The two Tevis-crazed girls rode daily on the Western States Trail with local endurance legends. As a result, riding the Tevis turned into a lifelong passion. To date, Barbara holds the record for earning the most Tevis buckles – 32 and counting. Martha and Charlie became close friends and spent much time together through the years, attending endurance rides and exploring pioneer cemeteries of the West.

Martha satisfied her life's dream and covets her only Tevis buckle earned in 1969, in the day when the Ride could be read about on the society page of the *San Francisco Chronicle*. She has maintained her interest in the sport, becoming one of the many people who moved to the Auburn area to be closer to the Western States Trail, where she still resides today. Martha completed eighteen 50-mile endurance rides and numerous limited distance rides on a 17-hand Hanoverian gelding named Duncan whom she calls her 'heart horse,' all after he turned 20. She continues to trail ride with her daughter, Sarah McGinn, on their half-Arabian geldings and Hanoverians, occasionally participating in endurance rides. Following in her parents' footsteps, Martha became a geologist, earning a master's degree in geology at the University of California, Davis. Today she evaluates seismic hazards at bridges for the State of California, and is a doting grandmother of three.

SUSAN MAYO - Denton, Texas

Susan Mayo has spent her life as a teacher of both art and equitation. In 1970 she formed Susar Farm in Denton, Texas where she continues to breed, raise and train numerous Asil Arabian horses. Susan was fortunate enough to serve as Linda Tellington's assistant at the Chadwick School in Rolling Hills, California. She was one of the original students at the Pacific Coast School of Horsemanship in the early 1960s at Hazard Canyon, California.

It was there that she was introduced to the straight Babson Egyptian stallion,

Shannon Yewell Weil

Lothar, with whom she fell in love as a young girl. So inspired by Lothar, she has thoughtfully managed her breeding program by carrying his Asil, Blue List bloodlines forward to the Arabians she breeds today. Susar Arabians have gone on to great success in the Region 9 horse show arenas. To learn more about the Asil Arabians preservation breeding program at Susar Farm please go to http://www.susarinc.com/bucky.html.

MICHELE POULIOT - Portland, Oregon

Michele Pouliot has been a professional guide dog mobility instructor since 1974. Before entering the guide dog field Michele trained under Linda Tellington-Jones and Wentworth Tellington, becoming a professional in the equestrian field for four years. Once Michele began training her pet Labradors, she became fascinated with the comparisons of how dogs and horses learn. This sparked a keen interest in working with dogs, resulting in Michele turning dog training into her profession while horses became her hobby. "Everything I learned at the Research Farm, I applied to dogs," Michele said.

Michele is the Director of Research and Development with Guide Dogs for the Blind, the largest guide dog school in North America. Michele has served as International Assessor for the International Guide Dog Federation, certifying the quality of guide dog schools in Norway, Austria, Czech Republic, France, Japan, and the United Kingdom.

Michele is recognized internationally for her innovation and creativity in dog training for service work and competitive sports by clicker training methods. Michele has been on Karen Pryor's faculty for Clicker Expo conferences since 2008 and has an online training course through the Karen Pryor Academy.

Michele is active in her hobby sport of canine musical freestyle and continues to enjoy working with her horses in her free time. To learn more go to www. guidedogs.com; www.karenpryoracademy.com/catalog. To see Michele's phenomenal performances with her dogs and be sure to watch "Smile" by going to: www.cdf-freestyle.com

LAURIE JURS – Green Valley, Arizona

Laurie spent the summer of 1967 at PCERF and was one of the five Tellington Girls at the Bitter Root Competitive Trail Ride. Thereafter her horse related-life revolved around endurance riding until 2005. As the founder of the Cobre Ridge

Endurance Rides (50 and 25 mile distances), she was its manager for 20 years. It was a no-frills ride held on a strenuous and glorious trail in the rugged border region of Southern Arizona.

Her endurance riding experiences cover the Southwest, but her personal point of pride was two successes at California's Tevis Cup Ride in 1984 and 1994, finishing strong on two magnificent horses.

In 2001, a challenging mare led her to a teacher named Peggy Cummings and her "Connected Riding" program. "Peggy, a Certified TTouch Practitioner, helped me transform my horse related life and thereby, my whole life."

Thanks to the Connected Riding network, Laurie was part of a team that established a horse-related curriculum for a summer leadership program for teenage girls in rural West Virginia. This effort, now seven years old, gets better every year.

During Laurie's professional career, she served for 22 years as the director of the United Community Health Center. It is a network of community-based primary health care clinics and programs in multiple locations in Southern Arizona. In 2006, Laurie retired and continues to live in the borderlands region of Southern Arizona.

The Southern Arizona Borderlands are where she will live out her days.

DIANE WOODARD SCOTT – Elverson, Pennsylvania

"It's hard to believe that 43 years have passed by since I was at PCERF from 1967 to 1968," Diane reflects. She married farrier Bruce Scott and moved to Pennsylvania where she still calls home. They had two children who are now married and live in California.

In her 70s now, Diane no longer rides but still loves being around horses. "I volunteered at a Horse Therapy program called 'Sebastian' where I was able to groom, tack and lead horses for children who had cerebral palsy or other conditions."

Diane volunteers at the Ryers Horse Farm for Aged Equines in Pottstown, Pennsylvania http://ryerssfarm.org/ where over 70 horses reside with hundreds on a waiting list. The population includes former race and show horses as well as rescued horses. Diane, in addition to the staff and other volunteers, cares for these horses and understands the importance of love and respect for the service they have given. She is especially attentive to rescued horses that have suffered from abuse.

This photo of Diane is with 17-year old Matisse, a 17-hands high black Westphalen, who was a high-level dressage horse in his day. She tends to his needs while he happily lives out his retirement with in the rolling hills of Chester County.

"Our biggest horse here is Stanley, an 18-hand Belgian who spent many years in a stall giving blood for snakebite venom research, never seeing grass or the sky. He is now able to live out his life in comfort." She feels blessed to be a small part of Ryers Horse Farm, confirming that spending time with horses makes a difference in her life.

She says, "I am so privileged to be a part of this tribute to Linda who has given so much to the animal world, and to us who knew she was destined for great things."

PAM PARKER – Bellevue, Washington

After graduating from PCERF, Pam went to the University of Washington and galloped racehorses at Longacres Racetrack in Renton, Washington. Pam converted a tack room into her studio where she could paint; soon she was selling her horse portraits to the shedrow visitors.

She painted the world-famous Thoroughbred Exceller and entered the painting into the Washington Horse Breeders Association Art Show where it won "First Prize for Best Oil" and the "People's Choice Award." Veterinarian Dr. Chris Cahill happened to see the painting and suggested that Pam call Exceller's owner, Mr. Nelson Bunker Hunt, who then enthusiastically bought the piece. Pam traveled to Texas to deliver the painting to him, which led to many other commissions including Palace Music, the sire of Cigar, and six stakes winners.

With ample racetrack experience, coupled with her Pacific Coast School of

Horsemanship education, she acquired a Trainer's License in 1976 and continued at the track until 1980.

Pam worked for a bloodstock agency preparing and selling Thoroughbreds at public sales in Arkansas, Northern California, Kentucky and Canada. She continued to paint, which led to even more commissions.

In 1986 she moved to Carmel, California where she was accepted as a student under Italian painter Roberto Lupetti, who proved to be an extraordinary teacher for Pam. Soon she was painting portraits for many professional golfers who played at Pebble Beach.

From a brilliant rail shot photograph captured at the inaugural 1984 Breeders' Cup Classic at Hollywood Park race track, Pam painted the exciting instant when Wild Again, piloted by jockey Pat Day, dug deep to win a three-way battle to beat out Gate Dancer and Slew of Gold. There she met Mrs. Fred Hooper, who commissioned her to paint Eclipse Award winner Precisionist. This led to painting well-known horses including Affirmed, Spectacular Bid, Shampoo and Never Knock, the dam of Go For Gin.

Pam's paintings hang in the Favell Museum of Western Art and Artifacts, in Klamath Falls, Oregon and she exhibited at the Kentucky Derby Museum in 1986 where she won the People's Choice Award. She has painted portraits of Willy Shoemaker and renowned Thoroughbred horse trainer Woody Stephens, which is on permanent display at the Kentucky Derby Museum in Louisville, Kentucky.

One of her best-known paintings is of a little girl leading a white horse that won the People's Choice Award at the 1992 American Academy of Equine Art Show held at the Kentucky Horse Park and is a popular image on greeting cards. Pam's work has appeared on over 12 magazine covers and she has had greeting cards published by companies such as Leanin' Tree, Tolten, Cabela's, and Wildwood. Her work can be found at TheParkerCollection.com.

Today Pam lives in Bellevue, Washington where she a practicing animal communicator. Her gratitude runs deep for the persistent study of good conformation in horses that she learned from Linda, which she has applied directly while training horses, training dogs, or painting animals. Pam's many talents have flourished as a direct result of the excellent foundation she acquired at the Tellington's PCERF School of Horsemanship.

Shannon Yewell Weil

ALEXIS FLIPPEN VON ZIMMER – Woodside, California

Elegrantly dressed, Alexis is riding sidesaddle on her horse Panache.

"Since graduating from PCERF, life has taken me down many paths, professionally and personally, and horses were put on hold for a time. I found horses again in my early 30's and have since been blessed with wonderful equine companions that I've had for the past three decades. One was a stunning grey Thoroughbred, Freedom Pass by Gulch, who produced Kentucky Derby winner Thunder Gulch and who was many times show hunter champion. Another Thoroughbred show champion, Panache, became my champion ladies sidesaddle horse that carried me to the National Horse Show at Madison Square Garden. Through many of the basics learned at PCERF about health, nutrition, massage and fitness, I was able to keep these horses happy and sound throughout their lives and into their 30s.

"At the time of this writing, I have co-bred and own the reserve National Champion Hunter Breeding Yearling, having won at the top shows in the nation, including at Devon, 'where champions meet.' I own and show a 17.3hh 1600 pound Thoroughbred, Devoncourt, who has had the most challenging behavior issues of any horse I have ever encountered. Without the mindset and basic skill set instilled from those early days at PCERF, I could never have managed this horse that has taught me so much about maintaining a calm and caring demeanor. He was twice Grand Champion at the Grand National in San Francisco and he has won many classics in his career. He is still teaching me to be vigilant, yet always fair and kind. He has the heart of a Thoroughbred and has given me so much joy.

Alexis on Toon Town.

"Decades later and now in my sixties, I still ride and show, and for many years I've driven a Ferrari – just like my mother – with the signature prancing horse emblem, of course. And after 44 years, I have had the good fortune to reconnect with Linda Tellington for her insight and intuition."

Shannon Yewell Weil

VAL PRUITT SIVERTSON – Eatonville, Washington

Brado nonchalantly denies responsibility of any wrong-doing.

Val stayed in touch with Linda for many years and ultimately purchased several Hungarian mares from Margit Bessenyey. She is an active member of the Hungarian Horse Association of America (www.hungarianhorses.org/ an excellent place to learn more about these wonderful horses). Her Ohop Valley Hungarian Horse Farm in Eatonville, Washington can be viewed at www.ovhhf.com

Val has taken over the reins as manager of the Pioneer Farm Museum and Ohop Indian Village that her mother initially founded. The Pioneer Farm Museum program provides hands-on pioneer activities for children who come to the exhibit. Kids can churn butter, grind grain, wash clothes on a washboard, use a curling iron for curling hair, cut wood with a bucksaw, remove bark from poles with a spud – a chisel-like tool, and play with pioneer toys.

PAULA STOCKEBRAND FABINAR – Stockton, California

Today, Paula Stockebrand Fabinar is the equivalent of Mother Teresa for canines.

In the early 1960s, Paula began her journey with the Tellingtons at the PCERF summer school at Hazard Canyon as a 14-year-old girl. Her parents, Archie and Bunny assisted the Tellingtons with building the infrastructure at the original PCERF at Hazard Canyon, on the California Coast near San Luis Obispo. When PCERF moved to Badger, the Stockebrand family followed closely. Archie and Bunny then managed the nearby M Bar J Guest Ranch, which had been purchased by Margit Bessenyey as an extension of PCERF. Archie then applied his knowledge as a retired US Navy Commander and maintained Went's vintage Stearman biplane that was housed in a hanger in Visalia, nearly 40 miles from Badger.

The Stockebrands ultimately bought the M Bar J where Paula's mother, Bunny and her brother still reside.

Today Paula is a stalwart volunteer at the Stockton Animal Shelter where she cares for dozens of rescued dogs. Her love for dogs is still center stage in her life.

Shannon Yewell Weil

LYNN BLADES – Arkport, New York

When Lynn left Badger, she moved to San Francisco for a few months to assist Wentworth with his endeavors marketing Whitehurst Products. Soon she realized that was not for her and she left to spend time in Auburn among the endurance riding set. Later she returned to her home in New York where she again joined her family's construction business.

She continued to hunt and show horses after she left the Research Farm. Lynn went on to say, "Of all the many equestrian competitions that I've been to over the years, there is no venue that compares to the spectacular setting at Pebble Beach." Lynn remembers that, "Just like Brado, my horse today, Howie, has the same kind eye that he had." Lynn is pictured above riding Howie.

Recently retiring from the family business, Lynn resides in Upstate New York. The PCERF experience has remained a high point in her life.

Summer Class of 1967 *First Row: Janice Barr, Linda Ferguson, Peta Wiley, Silver Brandon, Terry Duncanson, Manny Knox. Second Row: Paula Jacobs, (unknown), Diane Woodard Scott, Laurie Jurs, Pam Parker, Faith-Ann Arnold, Sara Engle, Lucy Diehl, Kathy Young, Peggy Wherry. Top Row: Shannon Yewell, Carolyn Woltjes, Nancy Maddock, (unknown), Bruce Scott, Jim McArthur Linda Harpster, Martha Merriam, Ann Greer, Linda Tellington.*

Winter Class of 1968 *(back row: l to r) Carol Cook, Linda Tellington, Diane Woodard, Beth Preuss, Sylvia Jordan (middle row: l to r) Silver Brandon, Pam Cameron, Hara, Crystal Sandberg, Roberta Wiebe, Tiger (front row: l to r) Linda Day, Shannon Yewell (with Great Dane puppies everywhere)*

Fall Class of 1969: *Vicki Bailey, Kathy Barbarowicz, Nettisea Bellah, Diane Gerhardt, Cindy Greer, Jo Hagerud, Judy Hale, Birch Jones (far right), Beth Klein, Janet Lay, Albert Lo, Susan Magliano, Kathy Mergler, Pam Miller, Michele Pouliot (third from left, back row), Sandi Simms, Debbe Stemmler, Paula Stockebrand (fourth from left, back row), James Weir, Lisa Wood. Instructors: Linda Tellington (center front row) and Lynn Blades (second from right, front row) Assistant: Melissa Murchison.*

Student Albert Lo from Hong Kong, is seen here with Linda in the late 1960s. He was an inexperienced rider when he arrived at PCERF but soon acquired a confident seat. The first week he was there, the riding lessons were conducted entirely without the aid of stirrups. Albert later majored in Physics at the University of California, Davis.

APPENDIX

APPENDIX A

These **33-Points of the Balanced Seat Position** were originally created and used as a teaching tool by the Pacific Coast Equestrian Research Farm School of Horsemanship. This list provided students with a solid seat while riding over a variety of obstacles on cross-country courses. Linda evolved the position based on what she learned after her 4-years study with Moshe Feldenkrais.

1. Eyes looking in the direction where you are going while you are seeing your horse and surroundings.
2. Chin up and in.
3. Jaw relaxed.
4. Back straight and supple. Relaxed erectness.
5. Shoulders back and down.
6. Chest out.
7. Upper arm perpendicular to the ground.
8. Elbow relaxed and bent and at point of hip (except at rising trot and Two- Point Position when it is forward.)
9. Straight-line vertical and horizontally from bit to hand to elbow.
10. Straight line along back of wrist.
11. Hands 30% angle inside the vertical.
12. Fingers cupped and relaxed. The rein is held in two hands, passing up through the palms and over the index fingers.
13. Hold reins over the first joint of index finger between first and second digit of fingers.
14. Thumbs lightly bent, light and secure contact on top of reins,
15. Knuckles even.
16. Hands 6 to 8 inches apart.
17. Three Point Position – Crotch in deepest part of saddle at a sitting trot, between pubis and seat bones at the walk and canter, and the pubis bone over the deep part at the rising trot, buttocks. Sit straight at the rising trot, a slight angle at the hips at the walk, more of an angle at the canter, a greater angle at the rising trot, and the greatest angle in the jumping position

    Two Point Position or Half Seat –by bending at the hip (not the waist), the rider creates a greater angle in the body. This jumping position is used while riding over obstacles such as going up or down banks, crossing ditches. Contact is balanced from inner thigh to knee and knee to lower leg down to stirrup.

18. Seat (ischium) bones spread.
19. Thigh rolled in.
20. Center of kneecap pointing forward.
21. Contact with the inner thigh and upper 1/3 of lower leg below the knee.
22. Lower 2/3 of leg close to horse and used for aids.
23. Heels thrust down for the most stable cross-country or jumping seat (for dressage or casual riding the heal is kept level)
24. Straight line from shoulder through hip to heel.
25. Stirrup leather hanging naturally at the middle or towards back of girth.
26. Foot on the inside of the stirrup.
27. Weight on the inside of the foot.
28. Iron on the ball of foot (widest part.)
29. Iron perpendicular to foot.
30. Angle flexed in at trot and Two-Point Position – relaxed at walk, canter and sitting trot.
31. Toes up to 15% outside of vertical.
32. Toes relaxed (little toe slightly raised.)
33. Pressure on the inside of stirrup.

These points of contact in the Three-Point Position (flat seat)
1. Seat.
2. Thigh to knee.
3. Knee to upper 1/3 of lower leg.

Two points of contact in the Two-Point Position (Jumping position or Half Seat)

1. Thigh to knee.
2. Knee to upper 1/3 of lower leg.

APPENDIX B

Pacific Coast School of Horsemanship
Badger, California
March 1971

PRE-SILVER MEDAL WRITTEN TEST

PART A: COMPLETION

1. _____ hay has a tendency to cause white sweat and kidney problems.
2. _____ hay contains the most protein.
3. The best and least expensive grain for fattening a horse in the summer is _____.
4. _____ is fed as a concentrate in the mid-west during the winter because it is cheap and produces heat.
5. The best grain for producing energy and hard flesh is
   _____.
6. If a horse gorges on pellets and then drinks a great amount of water, the pellets are likely to swell and cause an _____
   _____.
7. _____ hay is low in digestible nutrients, low in energy and produces a clear sweat.
8. A soft swelling on the front of the hock, which seldom causes permanent lameness is _____.
9. A horse, upon leaving the stable, suddenly shows a distinct stiffness of the loins, profuse sweating and tenderness in the muscles of the loins and quarters may have _____.
10. A calcification on the fetlock joint is called
    _____.
11. A calcification on the front of the hock, which usually causes permanent lameness is called _____.
12. When a horse is foundered, the _____ bone shifts downward pushing on the sole of the foot.
13. A large donut-shaped boot is used on the pastern of the horse to prevent a _____.
14. The legs of the rider are principally used to control the
    _____ of the horse.
15. When the rider is using the right lateral aids, he is using the
    _____ hand and the _____ leg.
16. When holding your reins in a hunt seat equitation class, the AHSA

rulebook says you should turn your hands_____ degrees inside the vertical.

17. The 2 points of contact of the Two-Point Position are _____ and _____.

18. The term used to describe any injury to the front of the knees, generally occasioned from falling. is _____ _____.

19. Another name for sore shins, an inflammatory condition of the membrane of periosteum of the cannon bones, is _____.

20. Another name for founder is _____.

21. A condition, which the glands of the sensitive frog "sweat" excessively due to irritation from dirt and stale urine, is called _____ _____.

22. The test of holding the hind limb up by the toe for 30 seconds, thereby forcibly flexing it and releasing it and immediately trotting the horse out, _____ is used to determine if the horse has _____.

23. A term used by horsemen to mean abdominal pain is _____.

24. A common rule for feeding horses is to feed _____ of grain per 100 pounds of horse and _____ of hay per 100 pounds of horse.

PART B. TRUE OR FALSE

_____1. Oat hay should be cut before the oat is fully matured.

_____2. Horses' teeth will not need to be checked for floating until they are at least 3 years old.

_____3. Thick, cloudy urine may indicate digestive disorders or kidney problems.

_____4. If a horse has a great deal of sound in his side, one would suspect colic.

_____5. A splint may occur on either side of the cannon bone and on any or all of the legs of the horse.

_____6. The two jumps comprising an "In and Out" are sometimes set from 24' to 27' apart in a show.

PART C: SHORT ANSWERS

Value

5   1. List 5 important things to look for in selecting hay for horses.

3   2. List 3 things that could eliminate you from a hunt seat equitation class.

5   3. List 5 points of basic show ring etiquette.

5   4. Name 5 types of stall bedding.

13   5. List 26 points of position for the balanced seat.

8   6. On the accompanying diagram locate and label 16 undsoundnesses or blemishes.

20   7. Write in outline form a plan describing the principles of caring for stabled horse, considering; diet, periodic procedures (parasite control, dental care, etc.) stable hygiene and exercise.

12   8. List the symptoms of the following:

    a. Colic

    b. Azoturia

    c. Sleeping sickness

    d. Founder

3   9. List 4 causes of colic.

3   10. List 3 causes of founder.

2   11. List 2 causes of azoturia.

Shannon Yewell Weil

ANSWERS to PRE-SILVER MEDAL EXAM

Part A: Completion

1. Alfalfa
2. Alfalfa
3. Barley
4. Corn
5. Oats
6. Impaction Colic
7. Oat
8. Bog Spavin
9. Azoturia, Monday Morning Sickness, Tying Up
10. Osselets
11. Bone Spavin
12. Coffin bone
13. Shoe Boil
14. Hindquarters
15. Right Hand and Right Leg
16. 30° inside the vertical.
17. Thigh to knee; Knee to upper 1/3 of lower leg.
18. Hygroma or "Big Knee"
19. Shin Splints, Bucked Shins
20. Laminitis
21. Thrush
22. Flexion Test, joint lameness issues
23. Colic
24. ½ pound of grain; ½ pound of hay per 100 pounds of horse's weight or 1% of horse' body weight

Part B: True or False

1. False
2. True

3. True

4. False

5. False

6. True

Part C: Short Answers

1. Green, Not rained on, No dust or mold, Fine stems and lots of leaf, No weeds. Suitability for the intended purpose (hunter, jumper, dressage, endurance, etc.)

2. Use of standing martingale, sue of a crop (assuming a flat equitation class), use of 3-ring bits or gags.

3. Passing to the inside track; say "rail" if you must pass on the outside; don't' crowd, allow a minimum of one horse distance between you and the next horse/rider, don't ride between another rider and the judge (called "shielding")

4. Straw, Wood shavings, Rice Hulls, Wood Pellets, Rubber mats

5. Balanced Seat Position – See Appendix A

6. Blindness, Poll evil, Parrot mouth, Fistula, Sweeney, Knocked down (dropped) hip, Scars, Hernias, Roaring (whistling), Heaving, Cribbing, Weaving, Biting, Kicking, Tail rubbing, Halter pulling/Pulling back on halter and lead rope.

7. Write an overall plan for a stabled horse.

8. a. Colic. Loss of appetite, shallow breathing, kicking at abdomen, no gut sounds, lying down groaning and rolling, turning head toward flank, standing stretched out, pawing ground, sweating in loin area.

    b. Azoturia: Cramping and pain upset by muscle chemistry, stiffness in movement, unwillingness to move,

    c. Sleeping Sickness: Profoundly depressed; Lack of appetite; Aggressiveness, circling, or hyper-excitability; Facial nerve dysfunction or blindness; Head tilt, and paralysis of the muscles of the face, mouth and throat. Some horses become comatose, seizure, or even die suddenly.

    d. Founder: Lameness; shifting weight when standing; Heat in the feet; Separation of the laminae in hoof wall; Increased digital pulse in the feet; Pain in the toe region when pressure is applied with hoof testers; Reluctant or hesitant gait; Pointing a foot at rest or "camped out" feet positioned farther back to redistribute weight; Rings in hoof wall; Widened white line; dropped soles or flat; Bruises, abscesses in sole of feet; Thick "cresty" neck; Dished hooves.

9. Colic: Bad feed; Sudden changes in feed; Over feeding; Poisons; Parasites; Sand Colic; Impactions from too much dry food, such as pellets; Twisted intestines.

10. Founder: Too much grain; Too much water in an overheated state; Sudden access to lush pasture (clover); High fever; Excessive concussion from walk, trotting or cantering on pavement "Road founder"; Obesity; Excessive weight bearing on one leg due to compensation of an opposite injured leg; Retained placenta in mares.

11. Azoturia: Overfeeding of non-structural carbohydrates (grain and pellets, for example); poor conditioning or fitness; sudden increase of workload; work of a horse after a period of rest, if the concentrate ration was not reduced; electrolyte or mineral imbalances, especially seen with potassium; deficiency in selenium or vitamin E; wet, cold, or windy weather conditions.

Pacific Coast Equestrian Research Farm

Badger, California

REQUIREMENT FOR THE SILVER LEVEL PROFICIENCY

The Silver Level horseman has the presence of mind and enough experience to be able to help a horse improve or help a rider improve. This level of horseman is able to compete successfully in the areas of his choice. The experience implied at this level is both broad and deep and covers both the academic and the practical physical side of the subject. The Silver Medal person has demonstrated his ability in and around the stable with normal horses under a variety of conditions including momentarily adverse or ordinarily frightening circumstances. He is also skillful in detecting various types of difficulties with horses including injuries and ailments.

Excellent	10
Very Good	9
Good	8
Fairly Good	7
Satisfactory	6
Sufficient	5
Insufficient	4
Fairly Bad	3
Bad	2
Very Bad	1

A minimum grade of 5 for each phase is necessary to earn the Silver Medal.

Name:_____ Date _____

RIDING	SCORE	REMARKS
Satisfy Pre-Silver Prerequisite. (written examination)		
DEMONSTRATE:		
Classical Balanced Seat position at all gaits.		
Superior coordination of leg & rein aids.		
Tactful use of aids for turns, circles, and canter departs.		
Seat independent of reins.		
Turn on forehand.		

Schooling movements at posting trot without stirrups.		
Vault off either side at trot upon command.		
Figure 8 at canter with simple change of leads.		
Rein Back.		
Adjust stirrup length at walk.		
Be able to rate cross-country at 8, 12, 16, m.p.h.		
Negotiate: Cavaletti without stirrups or reins.		
Banks and slides with and without stirrups.		
A 3-foot cross-country course safely.		
BAREBACK RIDING REQUIREMENT:		
Mount bareback.		
Ride safely and comfortable a the walk, trot, and canter bareback		
Jump cross-country bareback.		
Demonstrate control on banks and slides bareback.		
Compete in a horseshow jumping class at 3 feet demonstrating control and style.		
DRESSAGE:		
Compete successfully in AHSA Level 1 Dressage test.		
Demonstrate the riding ability, tact and basic understanding of training principles necessary to improve the performance of a riding horse.		
STABLE MANAGEMENT:		
Demonstrate ability and maturity to take complete charge of a small stable of horses:		

Mucking out		
Organization		
Fly Control		
Care of Tack		
Be observant to first signs of trouble, i.e., Check feed consumption, water intake, and droppings and give necessary aid.		
Understand the use of a bran mash and be able to make various types.		
Understand normal temperature, pulse, and respiration and be proficient at taking them.		
Understand the principles and techniques of lunging a horse.		
HORSES FOR SHOW:		
Demonstrate ability to give a horse a body clip and trim for show.		
Understand principles and techniques of bandages for a variety of conditions.		
Be able to twitch a horse correctly.		
THEORY:		
Demonstrate a thorough knowledge of the principles of the Balanced Seat style of riding, including:		
Basic dressage – terms, letters, movements.		
The Field Seat.		
Obstacles – Jumping, banks, water.		
AILMENTS:		
Understand causes, symptoms and cures for common ailments, e.g. colic, laminitis, azoturia, thrush, colds, cuts, etc.		
Recognize symptoms and causes of common unsoundnesses and blemishes, e.g., side-bone, ring-bone, curb, splint, wind puffs, spavins, thoroughpins, etc.		

Shannon Yewell Weil

CONFORMATION:		
Understand conformation faults, ideal characteristics in general and distinguishing characteristics of the major breeds.		
FEEDING AND CARE OF HORSES:		
Demonstrate the ability to plan and execute a feeding program taking into account:		
Geography		
Climate		
The character of the physical plant		
The type and use of the horses.		
COMPETITION RIDING:		
Know ring etiquette.		
Know AHSA rules for Hunter, Jumper, and Equitation and Western Classes.		
Know required clothing and equipment for show classes.		
Know the anatomy of the lower leg and foot.		
PARASITES:		
Know problems and prevention methods.		
Understand shoeing problems and corrections.		

The Silver Medal final written examination counts for 30% of the overall score.

Passing Grade   60%   Student Score   _____

Honor   85%   Notebook Grade   _____

Date examined   _____

Suggested booklist for Silver Medal examinations:

(Check off books read.)

THE ART OF HORSEMANSHIP – Xenophon

BREEDING THE RACEHORSE – Tesio

LAMENESS IN HORSES – Adams

SCHOOLING THE WESTERN HORSE – Young

AMERICAN HORSE SHOW RULE BOOK

TRAINING HUNTERS, JUMPER AND HACKS – Chamberlin

THE BACKYARD HORSE – Pittenger

THE HORSEMANS ENCYCLOPEDIA – Self

RIDING AND JUMPING – Steinkraus

VETERINARY NOTEBOOK – McGee

DRESSAGE – Wynmalen

HORSEMANS TAX GUIDE – Humphreys

TRAINING THE HORSE AND RIDER – Podhajsky

CONDITIONING AND TRAINING THE ENDURANCE HORSE –
Tellington

LEARNING TO RIDE HUNT AND SHOW – Wright

ETIQUETTE – Vanderbilt

ELEGENCE – Dariaux (for women students)

REQUIRED READING

HORSEMANSHIP – Gordon Wright and The U.S. Equestrian Team

KNOW YOUR HORSE – Codrington

OTHER TEST SCORES:

HORSE SHOW WINNINGS:

BIBLIOGRAPHY

Internet Websites

www.hungarianhorses.org/

hungarian.hvyhorse.com/DisplayHorse.asp?horsenum=859&tab=1

www.ansi.okstate.edu/breeds/horses/kisberfelver/index.htm

en.wikipedia.org/wiki/Nonius_(horse)

query.nytimes.com/mem/archive-free/pdf?_r=1&res=990DE1D91439E133A25751C0A9669D946095D6CF

www.travelmt.com/mt-cities-Hamilton.html

hamiltonmontana.com/montana/hamilton_montana_history.html

www.walkercustomboots.com/cooksley.htm

www.westwindbarn.com/History.htm

dnr.maryland.gov/publiclands/southern/chapman.asp (Mt. Aventine Manor House, Indian Head, Maryland)

www.uffdafarmhungarianhorses.com/abouthungarians.htm

www.wineglassfarm.com/mares.html

www.horseplaza.com/cfusion/template/hhaa/history.cfm

www.equinenow.com/hungariantraining.htm

www.saddleupnebraska.com/index.php/tag/rider/

www.cstone.net/~magyar/services/history.htm

www.morgandressage.org/history/timeline.html

www.ttouch.com/tteamConnections/JanMar11.pdf

www.hungarianhorse.com/hha_news_sep98.html

www.hungarianhorse.com/hha_news_sep98.html#margit

www.hungarianhorses.org/docs/HHA_newsletter_2010-11_Winter.pdf

www.pedigreequery.com/moon+king2

xprides.com/history/

www.teviscup.org

Shannon Yewell Weil

Books

Physical Therapy for the Athletic Horse, Pacific Coast Equestrian Research Farm

The Arabian War Horse to Show Horse, Gladys Brown Edwards

The Heavenly Horses, Virginia Weisel Johnson

Mark of Clover, Judith Barczy Kelly (aka) Countess Judith Gyurky Kelly

Beyond Spirit Tailings — Montana's Mysteries, Ghosts and Haunted Places, Ellen Baumler

The Hundred Milers, Jo Stanchfield, S.I. Hayakawa, Ralph Kellogg, Frank Hutchinson

Competitive and Endurance Riding Manual – Tellington, Wentworth and Linda

Endurance and Competitive Trail Riding – Tellington, Wentworth and Tellington-Jones, Linda

Crazy in America, Book I: 1766 – 1776 The Seeds of Freedom, Wentworth Tellington

Military Maps and Air Photographs, Their Use and Interpretation, A.K. Lobeck and Wentworth J. Tellington

And Miles to Go, The Biography of a Great Arabian Horse Witez II, Linell Smith

Books and School Study Course

Horsemanship – Gordon Wright and the U.S. Equestrian Team Illustrated, Sam Savitt

The Complete Training of Horse and Rider in the Principles of Classical Horsemanship ~ Alois Podhajsky (Author), Eva Podhajsky (Translator), Colonel V. D. S. Williams (Translator)

Magazines and Publications

Western Horseman Magazine, 1961; April 1961; January 1963; May 1963 – first Let's Go article; August 1964; September 1966; March, 1967

Hungarian Half-Breds in the Bitterroot Valley, Western Horseman Magazine by Helen Clark, January 1963

Arabian Horse World, Feb. 1972, Competitive Trail and Endurance Riding in the U.S.A by Gladys Brown Edwards

Remount Magazine, Nov/Dec. 1946

Western States Endurance Run program, 2002

Western States Trail Ride – The Tevis Cup 100-Miles One Day Participants Guide

Newspaper Articles and Letters

"Defier of League Married American" by Frederick Cunliffe-Owen, C.B.E October 02, 1921, New York Times, regarding the marriage of Count Sigray to Miss Harriot Daly.

Hungarian Horse Association Newsletter, Winter 2010-2011

Letter to author from Danica Cuckovich DuBois, March 17th, 2008, regarding Bint Gulida and Cougar Rock.

Photo Credits

David Wolfgang Photography

Ed Lawrence Photography

Ernst Peterson, Hamilton, MT

Gifts from Charles Barieau

Ira Hass Photo

Jan Dickersen Photo

Martha Merriam Archives

R.S. Kilburn Photo

Shannon Yewell Weil Archives

Tellington-Jones Archives

PCERF Archives

Gabriele Boiselle p. 284

Sylvia Jordan

Family of Judith Gyurky

INDEX

A

Al-Marah Rainbow 41, 75, 76, 77, 79, 80, 83
Anaconda Copper Mining Company 153

B

Bailey
  Rho 41, 171
Banat Ar-Rih Ranch 49
Barieau
  Charles 75, 172, 175, 300, 331
Barner
  Dru 59, 199
Barsaleau, DVM
  Richard 100, 169-171, 173-175, 200, 205
Becker
  Claus 257-259, 261, 266, 270
  Ullu 257-259, 261, 270, 276
Bessenyey
  Baron George 97
  Countess/Baroness Margit Sigray iii, iv, x, 85-87, 94, 109, 115, 150, 152-154, 155,
      158, 159, 170, 179, 195, 205, 206, 211, 212, 231, 215, 221, 222, 224, 225,
      226, 233, 237, 244, 245, 250, 251, 292, 310, 311
Bezatal 115, 234, 292
Bint Gulida iii, v, vii, ix, 35-41, 54-61, 65, 77, 85, 107, 115, 144, 151, 215, 220,
      234, 292
Bitter Root Competitive Trail Ride 149, 150, 156, 159, 178, 303
Bitter Root Stock Farm 85, 86, 93, 96, 152-155, 157, 159, 224, 250
Blades
  Lynn iii, 102, 135, 147, 171, 181, 187, 215, 216, 219, 221, 223, 226, 228, 312, 314
Bouncing Buster 28, 29
Briarcrest Stables 18, 19, 295
Brislawn
  Bob 158
  Emmett 158
Brown
  Colonel W.R. "Pinky" 37, 43

C

Calgary Horse Show 29
Caywood
  Will iv, 17, 51, 52, 53, 54, 166, 181, 293, 296
Chadwick
  Mrs. Margaret 2, 6, 33
Chadwick School iii, 2, 32, 33, 34, 38, 39, 40, 43, 44, 46, 47, 49,54, 66, 69, 179,
      225, 231, 246, 252, 290, 301
Churchill
  Doris 10
Cook
  Carol 8, 107, 313
Cooksley
  Steve and Wanda 96, 292
Cougar Rock
  (place) 190, 207
  Arabian horse 234, 292, 331
Czar Nicholas II 293

D

Daly
  Harriot 89, 146, 331
  Marcus 88, 93, 153, 154, 155
Dardi
  Bud 200, 202, 203, 205
Doyle
  Dr. John L. 36, 38, 45
  Mrs. Ellen C. 36, 38, 45

E

Edmonton Spring Horse Show 22, 24, 294, 295
Edwards
  Gladys Brown 61, 330, 331
  Jim 95, 96, 292
  Patty 76, 79, 80
  Rob iii, 37
Esalen 247, 248, 249, 251, 254, 293

F

Feldenkrais
  Dr. Moshe xi, 254, 255, 275, 277, 287, 288, 289, 297, 315

Shannon Yewell Weil

L

Lothar (Arabian horse) 41, 292, 302

M

Mackay-Smith
  Matthew 58, 84, 100, 163, 166
Maddock
  Nancy 10, 150, 151, 313
Mark of Clover 90, 91
Marsden
  Captain 43, 126
Mayo
  Susan iii, 33, 39, 40, 44, 59, 60, 68-70, 301
M Bar J Guest Ranch 4, 179, 206, 234, 311
McKillip
  Lyn 168, 190
Merriam
  Martha 41, 47, 69, 74, 77, 81, 117, 134, 175, 299, 300, 301, 313, 331
Miller
  Cherie 76, 79, 80, 97
  Jack 97
Moon King 30, 31
Moscow Hippodrome 51, 52

N

NATRC 100, 150, 151, 190
Nicholson, DVM
  Dave 200, 262, 269, 272, 274, 285

O

Oakland National Horse Show 167, 168, 194
Ott
  Miss Jane Llewellyn 38
  Mrs. John Ekern 41, 49

P

Parker
  Pam iii, 10, 150, 151, 154, 159, 161, 163, 164, 165, 166, 198, 199, 200, 202, 205,
      306, 307, 313
Patee House 273

Sigray
  Count Anton 89, 246
Smith
  Roy 206, 208, 225
Snyder-Smith
  Donna 168
Sproul
  Curt 287
Steere, DVM
  James 100, 200
Stewart
  Lori 262, 265, 270, 271, 283, 284
  Rick 262, 265, 270, 271
Stockebrand
  Archie iii, 67, 179, 311
  Bunny iii, 67, 179, 311
  Gwen 66, 67, 293
  Paula iii, 66, 67, 117, 179, 180, 221, 211, 314
Susar Arabians iii, 33, 301, 302

T

Tankersley
  Bazy 41, 77
Tellington
  Jay 229, 233
Tevis
  Lloyd 56, 153
Tevis Cup Ride iii, x, 41, 55-58, 75-77, 79, 85, 97-100, 112, 113, 151, 152, 161, 169, 182, 188, 190, 195, 196, 199, 200, 204-207, 209, 212, 213, 224, 287, 291, 299, 304
Turner
  Joan 148

V

Varian
  Sheila 100

W

Wall
  Colonel John F. 26
Western Horseman Magazine ix, 75, 85, 99, 181, 330